National Forest

Scenic Byways

By BEVERLY MAGLEY

FALCON PRESS®

Helena, Montana

ACKNOWLEDGMENTS

This author could not have custom-designed a more enjoyable way to spend time than writing and editing this guidebook. I wish to thank the many people with the Forest Service who spent hours giving me, and the other writers, valuable and insightful information about the scenic byways, and who then proofed the final write-ups for accuracy. This book reflects the dedication and genuine interest of Forest Service rangers and employees who shared their knowledge so willingly.

I also wish to thank those people whose confidence in me enables me to continue with many and varied writing projects: Bill Schneider, DD Dowden, and Chris Cauble of Falcon Press; and Carolyn Cunningham of *Montana Magazine*.

Sincere thanks to the writers and photographers who contributed byway descriptions and photographs. It was a pleasure to work with them and to learn about the scenic byways in their regions.

Last, but not least, the support of family and friends is essential and was freely given. I am grateful.—Beverly Magley.

Front cover photo

DAN PEHA San Juan Skyway, San Juan and Uncompahgre national forests, Colorado.

Back cover photos

JIM HUGHES/PhotoVenture Mount Washington, McKenzie Pass-Santiam Pass Loop, Deschutes and Willamette national forests, Oregon.

MICHAEL S. SAMPLE Beartooth Highway, Montana.

DICK SMITH Autumn foliage, Kancamagus Highway, White Mountain National Forest, New Hampshire.

Inside photos

All photos are by BEVERLY MAGLEY, unless otherwise indicated.

To my father, who inspired an enduring love of travel
and interest in the natural world,
and to my mother,
whose ability to stretch a dollar
made family travel possible.

CONTENTS

East

South

FOREWORD

Driving for pleasure is the most popular form of outdoor recreation in America and the most often chosen activity of the millions of visitors to the National Forests each year. These Forests—156 of them in 44 states—offer a wide array of outdoor recreation opportunity from camping and hiking to boating and birdwatching. All this and more is offered amid the breathtaking splendor of the natural beauty of our nation. Now the Forest Service has developed a system of Scenic Byways to help you explore and enjoy America's Great Outdoors—our National Forests!

Forest Service employees are proud to be the managers and caretakers of these lands. Along with the natural resources upon which this country has come to depend, we are eager to share the story of rich cultural, historic and geological heritage the National Forests offer our visitors. From Alaska on the Pacific to Florida on the Atlantic, these Byways offer some 3,000 miles of driving pleasure in 28 states.

Catch the fever of the gold rush days along Oregon's Blue Mountain Scenic Byway or encounter the drama of a Tennessee Civil War battlefield on the nation's first Scenic Byway, Ocoee - U.S. 64. Experience the vast arid desert of New Mexico, enjoy the painted finery of fall color in New Hampshire or visit the swamps and savannahs of Florida—all along the National Forest Scenic Byways.

Whether you are an armchair traveler or an on-site visitor, you may use this book to learn more about the Scenic Byways and the National Forests through which they wander. However you travel, we especially invite you to learn about and become involved in the management and care of your National Forests. We invite you to join us in enjoying the National Forests—America's Great Outdoors.

F. Dale Robertson, Chief
USDA Forest Service

PARTNERS IN SCENIC BYWAYS

The national forest scenic byways program has benefitted from a unique partnership between the Plymouth Division of Chrysler Corporation and the Forest Education Foundation. This partnership represents a new era of cooperation between government and the private sector to promote recreation on public lands.

The Forest Education Foundation is a non-profit educational foundation chartered to raise funds through public donations and commercial sector grants. Funds are disbursed through program grants to support worthy projects, primarily in the area of recreation on public lands.

The Foundation engineered the partnership between the Forest Service and Plymouth and administers several key elements of the Scenic Byways program.

Plymouth recognizes the critical role passenger cars play in the enjoyment of America's scenic roads. Plymouth has designated the National Forest Scenic Byways program as a major theme in its efforts to operate as an environmentally conscious and responsible corporate citizen.

Plymouth supports national promotion of the scenic byways, provides funds for byways signage, turnouts, and site improvements in the forest. The Plymouth exhibit promoting national forest scenic byways visitation travels the length and breadth of America each year.

Plymouth has also funded production of the scenic byways brochure for the Forest Service.

The Forest Education Foundation, Plymouth, and the Forest Service demonstrate how working together can enhance the recreational opportunities for all Americans.

For more information about Plymouth's sponsorship of the scenic byways program, please see your local Plymouth dealer. For information about the Forest Education Foundation, contact the Forest Education Foundation, P.O. Box 25469, Anaheim, CA 92825-5469, phone 714-634-1050.

INTRODUCTION

The most popular form of outdoor recreation on our national forests is scenic driving. In response to this enjoyable pastime, the Forest Service established the national forest scenic byways program in May, 1988.

Across the nation, national forest employees were invited to select their favorite roads, and their choices were wonderful. These spectacular routes take visitors alongside trout-filled sparkling streams, through diverse hardwood forests, over 13,000-foot passes, and to high alpine meadows, peaceful lakes, far-ranging views, cypress swamps, and much more.

These are the nation's first fifty national forest scenic byways, some of the most beautiful and interesting places in the United States. The byways cover 2,668 miles in 26 states. Each is described in detail in this book.

Americans often think of national parks when planning a vacation, but national forests are the foremost providers of outdoor recreation in the country. Americans visit national forests *twice* as often as they visit national parks.

One reason is that national forests are usually much more accessible. There are 156 national forests in 44 states, covering a total of 8.5 percent of the United States. Most Americans live within a day's drive of one or more national forests.

Another reason is that national forests have so much to offer. About half of the nation's big game animals reside on national forests, along with a wide variety of other animals and plants, including rare and endangered species. These lands also contain 329 wilderness areas, 99,468 miles of trails, more than 6,000 campgrounds and picnic areas, over 1,100 boating sites, and 307 winter sports areas.

In addition to traveling through magnificent countryside, national forest scenic byways provide access to varied recreational activities. Visitors can simply enjoy the scenery from the car, or get out and meander along interpretive nature walks, picnic at a scenic overlook, boat on the many lakes and rivers, camp in secluded sites, or hike into wilderness areas for days or weeks.

Byway travel also is educational. Through brochures, interpretive displays, visitor centers, and their own experiences, byway travelers have many opportunities to learn about natural history, human history, archaeology, geology, and national forest management, to name just a few subjects.

The byways are as varied as the landscape. Zilpo Road winds nine miles across forested ridges to a lovely lake in eastern Kentucky, while the San Juan Skyway travels 236 miles through southwest Colorado's highest, most rugged peaks. Apalachee Savannahs Scenic Byway offers visitors to Florida's pine forest an opportunity to see odd, insect-eating pitcher plants and Venus flytraps, while Cascade Lakes Highway in Oregon provides great fishing and outstanding views of volcanic peaks. Travelers on Montana's Wise River— Polaris Road can dig for crystals in the Pioneer Mountains, while motorists in Arizona's Kaibab Plateau—North Rim Parkway end their route overlooking the Grand Canyon.

This brand-new program also is exciting as a way people and businesses can form productive partnerships with the Forest Service. Various community organizations, volunteers, and national and local businesses are helping with the byway program. Their efforts in the next few years will make your trip more pleasurable and enlightening, as such facilities as interpretive signs, paved overlooks, and hiking trails are installed. In this way, the scenic byways program not only invites us to visit the national forests, it provides opportunities to get involved in conservation.

Whether you seek solitude or active participation, enjoy the national forest scenic byways.

Bear grass adorns the forest floor along Deadhorse Grade, a historic section of highway on the McKenzie-Santiam Pass Loop. This 81.5-mile loop crosses two mountain passes in the heart of the Cascade Range, on the Deschutes and Willamette national forests in central Oregon.

HOW TO USE THIS BOOK

National Forest Scenic Byways describes fifty byways all across the United States with maps, photos, and informative text.

Each byway description features a travel map that shows the byway, campgrounds, special features such as visitor centers and recreation areas, connecting roads, and nearby towns. Each map also displays a mileage scale and a state map that shows the general location of the byway. All byways are marked on the United States map on pages xiv and xv, and a legend to map symbols appears on page xiii.

Each text description is divided into ten categories. Most are self-explanatory, but the following information may help you get the most from each description:

General description provides a quick summary of the length, location, and scenic features of the byway.

Special attractions are prominent and interesting activities and natural features found on the byway. Additional attractions are included in the description. Some activities, such as fishing and hunting, require permits or licenses which must be obtained locally.

Location gives the name of the national forest, and the general area of the state in which the byway is located. It also describes exactly where the scenic byway designation begins and ends. The road numbers are normally found on a state highway map and are posted along the route. Occasionally, the scenic byways are on back roads that are not numbered on the state highway maps. In that case, the map of the byway includes primary routes from a nearby city or primary highway.

Byway route numbers are the specific highway numbers on which the scenic byway travels, such as U.S. Hwy 12, or Arkansas Route 23, or Forest Road 1243.

Travel season notes if the byway is open year-round or closed seasonally. Many byways are closed to automobiles in winter, due to snow cover, but are delightful for snowshoeing, cross-country skiing, and snowmobiling. Opening and closing dates are approximate and subject to regional weather variations. Always check for local conditions.

Camping on the national forests can be a rich and varied experience. Services basic to all developed national forest campgrounds along the byway are listed in this category. Individual national forest campground names and their additional services or features are noted in the **Description.** Many campgrounds charge a fee, noted at the campground entrance. National forest campgrounds generally provide the basics: toilets, picnic tables, and fire grates. Drinking water and garbage pickup are found at some, and electrical, water, and sewer hookups are rare.

Primitive dispersed camping is permitted on all national forests, subject to local and special restrictions. Check with the individual national forest for details.

Selected campsites may be reserved on some national forests, through the

MISTIX computerized reservation system. Call 1-800-283-CAMP for campsite availability information. A fee is charged for the service.

Privately owned campgrounds, usually with full hookups, showers, and other amenities, are often located near the byways. Check with the local Chambers of Commerce for details.

Services lists communities with at least a restaurant, groceries, lodging, phone, and gasoline. When a community has each of the services, but perhaps only one motel, and a small cafe, it is noted as having services with limited availability.

Nearby attractions are major features or activities found within about fifty miles of the byway. Many of these make an interesting sidetrip and can be combined with byway travel.

For more information lists the names, addresses, and phone numbers of the national forest(s) for each scenic byway. The supervisor's office is first, followed by ranger districts. Travelers may wish to contact the district rangers for detailed area maps and information on specific subjects.

The maps in this book cover each byway thoroughly. However, if you plan to take side trips or explore the area further, a Forest Service map is invaluable and can be obtained at all national forest offices for a small fee.

Description provides detailed traveler information, along with interesting regional history, geology, and natural history. Attractions are presented in the order a traveler encounters them when driving the route in the described direction. If you travel the route from the opposite direction, simply refer to the end of the byway descriptions first.

A steep escarpment towers over an alpine landscape of lakes and wildflowers along the Snowy Range Highway, on the Medicine Bow National Forest in southern Wyoming.

SCENIC BYWAY SIGNS

Look for these distinctive road signs along every national forest scenic byway. Each byway will be marked with the basic scenic byway sign, shown below, and some of these signs will carry a plate with the name of that byway. The smaller "blaze" sign will appear as a reminder sign along the route. The signs are in color—purple mountains, dark green trees and lettering, and pale, bluish-green foreground.

The Blue Ridge Mountains on the Sumter National Forest has many swift-moving streams. This one runs near the South Carolina State Highway 107 Scenic Byway. There is excellent trout fishing, hiking, and hunting in this area. Larry Cribb photo.

LOCATIONS OF THE SCENIC BYWAYS

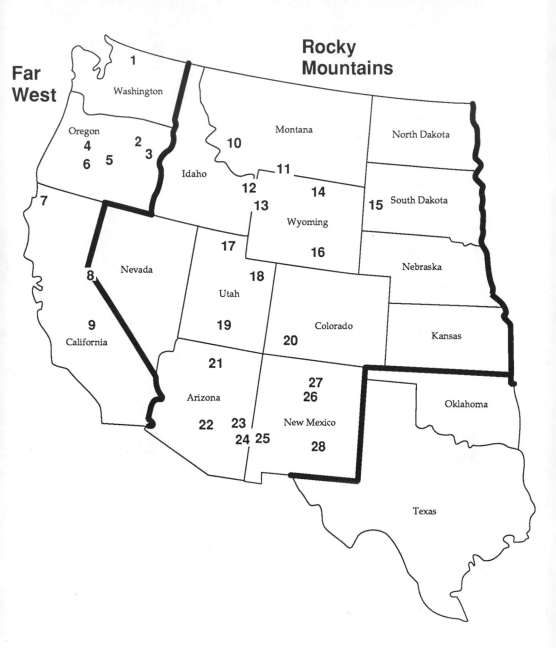

Far West

Rocky Mountains

Washington 1

Oregon 4 2 3
6 5

7

Idaho 10

Montana

North Dakota

11

12
13
Wyoming 14

South Dakota 15

Nevada 17
18
Utah

16

Nebraska

8

California 9

19

20
Colorado

Kansas

21
Arizona

27
26
New Mexico

Oklahoma

22 23
24 25

28

Texas

MAP LEGEND

Byway	▬▬▬	Interstate	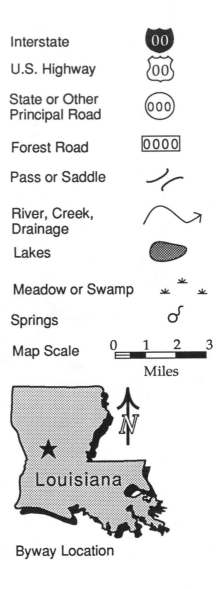
Interstate and Four Lane Highways	⟹	U.S. Highway	
All Other Roads	⟹	State or Other Principal Road	
Point of Interest	❶	Forest Road	
Overlook	▣	Pass or Saddle	
Hiking Trail	🚶·····>	River, Creek, Drainage	
Ranger Station	♟	Lakes	
Ski Area	⛷	Meadow or Swamp	
Picnic Area	⛢	Springs	
Campground	▲ ▲	Map Scale	

There is no difference between campgrounds designated ▲ *or* ▲.

·······························≫
NATIONAL FOREST BOUNDARY

– – – – – – – – – ➤
WILDERNESS BOUNDARY

— – — – — – — – — – —
S T A T E   B O U N D A R Y

Byway Location

General description: A 24-mile road through the northern Cascade Mountains, from rain forest up to rugged timberline.

Special attractions: Salmon and trout fishing, old-growth forests, hiking, alpine and cross-country skiing, river rafting, magnificent scenery.

Location: Northwestern Washington on the Mount Baker-Snoqualmie National Forest, east of Bellingham. The byway travels Washington Route 542 between Glacier and the end of the road at Artist Point.

Byway route number: Washington Route 542.

Travel season: The highway is open year-round to Mount Baker Ski Area. The last 2.6 miles from the ski area to the road's end at Artist Point is open from about mid-July through the end of October, depending upon snowfall.

Camping: Two national forest campgrounds with drinking water, picnic tables, and vault toilets. Suitable for tents and trailers. No hookups. One group campground with 13 sites.

Services: The nearest gas station is at Kendall. Food, lodging, convenience store, and cross-country ski rentals available in Glacier.

Nearby attractions: North Cascades National Park, Mount Shuksan, Mount Baker Wilderness, Nooksack Falls.

For more information: Mount Baker-Snoqualmie National Forest, 1022 First Ave., Seattle, WA 98104, (206) 442-5400. District Ranger: Mount Baker Ranger District, 2105 Highway 20, Sedro-Wooley, WA 98284, (206) 856-5700. Glacier Public Service Center (USFS-NPS), Mount Baker Ranger District/North Cascades National Park, Glacier, WA 98244, (206) 599-2714.

Description: Mount Baker Scenic Highway begins at the Glacier Public Service Center, elevation 932 feet, and climbs to 5,200 feet at Artist Point.

The first 14 miles are mostly straight with a gentle ascent through thick old-growth and second-growth forest. As the highway gains 3,200 feet during the final 10 miles, a series of switchbacks affords outstanding views of glacier-carved horns and the awesome face of Mount Shuksan. Traffic on this two-lane road is light on weekdays and after Labor Day, but it can be heavy on holidays and during August and September weekends. The route has some sharp drop-offs and steep cliffs and is not for the fainthearted. Paving will be completed in October 1990. There are frequent turnouts for scenic viewing.

A local axiom holds that summer starts after July 4, for rain invariably falls on Independence Day. Summer temperatures are generally in the pleasantly high 70s and low 80s, with nights in the 40s. The best months to visit are August and September, when there are fewer people and annoying insects have left the high country. Winter snow accumulations range from two feet at Glacier to 300 inches in the Heather Meadows area.

Glacier Public Service Center was built in 1938-39 by the Civilian Conservation Corps. It is on the National Register of Historic Places. The design is a classic example of "Cascadian" style architecture unique to the Pacific Northwest, with massive squared timbers, cedar-shaked gable roof, and double-hung sash windows. An outdoor plaza, information kiosks, and restrooms were added in 1989.

Picture Lake and Mount Shuksan are scenic highlights along the Mount Baker Highway.
Tom Barr photo.

To begin your trip, leave the center and head east into a typical western Washington forest dominated by Douglas-firs and western hemlocks, mixed with red alders, western redcedars, and bigleaf and vine maples. Watch for blacktail deer in the ground cover of salal, maidenhair, and sword and bracken ferns. Chipmunks and ground squirrels are common in the forest, and wolverines, rarely seen, inhabit riverbanks.

A side trip on Glacier Creek Road (Forest Road 39) leads nine miles south to a spectacular view of Coleman Glacier on Mount Baker.

Douglas Fir Campground, two miles east of Glacier, has 30 sites in a picturesque setting along the North Fork Nooksack River. Twenty sites are open year-round. The "community kitchen" picnic shelter is a National Historic Landmark and exhibits typical CCC pole and stonework architecture. For a short walk through the cool forest, take the half-mile Horseshoe Bend Trail.

Rafters put into the North Fork Nooksack River off the Horseshoe Bend Trail and float 10 miles to Maple Falls. The class III river is fed by glaciers and can be rafted into late summer. In January and February, this is a prime spot to watch bald eagles feast on salmon. Five species of salmon spawn in the North Fork Nooksack, offering anglers a good chance of catching sockeye, king, chinook, and cohos. Strong runs of pink salmon occur every odd-numbered year. Trout catches include rainbow, brown, brook, and cutthroat.

The byway continues east, paralleling the North Fork Nooksack for 14 miles. Side roads lead to fishing and salmon-spawning banks, and pullouts allow time to photograph the river's 400-foot-deep gorge.

Turbulent Nooksack Falls plunges 175 feet in two raging columns. The wooden pipeline behind its parking area still carries water to the Excelsior power-generating plant, which was completed in 1906 and is the oldest in Washington.

Excelsior Trail is a four-mile hike to the High Divide and outstanding views of Baker, Shuksan, and the remote Tomyhoi country. The trail leads into the Mount Baker Wilderness. Eighteen trails, ranging from a half to six miles long, begin on the byway or on adjacent spur roads. Their varied pleasures include picturesque alpine lakes known for excellent fly fishing, unusual rock formations, remnants of past mining activity, and a chance of seeing black bears, coyotes, and other wildlife.

About 11 miles from Glacier is the delightful North Fork Nooksack Research Natural Area. Research natural areas are lands on which certain natural features are preserved in an undisturbed state solely for research and educational purposes. Enjoy the brilliant sulphur yellows and dark greens of a 500-year-old western redcedar forest, where varied thrushes serenade. South of the byway is a four-site primitive campground on the riverbank.

In 1897, gold was discovered in the surrounding mountains. An original miner's cabin still stands about half a mile off the byway on Hannegan Road. Also known as Forest Road 32, the route accesses a popular 47-mile hike that travels from national forest land through North Cascades National Park and ends at Ross Lake National Recreation Area. The well-designed trail is an easy, leisurely week's walk. En route, it meanders through the Nooksack, Chilliwack, Beaver Creek, and Big River drainages and crosses Hannegan, Whatcom, and Beaver passes.

Silver Fir Campground has 21 sites near the river, some with barrier-free access. The day-use picnic area has a unique CCC-built shelter. In winter, the Salmon Ridge cross-country ski area is located here, with 20 miles of groomed trails for skiers at all levels of experience. Across the road is an overflow camping area. Anderson Creek Road, near the campground, leads four miles south to large beaver ponds and good trout fishing. At 2,000 feet in elevation, this is a transition zone where silver fir mixes with Douglas-fir, western hemlock, and alder.

As the byway clings to cliff sides and rises in a series of dramatic switchbacks, lofty mountain peaks and jagged horns stand in sharp contrast to the deep, forested valley below. Watch roadside cliffs for excellent examples of columnar basalt, small waterfalls tumbling from alpine creeks, and tiny lake tarns.

Mount Shuksan fills the horizon to the east. The multifaceted peak is a mass of imposing rock outcroppings, hanging glaciers, and steep snow-covered ridges. Approximately 20 climbing routes lead to the 9,127-foot summit. None are easy and most require intermediate to expert knowledge in handling ropes, ice axes, and crampons. Picture Lake, near the byway, is often photographed with Mount Shuksan in the background. Photos are particularly striking when taken in early October to include the brilliant autumn foliage.

Heather Meadows, near the end of the byway, is one of two major accesses to the 117,900-acre Mount Baker Wilderness. It is also the site of the Mount Baker Ski Area. Facilities include a ski shop, six chair lifts, rope tows, and groomed cross-country ski trails. A day lodge with snack bar is open during summer weekends, and a guided nature walk is offered. Weekend walkers learn local history, biology, and geology from the naturalist at Heather Meadows. This country may look familiar because it is often featured in television commercials and films. The Clark Gable-Loretta Young version of "Call of the Wild" was filmed at Heather Meadows and Artist Point.

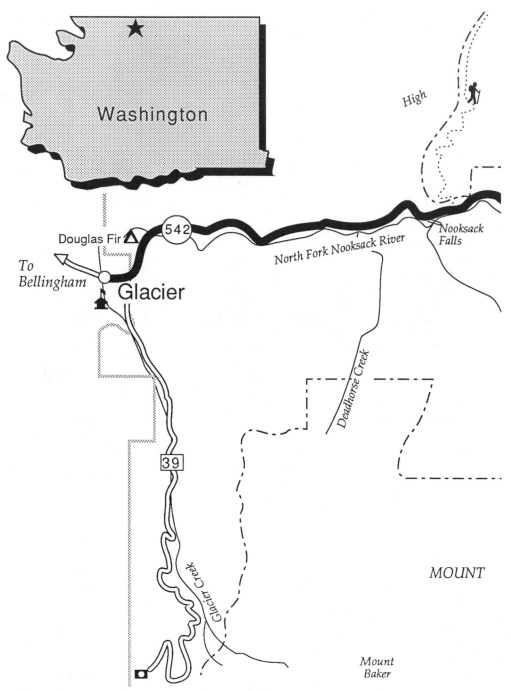

Washington

High

Douglas Fir

To Bellingham

Glacier

542

North Fork Nooksack River

Nooksack Falls

Deadhorse Creek

39

Glacier Creek

MOUNT

Mount Baker

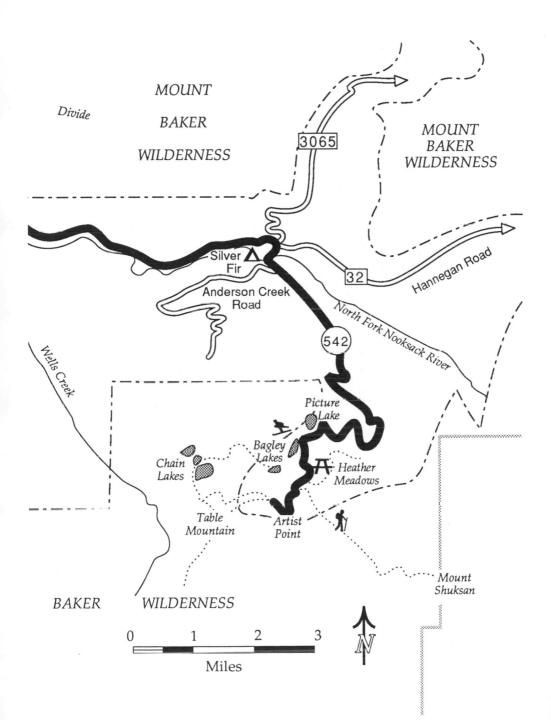

MOUNT

BAKER

WILDERNESS

Divide

3065

MOUNT
BAKER
WILDERNESS

Silver
Fir

Anderson Creek
Road

32

Hannegan Road

North Fork Nooksack River

542

Wells Creek

Picture
Lake

Bagley
Lakes

Chain
Lakes

Heather
Meadows

Table
Mountain

Artist
Point

Mount
Shuksan

BAKER   WILDERNESS

0   1   2   3

N

Miles

5

Austin Pass Picnic Area was built by the CCC in the late 1930s. A network of trails spreads to several small fishing lakes and the surrounding peaks. Picnic in the huge bowl-like valley, hike through the heather, and watch for mountain goats cooling off on the snowy slopes. In September, this area offers the added treat of mountainsides filled with bushes of ripe blueberries and huckleberries. A self-guided interpretive trail tells how glacial action and volcanism shaped the landscape.

Artist Point is the end of the scenic byway. From here, view snowcapped Mount Baker rising to 10,778 feet across a wide valley to the south. North Cascades National Park can be seen to the east, as can Canada to the north. Artist Point is situated on a divide between Mount Shuksan and Mount Baker. Shuksan was formed between 200 and 300 million years ago when tectonic plates collided and forced earth and rock upward. Baker is a volcano, about 300,000 years old. It is still active, and on clear cool days steam clouds are sometimes seen rising from a crater near the summit.

Winter snows usually linger at Artist Point well into summer months. Stroll out the half-mile self-guided interpretive trail to learn about the natural surroundings and history of the area. A more challenging hike leads up the front face of Table Mountain to the top. Other hiking trails lead from here to the Chain lakes and Ptarmigan Ridge.

Returning along the same route affords you a second chance to enjoy the magnificent scenery and to explore sites that you missed on the way up. It's an opportunity most travelers welcome.—*Tom Barr* □

2 BLUE MOUNTAIN SCENIC BYWAY
Umatilla National Forest   Oregon

General description: A 130-mile paved route from the arid Columbia River grasslands up into the forested Blue Mountains.

Special attractions: Elk herds, North Fork John Day Wilderness, historic sites, forest views, Wild and Scenic North Fork John Day River.

Location: Northeast Oregon on the Umatilla National Forest, southwest of Pendleton. From the north, exit Interstate 84 onto Oregon Route 74 at Heppner Junction. The byway begins here and travels southeast on Oregon Routes 74 and 207/74 from Heppner Junction to Heppner, then on Forest Road 53 from Heppner to Ukiah, and on Forest Road 52 from Ukiah to North Fork John Day Campground, near the junction of Forest Roads 52 and 73.

Byway route numbers: Oregon Routes 74 and 207/74, Forest Roads 53 and 52.

Travel season: Portions of the byway are open year-round, but the sections crossing national forest lands are unplowed in winter and usually closed by winter snow from about mid-November through the end of May.

Camping: Four national forest campgrounds with picnic tables, vault toilets, and fire rings.

Services: All services in Heppner and Ukiah. Limited services in Ione and Lexington.

Far-ranging vistas mark the descent into Ukiah, on the Blue Mountain Scenic Byway.

Nearby attractions: Elkhorn Drive, Columbia River corridor, John Day Fossil Beds, Bridge Creek Wildlife Area, ski areas, state and county parks.

For more information: Umatilla National Forest, 2517 SW Hailey Ave., Pendleton, OR 97801, (503) 276-3811. District Rangers: Heppner Ranger District, P.O. Box 7, Heppner, OR 97836, (503) 676-9187; North Fork John Day Ranger District, P.O. Box 158, Ukiah, OR 97880, (503) 427-3231.

Description: The Blue Mountain Scenic Byway traverses a variety of terrain during its journey across northeast Oregon. When extended to include nearby Elkhorn Drive, the route nearly parallels Interstate 84, but it provides a more scenic, less hectic alternative for travelers. The two-lane road is paved and has frequent turnouts. Traffic is usually light, except during hunting season from Oct. 1 through Thanksgiving.

The weather in this region is generally moderate, with hotter summer temperatures up to 100 degrees in the lower elevations near the Columbia River and cooler temperatures in the mountains. Autumn and spring temperatures range from 30 to 70 degrees, while winters can dip to subzero in the mountains.

Beginning at the junction of Interstate 84 and Oregon Route 74, the byway climbs, following Willow Creek southeast through rolling grasslands and fields of wheat, potatoes, corn, and barley. The entire area is volcanic in origin, and occasional basalt outcrops are visible.

In Cecil, the byway crosses the Old Oregon Trail, which many pioneers traveled in the mid-1800s. The route then goes through Ione, Lexington, and into Heppner. Heppner has an interesting little museum with an old schoolhouse, post office, picture gallery, and other memorabilia. The picturesque county courthouse, listed on the National Register of Historic Places, was built in 1903 of locally quarried basalt. A ranger station is also

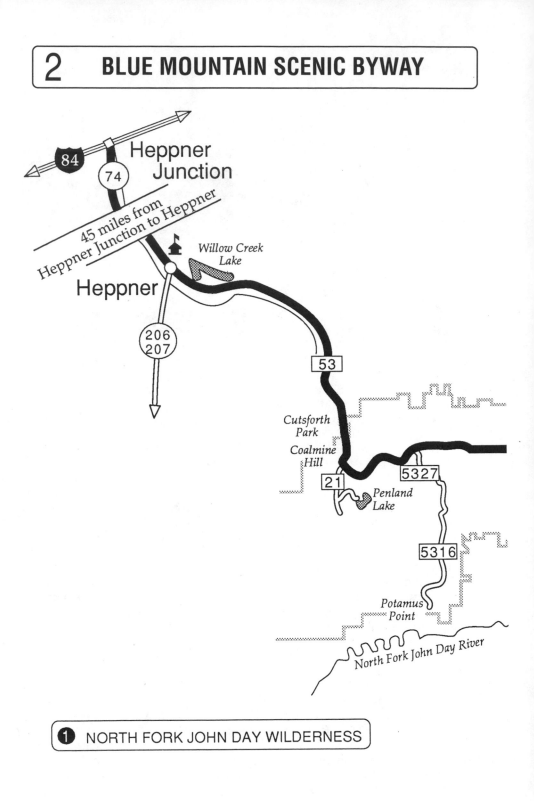

2 BLUE MOUNTAIN SCENIC BYWAY

84

74
Heppner
Junction

45 miles from Heppner Junction to Heppner

Willow Creek Lake

Heppner

206
207

53

Cutsforth Park

Coalmine Hill

21

Penland Lake

5327

5316

Potamus Point

North Fork John Day River

❶ NORTH FORK JOHN DAY WILDERNESS

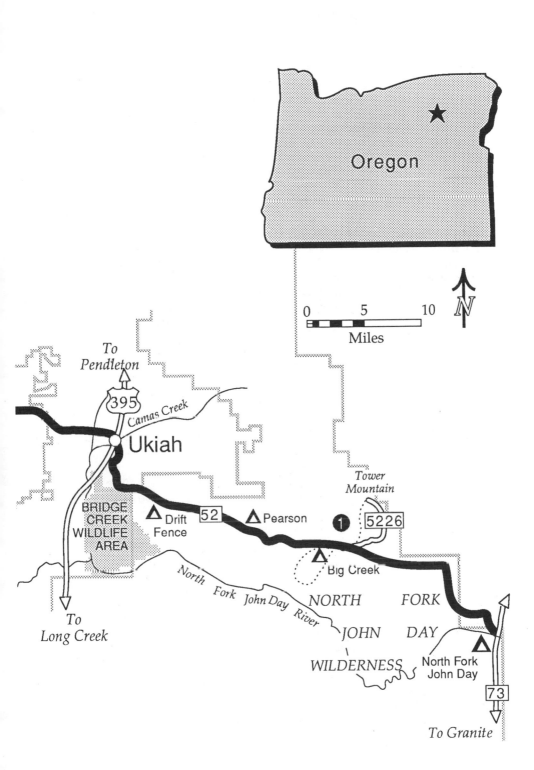

Oregon

0   5   10
Miles

N

To
Pendleton

395

Camas Creek

Ukiah

To
Long Creek

BRIDGE
CREEK
WILDLIFE
AREA

Drift
Fence

52

Pearson

1

Tower
Mountain

5226

Big Creek

North Fork John Day River

NORTH   FORK

JOHN   DAY

WILDERNESS

North Fork
John Day

73

To Granite

located in Heppner, offering information about the Umatilla National Forest and the region.

Just above Heppner on Forest Road 53, Willow Creek Dam and Lake offer boating, fishing, waterskiing, and swimming opportunities. The byway travels southeast to the national forest boundary, where you can walk downhill to Willow Creek and find relics and caved-in adits of old coal mines.

Nearby Cutsforth Park is located across from a brightly colored totem pole. This county facility has campsites, a playground, fishing, and hiking. Plowing stops between here and Ukiah, and the unplowed byway is popular with cross-country skiers and snowmobilers in winter.

The byway climbs Coalmine Hill, and a five-mile side trip on Forest Roads 21 and 2103 leads to Penland Lake for water-related recreation or picnicking at the refreshingly cool 4,000-foot elevation. Most of the shoreline is privately owned, but there is a public day-use area.

The byway travels through several miles of wet meadows with scattered stands of ponderosa pines, Douglas-firs, and grand firs. Heavy timber harvests on the Umatilla National Forest have left miles of clearcuts adjacent to, and visible from, this byway route. Wildflowers such as lupines, daisies, and Indian paintbrushes adorn the wet meadows and prairies, and it is very pleasant to walk among them and find the traces of old wagon-wheel ruts.

A 15-mile side trip south on graveled Forest Roads 5327 and 5316 brings you to Potamus Point, which overlooks Potamus Creek Canyon and the North Fork John Day River. Rock outcrops, palisades of columnar basalt, and sheer cliffs line the canyon, while the water sparkles 2,000 feet below.

The Umatilla National Forest hosts one of the largest elk herds in the United States. Spring calving grounds and winter range border this stretch of the byway. Hunting is a very popular activity in autumn. Other forest residents include mule deer, black bears, mountain lions, bobcats, coyotes, and many small mammals and birds.

The byway drops down to agricultural Ukiah, offering far-ranging vistas to the east during the descent. Ukiah has all services, as well as a ranger station. Nearby the Bridge Creek Wildlife Area is a good place to see elk in the winter, and Camas Creek has good fishing for rainbow and brook trout. The North Fork John Day River contains steelhead, salmon, and rainbow and brook trout.

The byway climbs Forest Road 52 south from Ukiah, again enters the national forest, and reaches an elevation of more than 5,000 feet. This section of the byway is also unplowed in winter. Drift Fence, Pearson, and Big Creek campgrounds each have a few sites. Big Creek is located between two sections of the North Fork John Day Wilderness. A seven-mile loop leads walkers on a moderately strenuous hike into the wilderness.

You can drive to 6,790-foot Tower Mountain Lookout via Forest Road 5226 for a good view in all directions. To the east, the peaks of the Elkhorn Mountains usually remain snow-covered until August and provide a pretty backdrop. The granitic Blue Mountains are part of an old coastal range that stood above later flows of volcanic rock. The broad valleys opened as blocks of the crust sank along fault lines. Early prospectors found a great deal of gold in the creeks of the Blue Mountains.

The byway ends at North Fork John Day Campground, which has 18 sites and drinking water. The Blue Mountain Scenic Byway connects with Elkhorn Drive at the campground. □

The Umatilla National Forest hosts one of the nation's largest elk herds. This bull elk's antlers are still in velvet. Christopher Cauble photo.

General description: A 106-mile loop to the crest of the Elkhorn Range, past historic mining territory, rivers, and lakes.

Special attractions: Narrow-gauge railroad, lakes and rivers, large elk herds, Oregon Trail Regional Museum, historic mining relics, North Fork John Day Wilderness, bright autumn foliage, alpine and cross-country skiing, museum in Haines, Bureau of Land Management Oregon Trail Interpretive Center.

Location: Northeast Oregon on the Wallowa-Whitman National Forest, west of Baker. The byway is a loop and travels Oregon Route 7 from Baker to the junction of Routes 7 and 410 (a few miles past Phillips Lake), County Road 410 to Sumpter, Forest Road 73 from Sumpter to the national forest boundary near North Powder, Baker County Road 1146 to Haines, and Oregon Route 30 back to Baker.

Byway route numbers: Oregon Route 7, County Road 410, Forest Road 73, County Road 1146, Oregon Route 30.

Travel season: Much of the loop is open year-round. The highway between Granite and Anthony Lake is closed by winter snows each year and is usually open from about mid-June to mid-November.

Camping: Eight national forest campgrounds with picnic tables, toilets, and fire grates. One campground has some hookups.

Services: All services in Baker and Sumpter. Limited services in Granite, Anthony Lakes, and Haines.

Nearby attractions: Hells Canyon National Recreation Area, Oregon Trail Monument, Wolf Creek and Pilcher Creek reservoirs, Blue Mountain Scenic Byway, and Eagle Cap, North Fork John Day, Monument Rock, and Strawberry Mountain wilderness areas.

For more information: Wallowa-Whitman National Forest, P.O. Box 907, Baker, OR 97814, (503) 523-6391; Umatilla National Forest, 2517 SW Hailey Ave., Pendleton, OR 97801, (503) 276-3811. District Ranger: Baker Ranger District, 3165 10th St., Baker City, OR 97814, (503) 523-4476.

Description: Elkhorn Drive encircles the southern portion of the Elkhorn Range in the Blue Mountains, passing through country rich in history, geology, and scenery. The paved, two-lane highway is lightly traveled and has frequent scenic and recreational turnouts. Watch for logging trucks.

Summer visitors can expect hot, dry weather, with temperatures ranging from 40 to 90. Spring and fall are mild, with temperatures ranging from 35 to 70 degrees. Winters are cold and snowy, with a temperature range of minus 10 to 37 degrees and an average snowfall of 31 inches.

This scenic byway can be entered at several places along the loop. The common starting point is Baker, a pleasant historic community situated in a broad valley on the Powder River. Mountains and hills rise in all directions, and it is easy to imagine the 1860s gold-rush activity in the area. Loggers came in the wake of the gold rush, and now Baker's primary industries are agriculture and timber harvesting. The offices of the Wallowa-Whitman National Forest and Baker Ranger District are located in Baker, and national forest and byway information is available at both.

Motorists along Elkhorn Drive enjoy views of the Blue Mountains and learn about logging and mining activities.

From Baker, travel south on Oregon Route 7 to Salisbury through low rolling hills dotted with junipers. There are scattered homes and farms, and cotton-woods line the Powder River.

The byway follows the Powder River, turns west, and continues on Route 7. The national forest boundary is approximately 13 miles from Baker. At 2.5 million acres, the Wallowa-Whitman is the largest national forest in the Pacific Northwest.

Visible from the highway are dark gray outcrops of the Miocene basaltic lava that covers much of the southern Elkhorns. Under the lava, the Elkhorn Range has a granitic core covered by sedimentary rocks of platy argillite and limestone layers. Glaciation and erosion sculpted the peaks and valleys. Many of the rock exposures show interesting folds, faults, and distortions.

Phillips Reservoir is a few miles west of the national forest boundary. This delightful man-made lake is set in the wooded hills at an elevation of 4,100 feet. The full moon reflects brightly across its quiet, sheltered surface. There is a boat launch, picnicking, fishing, and swimming in the refreshing water. Union Creek Campground has 58 sites in the ponderosa pines along the lake, restrooms with running water, a fish-cleaning station, and a trailer dumping station. Twenty-four sites have sewer, water, and electrical hookups.

Mason Dam is 167 feet high, and you can drive across its top and picnic nearby. Phillips Reservoir contains rainbow trout, coho salmon, and bass. Shoreline Trail leads along the shore of the lake for a gentle walk through riparian, lakeside vegetation. In spring, a pair of ospreys nest on a platform at the southwest end of the lake. There are two campgrounds on the south shore: Southwest Shore has 20 sites, and Miller Lane has six tent sites.

The Sumpter Valley Railroad is a restored narrow-gauge steam train museum that leaves from the depot at the head of Phillips Reservoir for a seven-mile

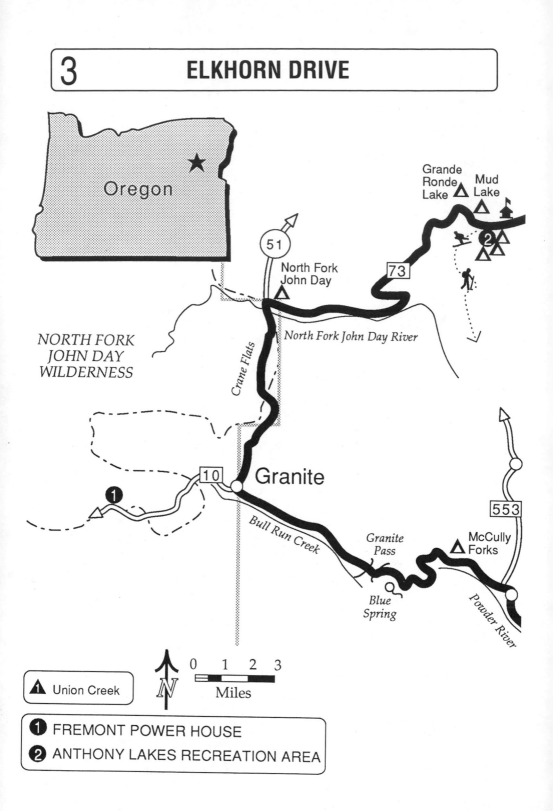

ELKHORN DRIVE

Oregon

Grande
Ronde
Lake Mud
Lake

51

North Fork
John Day

73

NORTH FORK
JOHN DAY
WILDERNESS

North Fork John Day River

Crane Flats

10 Granite

Bull Run Creek

Granite
Pass

Blue
Spring

McCully
Forks

553

Powder River

0 1 2 3
Miles
N

▲ Union Creek

❶ FREMONT POWER HOUSE
❷ ANTHONY LAKES RECREATION AREA

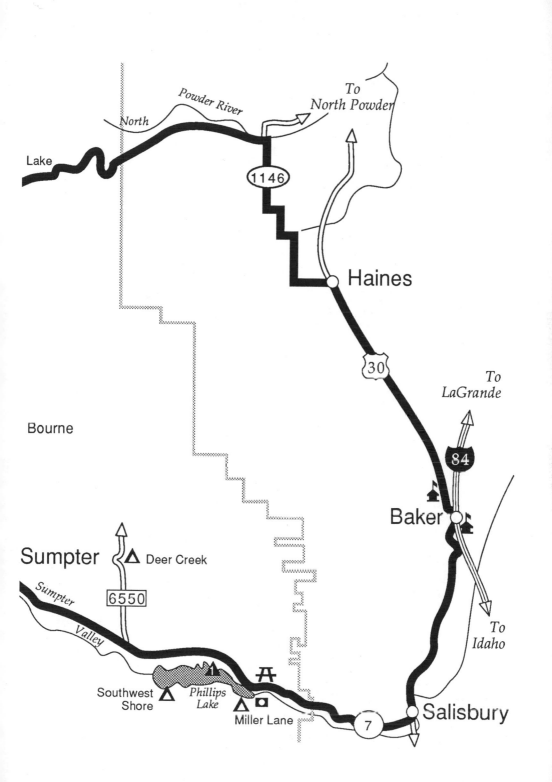

run through the gold dredge tailings and wildlife-rich Sumpter Valley. The train operates from Memorial Day weekend through the last week of September, with four runs a day plus an occasional moonlight ride. Visitors to the depot can picnic and go on nature walks through the wildlife area.

Deer Creek Campground and Picnic Area is about three miles off the byway, north on Forest Road 6550. There are six campsites in the ponderosa pines, and views extend north across the Sumpter Valley. This area of the national forest was and still is heavily logged, and there are active mining claims. Placer gold is present in Deer Creek. Unlike today's logging with motorized skidders, bulldozers, and trucks, early logging was done by hand. Logs were loaded onto horse-drawn wagons and brought to the Sumpter Valley Railroad for transportation to the mills in Baker.

Sumpter once was a booming mining town. Its population was 3,500 at the turn of the century, but now it is down to about 130 residents. You will find all services here, although availability is limited. An old dredge weighing 2.4 million pounds stands outside the town. Gold was found in significant quantities here, and piles of rock tailings are testimony to the dredging operations used in the Powder River and Sumpter Valley. Hard-rock mining was even more lucrative in the 1900s.

A side trip north on County Road 553 leads about seven miles to the ghost town of Bourne. Most of the buildings have been removed or destroyed, but some remain in the pretty forest setting. A handful of summer residents maintains homes here.

The byway travels west through ponderosa pines, Douglas-firs, and western larches. Views of the Elkhorn Range are extensive. McCully Forks Campground, elevation 4,600 feet, has seven sites. A few miles farther is Blue Spring, a winter snowmobile park. There are some interesting roadcuts near here. The red rocks are volcanic scorias or iron-stained quartz-rich argillites. The white rocks are highly weathered and eroded granodiorite. The rocks in this area are a chaotic assemblage of different compositions and ages.

Granite Pass sits at an elevation of 5,864 feet. The convoluted red rock visible below Granite Peak is volcanic rock called tuff or scoria. The byway descends for 10 miles along an old stagecoach route by Bull Run Creek to the townsite of Granite. There is a small store at the base of the hill there; it has a snack bar and gasoline pumps.

On July 4, 1862, miners struck gold in Bull Run Creek. The town of Granite sprang up, and a considerable amount of mining occurred for the next 80 years. Now the town has few residents and is mostly composed of abandoned homes and mine structures. It is interesting to walk around and view the old dance hall, drugstore, meat market, and more. Most buildings are locked, but you can get a satisfying look inside through the windows. The old schoolhouse is now the town hall, and the rope to ring the big bell dangles invitingly out front.

A side trip on Forest Road 10, across from the Granite store, leads five miles west on a gravel road to the old Fremont Power Plant. This historic building, built of andesite blocks, generated electricity for the town of Granite and most of the major mines in operation at the turn of the century. Outside is a section of the old wooden flume used to bring water eight miles from Olive Lake to the generators. If a staff person for the youth camp is around, ask to see inside the plant. You can view the inside workings of an early power plant, including the patented 1892 Westinghouse transformers and the instrument panel imbedded in a giant marble slab. A huge crack outlines the piece of the south wall that workers had to remove in order to bring the large machinery inside.

The byway turns north near Granite onto Forest Road 73. In the stream bottoms, you can see rock walls made by early Chinese gold miners. The route travels through long, grassy meadows and forested slopes.

Watch for mule deer and elk in the meadows along the way. Crane Flats is especially rich with wildlife. The Wallowa-Whitman National Forest hosts bald and golden eagles, egrets, sandhill cranes, kingfishers, great blue herons, and many species of hawks and waterfowl.

The byway crosses the North Fork John Day River and turns east, continuing on Forest Road 73. Early hydraulic gold mining is evident on the hillsides west of the bridge. The North Fork John Day Wilderness, visible on the east and west sides of the highway, encompasses a total of 122,296 acres. The wilderness protects the pristine headwaters of the river and its important anadromous fish runs, along with old-growth timber stands, big game, and many lakes and trails. The river canyon is accessible from the North Fork John Day Campground via Trail 3022. North Fork John Day Campground has nine sites adjacent to the road and along the river. The campground is the eastern terminus of the adjacent Blue Mountain Scenic Byway.

Clearcuts and logging activity border Elkhorn Drive as it travels east to Anthony Lakes Recreation Area. There are broad views of the forested Elkhorn Range, and the damage done by pine bettles and various fires is evident from Elkhorn Summit, at an elevation of 7,392 feet the highest point on the byway.

Anthony Lakes Recreation Area has three campgrounds with a total of 53 sites. There are also several picnic areas, two boat-launch areas, a Forest Service station, and a ski area. Gunsight Mountain, elevation 8,775 feet, is distinctive for its white rock and the tall, straight alpine firs and lodgepole pines on its slopes. Nearby Anthony Lakes Ski Area was established in 1938. A chairlift and lodge were added in the 1960s. The area features a day-use lodge, restaurant, ski rentals and school, and lounge, all open in winter.

A moderately easy half-mile footpath leads from the south side of Anthony Lake to Hoffer lakes. Alpine glaciation and plant communities are interpreted along the trail, and the lakes are very peaceful. Marsh marigolds, buttercups, wild strawberries, and shooting stars line the shores, while fish rise in the middle. There are logs to clamber over, dams and pools to investigate, and rocks to climb. The trailhead for the 23-mile Elkhorn Crest National Recreation Trail is located at the parking lot east of Anthony Lake Campground.

The byway descends through open forest and grassy ground cover. Vistas extend east over the Powder River Valley to the Eagle Cap Wilderness and south to include 8,897-foot Twin Mountain.

The byway emerges from national forest land and the Elkhorn Wildlife Management Area and crosses private agricultural land on County Road 1146 to Haines. From Haines, the route continues south on Oregon Route 30 and travels down the flat, broad agricultural river valley to Baker. En route, you are just south of the 45th Parallel, the halfway point between the North Pole and the equator. □

General description: A 93-mile highway through the alpine lakes and mountains of the Cascade Range.

Special attractions: Rugged mountains, alpine lakes, hiking, skiing, camping, Three Sisters Wilderness Area, Lava Butte Geological Area.

Location: West-central Oregon on the Deschutes National Forest, west of Bend. The byway travels Oregon Route 46 from the national forest boundary west of Bend to the junction of Routes 46 and 58, and it travels Oregon Route 42 from the junction of Routes 46 and 42 to Sunriver.

Byway route numbers: Oregon Routes 46 and 42.

Travel season: The byway between Bend and Mount Bachelor Ski Area is open year-round. The remaining miles of scenic byway are closed each winter by snow but are open most summers from early June until Thanksgiving.

Camping: Twenty-five national forest campgrounds with toilets, fire grates, and picnic tables. Most have drinking water. Additional national forest and private campgrounds located within a short drive of the byway.

Services: All services in Bend. Limited services of gas, food, and lodging scattered along the byway.

Nearby attractions: High Desert Museum, Lava River Cave, Newberry Crater, Lava Lands, Lava Cast Forest, Deschutes River, Crater Lake National Park.

For more information: Deschutes National Forest, 1645 Highway 20 E., Bend, OR 97701, (503) 388-2715. District Rangers: Bend Ranger District, 1230 NE Third St., Red Oaks Square, Bend, OR 97701, (503) 388-5664; Crescent Ranger District, Crescent, OR 97707, (503) 433-2234.

Description: Set in the heart of the towering Cascade Range, the scenic byway traverses the mountains past alpine lakes, forests, and wilderness areas. The two-lane highway is paved and has numerous turnouts for scenic and recreational opportunities. Traffic can be heavy on holidays and weekends, but there is little congestion unless a special event is being held. The byway is also a popular bicycle route.

Summer visitors can expect blue skies and warm days. Daytime temperatures from June through September average 60 to 80 degrees; evenings are cooler. Winter daytime temperatures average between 20 and 40 degrees, and snow accumulation at higher elevations is considerable. Nighttime temperatures are much colder.

The scenic byway begins at the national forest boundary just outside of Bend. This city is situated on the high desert plateau of central Oregon and enjoys 250 days of sunshine a year. The natural beauty of the Cascades forms a fitting backdrop to this delightful community, which revolves around the seasonal recreation opportunities that bring tourists.

Access to the byway through Bend goes alongside the Deschutes River and Drake Park, a popular spot for residents and visitors. There is a playground, a picnic area, waterfowl to watch and feed, and room to run. Outside the city limits, the route passes Meadow Picnic Area and begins to climb.

The Cascade Range is volcanic in origin, sculpted by glaciers and erosion.

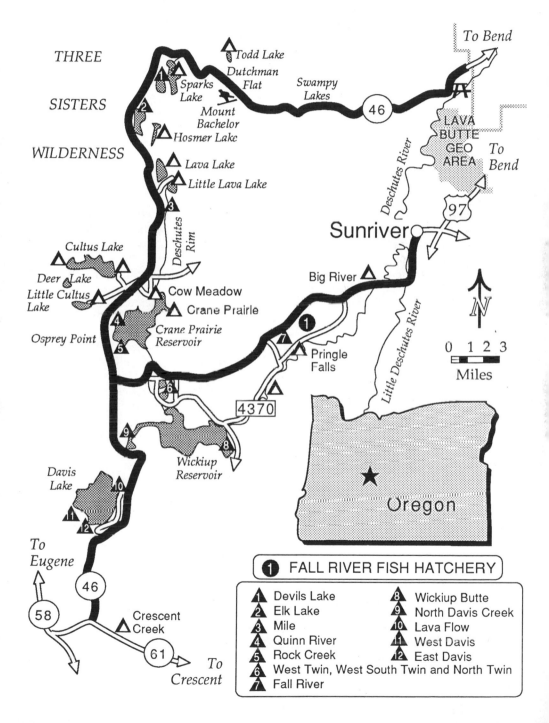

THREE

SISTERS

WILDERNESS

Todd Lake

Dutchman Flat

Sparks Lake

Mount Bachelor

Hosmer Lake

Lava Lake

Little Lava Lake

Deschutes Rim

Cultus Lake

Deer Lake

Little Cultus Lake

Osprey Point

Cow Meadow

Crane Prairie

Crane Prairie Reservoir

Swampy Lakes

46

To Bend

LAVA BUTTE GEO AREA

To Bend

Deschutes River

97

Sunriver

Big River

Little Deschutes River

N

0 1 2 3
Miles

Fall River

Pringle Falls

4370

Wickiup Reservoir

Davis Lake

To Eugene

46

58

Crescent Creek

61

To Crescent

★

Oregon

1   FALL RIVER FISH HATCHERY

1	Devils Lake	8	Wickiup Butte
2	Elk Lake	9	North Davis Creek
3	Mile	10	Lava Flow
4	Quinn River	11	West Davis
5	Rock Creek	12	East Davis
6	West Twin, West South Twin and North Twin		
7	Fall River		

Mount Bachelor probably formed about 14,000 years ago, when an 18-mile-long crack in the earth opened and lava spewed out. Evidence of flows is evident all along the byway, and many of the Cascade lakes were formed when volcanic flows dammed and diverted rivers, leaving water-filled basins. Sparks, Elk, and Lava lakes are examples of basins, while South and North Twin lakes are volcanic mars, or craters that filled with water.

On the byway, the first stunning closeups of Mount Bachelor come into view about 14 miles from Bend. There are a number of snowmobile trails in this area. Another mile leads to Swampy Lakes, elevation 5,600 feet, a recreation area featuring two- to 10-mile hiking, mountain biking, and cross-country ski trails.

Mount Bachelor Ski and Summer Resort features lodges, restaurants, shops, a nordic center, and nine chairlifts. The summit lift reaches the 9,065-foot top of Bachelor and is open Memorial Day through Labor Day for summer visitors, as well as during the ski season. The 360-degree view of the Cascades is absolutely splendid.

Dutchman Flat, across the byway from the ski area, is a desolate area with very little vegetation. Just a few miles away, however, Todd Lake is a photographer's paradise. Wildflowers such as elephant heads, columbines, penstemons, Indian paintbrushes, larkspurs, lupines, heathers, and phlox bloom here and elsewhere along the byway, and the secluded, pristine lake and snowcapped peaks are gorgeous. Todd Lake offers tent camping in its four forested sites away from the highway. It is a pleasant place to fish, swim, picnic, or simply walk around, but you will need your mosquito repellant.

Scientific investigations have revealed artifacts dating from before the eruption of Mount Mazama, indicating that humans were in the Cascades more than 8,000 years ago. Archaeologists are reasonably certain that a number of the campgrounds in use today were used as hunting camps thousands of years ago. Think about that while backing a trailer into a paved site!

Continuing west on the byway, you will pass Soda Creek Campground, which has 12 sites, fishing, and hiking. Sparks Lake Road winds nearly two miles through a lava flow and forest. The flow invites clambering around to explore the lava. Sparks Lake is stunning. The lake shimmers against the forested hills and snowcapped peaks. Tiny islands with grasses and a few subalpine firs offer secluded hideaways to boaters. Fishing is good, and you can also hike, swim, and picnic.

About 1.5 miles from Soda Creek Campground, pull off on the north side of the road near the large dacite flow from Devil's Hill. Indians painted a pictograph on a rock here, possibly 500 years ago. The pigment is red ochre mixed with animal fat. Continue walking east along the edge of the flow and look carefully for more pictographs. They may mark an ancient travel route or perhaps warn of impending danger. Nearby is a beautiful marshy area known as Devil's Garden, with an abundance of wildflowers, mosquitoes, and a small spring.

Devils Lake Campground has six tent sites, horse facilities, trails, and a tiny lake good for canoeing and fishing. Devils Lake is unusually clear, and the water appears emerald green.

The byway turns south and reaches Elk Lake, which attracts sailboarders and sailboaters to its breezy surface. A resort there features a restaurant, store, gasoline, boat rentals, and lodging. Winter visitors get here on snowmobiles

Trout fishing and boating are popular pastimes on the many lakes along the Cascade Lakes Highway.

or cross-country skis. A mostly gravel road circles the lake and gives access to 100 sites in several campgrounds, as well as picnic areas, viewpoints, and hiking trails. Elk Lake is surrounded by a thick forest of lodgepole pines, true firs, and mountain hemlocks, and Mount Bachelor and the South Sister rise majestically in the background.

Just east of Elk Lake, Hosmer Lake is stocked with Atlantic salmon for catch-and-release fishing. The lakes along the Cascade Lakes Highway are stocked with rainbow and brown trout and kokanee salmon. Fishing is a favorite recreational pastime because of the abundance of fish, the temperate climate, and the outstanding scenery.

West of the byway is Three Sisters Wilderness, a 200,000-acre wonderland of mountains, forest, glaciers, and wildlife. Numerous trails lead from the byway into the wilderness. Be sure to watch for mule deer, pine martens, yellow-bellied marmots, porcupines, black bears, and golden-mantled ground squirrels. Bald eagles soar overhead, as do ospreys and several other species of hawks.

Lava Lake has a resort with boat rentals, store, gasoline, and RV park. The picturesque lake is rimmed by tall reeds, a grassy picnic area, and 44 campsites. Nearby Little Lava Lake, with 10 campsites, is the headwaters of the Deschutes River, which flows south, east, and north before finally emptying into the Columbia to flow west to the Pacific Ocean. Mile Camp offers eight campsites.

The byway runs through a corridor of white and lodgepole pines, spruces, white firs, and mountain hemlocks to the Cultus Lake turnoff. The lake resort has groceries, store, boat rentals, and lodging. Cultus Lake and West Cultus campgrounds have a total of 69 sites, and the lake is warm enough for swimming in the summer. Little Cultus Lake, on the other side of Cultus Mountain, is less developed and has 10 campsites.

Crane Prairie and Crane Prairie Reservoir are a naturalist's delight. The 3,850-acre man-made lake offers fine fishing, and the shallow depths invite numerous species of birds and mammals to live nearby. Large snags in the water are used as perches by raptors, and the peaceful Osprey Observation Point is a fairly close location from which to watch eagles, ospreys, great blue herons, and double-crested cormorants. There are also Canada geese, several species of ducks, river otters, sandhill cranes, and occasional great egrets. You can bring a chair or perch on a log at water's edge. Electric-blue dragonflies buzz overhead, alighting on the tall grasses or even on your arm. Elegant cat's ears and Indian paintbrushes are just two of the many wildflowers. It is not unusual to see aerial acrobatics as an eagle tries to snatch a fish from a smaller osprey. Wildlife naturalists counted between 15 and 20 pairs of nesting ospreys here in the early 1960s. Now Crane Prairie houses one of the largest osprey populations in the world, with more than 100 nesting pairs. One Forest Service naturalist sat on Crane Prairie and counted more than 30 different species of songbirds in one afternoon.

Cow Meadow, Quinn River, and Rock Creek campgrounds are located on the west side of the reservoir, providing a total of 93 campsites. Quinn River features interpreted historical sites. On the east side of the reservoir, Crane Prairie Campground has 147 sites, several of which are barrier-free. There are boat launches, picnic tables, modern restrooms, and fish-cleaning stations.

Just south of Crane Prairie Reservoir, the road branches. Oregon Route 46 continues south to its junction with Oregon Route 58, while Oregon Route 42 turns northeast to Sunriver.

The route to Sunriver passes a side road leading to the Twin lakes and Wickiup Reservoir. The Twin lakes are surrounded by magnificent old-growth ponderosa pines. South Twin Campground has 21 sites and a fine swimming beach. West South Twin Campground has 24 sites. The private resort has lodging, restaurant, store, boat rentals, and laundry facilities available. North Twin Campground has 10 tent sites. Fishing is good in both lakes, and you may be lucky enough to see a few young anglers strutting about with a full string of trout slung between them.

Wickiup Reservoir is shallow, big, and open, with buttes and mountains enclosing the lower end. Here, you can fish, picnic, waterski, hike, and camp.

The byway descends through logged areas and experimental forest. Fall River Campground has 10 sites and good fly fishing nearby. A few miles farther is the Fall River Fish Hatchery. Visitors are welcome to walk around and see rainbow trout in all stages of growth, from fingerlings to big lunkers.

Big River Campground has 15 sites right on the Deschutes River. This is a popular put-in point for floaters. The byway then emerges onto mostly private land, crosses the Little Deschutes River, and ends in Sunriver. This town has a hands-on nature center that is excellent, especially for children. Follow the signs through a labryinth of streets to find the center and its small botanical garden at the far end of the resort community.

To complete the scenic byway tour, travel Oregon Route 46 and enjoy the views of the peaks from this direction. Turn south at the junction with Route 46. North Davis Creek has picnicking and 17 campsites. The route crosses an old lava flow, and birdwatching is very good at Lava Flow Campground.

West Davis Campground has 25 sites, while East Davis has 33 sites and a picnic area. Davis Lake is noted for good fishing. An early volcanic flow blocked the northeast corner of the lake, and naturalists are unable to discern where the water goes.

The remainder of the byway travels through a pleasant corridor of mixed conifers on rolling foothills. The byway ends at the junction of Oregon Routes 46 and 58. Traveler services are available in nearby communities. □

5 McKENZIE—SANTIAM PASS LOOP
Deschutes and Willamette National Forests   Oregon

General description: An 81.5-mile loop through the center of the Cascade Range, over two mountain passes, through lava flows and forests, and along rivers.

Special attractions: Volcanic features and lava flows; rivers and lakes; extensive vistas; Three Sisters, Mount Jefferson, and Mount Washington wilderness areas; Pacific Crest National Scenic Trail; developed and undeveloped hot springs; waterfalls.

Location: West-central Oregon on the Deschutes and Willamette national forests, west of Sisters. The byway is a loop and travels Oregon Route 126 from McKenzie Bridge to Sisters (U.S. Highway 20/Oregon Route 126 from the junction of 20 and 126 to Sisters), and Oregon Route 242 from Sisters to McKenzie Bridge.

Byway route numbers: Oregon Route 126, U.S. Highway 20, Oregon Route 242.

Travel season: Year-round on 126 and 20/126 between McKenzie Bridge and Sisters. Most of Oregon Route 242 closed by winter snows from about November until early July. When open, the steep gradient and sharp curves make it unsuitable for towed units or vehicles more than 22 feet long.

Camping: Fifteen national forest campgrounds with toilets, picnic tables, and fire rings. No hookups. Some campgrounds have drinking water.

Services: All services in Sisters and McKenzie Bridge. Lodging at Belknap Springs. Lodging, boat rental, and food at Clear Lake, Blue Lake, and Suttle Lake resorts. Suttle also has gasoline.

Nearby attractions: Cascade Lakes Highway and Robert Aufderheide Memorial Drive, numerous state parks, additional Cascade peaks, Crooked River National Grassland.

For more information: Deschutes National Forest, 1645 Highway 20 E., Bend, OR 97701, (503) 388-2715; Willamette National Forest, 211 E. Seventh Ave., P.O. Box 10607, Eugene, OR 97440, (503) 687-6521. District Rangers: Sisters Ranger District, P.O. Box 249, Sisters, OR 97759, (503) 549-2111; McKenzie Ranger District, State Highway 126, McKenzie, OR 97413, (503) 822-3381.

Description: The scenic byway travels through some of Oregon's most beautiful and varied mountain landscapes. The two-lane highways are paved and have frequent turnouts. One stretch of Oregon Route 242 is quite narrow and has very tight corners; it is unsuitable for towed units or large vehicles more than 22 feet in length. Traffic on the scenic byway varies with the seasons, and summer weekends and holidays are generally quite busy.

There is no real scenic difference when planning which direction to travel the loop. But you may want to think about keeping the sun out of your eyes and plan accordingly.

Expect variable mountain weather. Elevations range from about 1,600 feet to more than 5,300 feet. Summer temperatures average between 65 and 80 degrees, while spring and autumn range from the 30s to the 50s and 60s. Winter brings snow, with daytime temperatures in the 30s and 40s and nightime lows to 20. Early summer and midwinter are generally the wettest periods, but snow seldom accumulates at the lower elevations.

Begin the scenic byway loop in Sisters, a lively little community with an Old West theme. There are plenty of shops, and the annual rodeo in mid-June is renowned for its action.

Traveling west from Sisters on Oregon Route 242, the route passes pretty agricultural land and fields of throughbreds, cattle, and llamas. Central Oregon has a large population of llamas; they are popular as pack animals in the wilderness.

Lava Camp Lake offers nine campsites. A few miles west of Sisters is Cold Spring Campground, with 23 sites and a picnic area. A side road two miles farther leads to Whispering Pine Campground, situated on Trout Creek. The byway climbs through a forest of large ponderosa pines, and views of the Three Sisters are a continual delight.

Windy Point, elevation 4,909 feet, looks over an enormous lava flow and snow-covered Mount Washington. The Mount Washington Wilderness is adjacent to the byway here. It encompasses 52,316 acres of volcanic features and several picturesque lakes. Look closely at the apparently barren landscape from Windy Point and find the occasional shrub or tree that has found a hold on life in this harsh environment.

A few miles west is McKenzie Pass, elevation 5,321 feet, and Dee Wright Observatory. The 360-degree panorama includes 11,245-foot Mount Hood, 10,497-foot Mount Jefferson, 10,085-foot North Sister, and 10,047-foot Middle Sister. The adjacent lava flow covers 65 square miles and is about 2,700 years old. The Three Sisters Wilderness extends south of the road and is classified as a World Biosphere Reserve. Its 285,202 acres include spectacular old-growth Douglas-firs at lower elevations and numerous active glaciers on the Sisters themselves.

The Pacific Crest Trail crosses the byway at McKenzie Pass, and you may wish to hike some distance on this famous path. The short, interpretive Lava River Trail begins at the observatory and meanders through many volcanic features of the lava flow, such as cracks and chutes.

The Cascades are a chain of volcanoes extending from northern Washington's Mount Baker to California's Lassen Peak. Volcanism and glaciation created the landscape seen today. While most of the volcanoes are dormant, or dead, the Cascade Range still has active volcanoes that could erupt again.

The byway descends southwest from McKenzie Pass, crossing the old McKenzie, Salt River and Deschutes wagon route. Tiny lakes dot the roadside, and the campground at Scott Lake has 11 walk-in sites and several good footpaths nearby. Scott Lake is the subject of many a calendar picture hanging on walls across the nation. The old Scott Wagon Road passes through here, and a trail leads to nearby 6,116-foot Scott Mountain. Other trails of varying length and difficulty also lead into the Mount Washington Wilderness.

The byway descends Deadhorse Grade, a stretch of narrow highway with extremely sharp turns and a steep gradient. Several turnouts and a picnic area give you a chance to relax and enjoy the scenery, and in July tall plumes of bear grass adorn the roadside and forest glades. The route brings to mind travel in the 1930s, when the pace was slow and highway engineering was in its infancy. This is a designated Oregon Historic Highway.

At the bottom of Deadhorse Grade, Camp White Branch has a tubing hill open to the public in winter months. The byway follows White Branch and Lost creeks to Limberlost Campground, elevation 1,600 feet, which has 13 sites in a lovely forest setting. Just beyond the campground, the byway turns north onto Oregon Route 126. Travelers needing services should go on into nearby McKenzie Bridge before starting north on 126. Paradise Campground has 66 sites in the forest.

Belknap Springs is a resort with two developed hot-springs pools, cabins, and a campground with full hookups. The lodge is right on the McKenzie River, in an attractive forest setting. The McKenzie River National Recreation Trail begins near here and travels 27 miles along the west side of the river. There are 11 access points to the trail from the byway. Several undeveloped hot springs are scattered along the route and provide a delightful soak and rest from hiking.

The byway goes north through a corridor of old-growth Douglas-firs mixed with mountain hemlocks, madrones, redcedars, and dogwoods. Vine maples, oregon grapes, salal, huckleberries, and rhododendrons form a thick understory. Foliage colors are spectacular in autumn.

The byway follows the McKenzie River, popular for fishing and rafting. The river originates in the high country between the Mount Jefferson and Mount Washington wildernesses, and the McKenzie eventually empties into the Willamette River. The McKenzie River is nationally known for its native rainbow trout, locally called redsides.

Olallie Campground has 19 sites situated in the trees. This is a popular point for whitewater rafters to enter the river. A short distance farther, Trail Bridge has 37 campsites, picnicking, fishing, and a boat launch. There is excellent fishing for rainbows and an occasional bull trout of enormous size. A side trip on Forest Road 730 leads to Smith Reservoir, with more camping, fishing, and boating.

The byway then crosses a lava flow and enters a popular recreation area. Beaver Marsh is an excellent place to watch for ospreys, Steller's jays, and numerous small birds.

Koosah Falls bursts out of the forest and spills 70 feet over a basalt ledge. The ground shakes underfoot from the power of the falls. Frothy white Sahalie Falls pours over a 100-foot lava dam and then cascades another 40 feet downward. The adjacent vegetation is a soft, cushiony tangle of mosses, grasses, and bushes glowing a verdant green under the large hemlock and spruce trees. Visitors will enjoy snacking on the many edible berries that grow here.

Ice Cap Campground has 22 sites on Carmen Reservoir. The McKenzie River

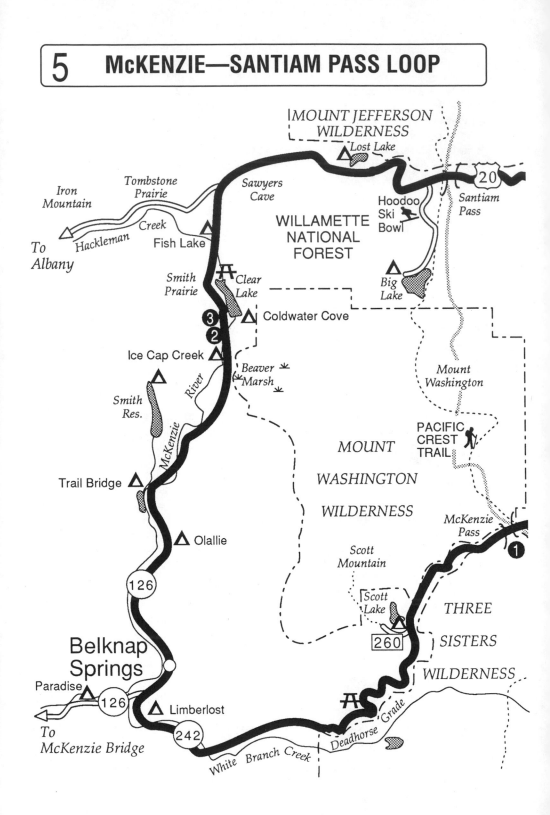

MOUNT JEFFERSON
WILDERNESS

Lost Lake

Iron
Mountain

Tombstone
Prairie

Sawyers
Cave

20

Santiam
Pass

Hoodoo
Ski
Bowl

WILLAMETTE
NATIONAL
FOREST

Creek

Hackleman

Fish Lake

To
Albany

Smith
Prairie

Clear
Lake

Big
Lake

3

Coldwater Cove

2

Ice Cap Creek

Beaver
Marsh

River

Mount
Washington

Smith
Res.

McKenzie

PACIFIC
CREST
TRAIL

MOUNT

Trail Bridge

WASHINGTON

Olallie

WILDERNESS

McKenzie
Pass

Scott
Mountain

1

126

Scott
Lake

THREE

260

Belknap
Springs

SISTERS

Paradise

126

WILDERNESS

Limberlost

To
McKenzie Bridge

242

Deadhorse Grade

White Branch Creek

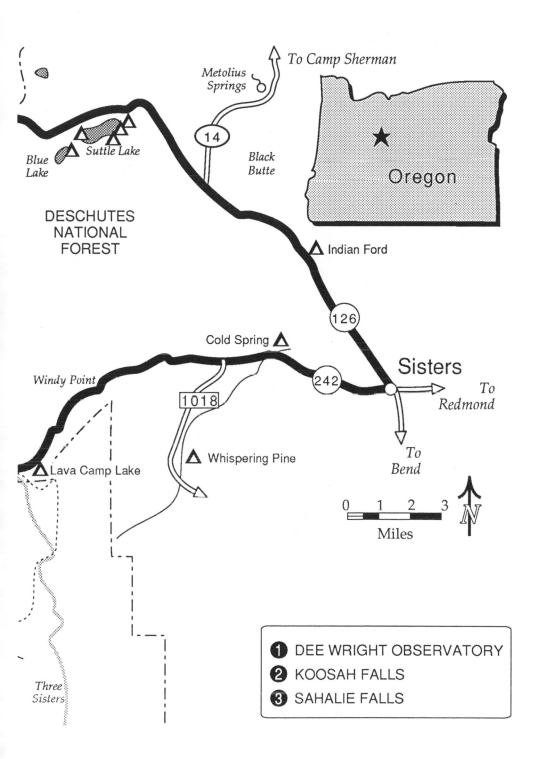

To Camp Sherman

Metolius
Springs

14

Black
Butte

Oregon

Blue
Lake

Suttle Lake

DESCHUTES
NATIONAL
FOREST

Indian Ford

126

Cold Spring

Sisters

Windy Point

242

To
Redmond

1018

Lava Camp Lake

Whispering Pine

To
Bend

0   1   2   3
Miles

N

Three
Sisters

❶ DEE WRIGHT OBSERVATORY
❷ KOOSAH FALLS
❸ SAHALIE FALLS

is diverted underground from here to Smith Reservoir and then into Trail Bridge Reservoir. Nearby Tamalitch Valley is a fascinating area. The McKenzie River disappears completely into the porous lava, and there are lava tubes, trenches, and tree casts.

Coldwater Cove Campground on Clear Lake has 35 sites on a hill above the lake. True to its name, Clear Lake has extraordinarily clear water, and boaters can look down in the deep waters at the north end and see 2,950-year-old trees still standing upright, drowned when the lava flow dammed the springs and created the lake. Clear Lake is the headwaters of the McKenzie River. A trail circles the lake and provides a lovely 4.5-mile walk on a path strewn with fir and hemlock needles, through the old-growth Douglas-fir forest, across a lava flow, and past Great Springs, the source of the lake. The lake temperature is a fairly constant 43 degrees, with the spring averaging in the high 30s. The peaceful lake is varying shades of transparent green, and the surface is usually dotted with the bright-colored clothes worn by anglers out in rowboats. The resort at the north end of the lake has lodging, food, rowboat rental, and a small store. There is also a national forest picnic area on the lake.

A few miles north, Fish Lake Campground, elevation 3,200 feet, has five sites. In spring there are lots of Canada geese, and in summer ospreys and bald eagles inhabit the area. Fish Lake dries up each summer, and its trout migrate up the creek. This isolation has created a hybrid fish named the Hackleman Creek trout.

The byway continues to climb through a lava flow, and you can escape the summer heat by walking into Sawyer's Cave, an interesting remnant of a lava tube.

The byway then turns east to its junction with U.S. Highway 20. A short side trip west on 20 leads to Tombstone Prairie. The wildflowers on the prairie and on Iron Mountain are unparalleled, particularly in July and August. More than 200 species of flowers have been identified. Hikers can walk up through knee-deep blossoms to the Iron Mountain Lookout, a strenuous but worthwhile climb.

Back on the byway, a major forest fire opened up extensive views of the Cascade peaks and jagged buttes. Continue on 126/20 east up Santiam Pass. En route, Lost Lake Campground has 14 sites and fishing for brook trout. This whole stretch of highway is a popular winter recreation area, with cross-country ski and snowmobile trails and Hoodoo Ski Bowl alpine ski area. Summer recreationists find hiking trails, and camping, waterskiing, and fishing at Big Lake on the crest of the Cascades.

Blacktail and mule deer and elk inhabit the byway area, as well as black bears, coyotes, and many small mammals and birds.

After crossing Santiam Pass, elevation 4,817 feet, you have views of Mount Washington, the Three Sisters, and the surrounding forests. Beaver ponds dot the foreground, and there are plenty of pullouts along the highway.

Footpaths lead into the wildernesses on either side of the byway, and tiny lakes dot the area. Permits are required for the wildernesses accessible from the byway and are available at the offices listed on page 23. Forest Road 2070 leads to rainbow- and brook-trout-filled Suttle Lake and Blue Lake, with picnic areas, campgrounds, and resorts. Suttle Lake is geared for the motorboater, while smaller Blue Lake is quieter. Blue Lake fills a volcanic crater, and the resort has a small store and horses for rent.

The McKenzie-Santiam Pass Loop cuts through the heart of a lava field. Visitors can walk on an interpretive trail through the ancient flow.

A side trip on County Road 14 leads north through an open ponderosa pine forest to Metolius Springs, Camp Sherman, and numerous Forest Service campgrounds. The springs are the headwaters of the Metolius River, and you can see water bubble out of the ground and flow through a meadow of wildflowers toward snowcapped Mount Jefferson. Camp Sherman, a few miles farther, has a lodge, gas, food, and store. The bridge there overlooks some huge fish not shy about wanting to be fed. Fish pellet dispensers make this easy.

The byway descends past prominent Black Butte, through an evergreen forest of ponderosa pines. Indian Ford Campground has 25 sites. A few more miles bring you back to Sisters, completing the scenic byway loop. □

6 ROBERT AUFDERHEIDE MEMORIAL DRIVE
Willamette National Forest   Oregon

General description: A 70-mile highway alongside cascading streams and through lush forests.

Special attractions: Old-growth forest, Cougar Reservoir, Wild and Scenic North Fork of the Middle Fork Willamette River, Waldo Lake and Three Sisters wilderness areas, colorful autumn foliage, horse and foot trails, camping.

Location: West-central Oregon on the Willamette National Forest, east of Eugene. The byway begins north of Oakridge and follows Robert Aufderheide Memorial Drive (Forest Road 19) from the community of Westfir north to the junction of 19 and Oregon Route 126.

Byway route number: Forest Road 19.

Travel season: The byway is generally open from May until the end of October, and then it is closed by winter snows.

Camping: Nine national forest campgrounds with toilets, drinking water, picnic tables, and fire grates. Also numerous scattered undeveloped sites.

Services: No services on the byway. All services in nearby Oakridge, Blue River, and McKenzie Bridge.

Nearby attractions: McKenzie Pass-Santiam Pass Loop and Cascade Lakes Highway; Crater Lake National Park; numerous Cascade peaks; and Diamond Peak, Waldo Lake Wilderness, and Three Sisters Wilderness.

For more information: Willamette National Forest, 211 E. Seventh Ave., P.O. Box 10607, Eugene, OR 97440, (503) 687-6521. District Rangers: Oakridge Ranger District, 46375 Highway 58, Westfir, OR 97492, (503) 782-2291; Blue River Ranger District, P.O. Box 199, Blue River, OR 97413, (503) 822-3317.

Description: Robert Aufderheide Memorial Drive travels north from Westfir along the North Fork of the Middle Fork Willamette River, crosses a small pass at Box Canyon, and descends along the South Fork of the McKenzie River, past Cougar Reservoir to the junction of Forest Road 19 and Oregon Route 126. The two-lane paved road has frequent turnouts for scenic and recreational access, and it is a popular bicycling route. Elevations range from 1,052 to 3,728 feet.

Summer visitors can expect infrequent rain and temperatures ranging from 30 to 90 degrees. Spring and fall temperatures are cooler—from 30 to 60

Cougar Reservoir offers boating, fishing, swimming, and camping opportunities. Three Sisters Wilderness, on the east side of the reservoir, is laced by hiking trails.

degrees. Most precipitation falls between November and May. Foliage along the byway is spectacular, particularly in autumn.

Oakridge has all services, a small museum, and ranger stations with information for travelers. Travel from there via Forest Road 19 to Westfir, past residential homes with lovely flower gardens. The byway begins at the covered bridge, a faded barn-red structure with giant timbers.

The road is named in memory of Robert Aufderheide, a former Willamette National Forest supervisor. The route follows the North Fork of the Middle Fork Willamette River, designated a Wild and Scenic River from Westfir to Waldo Lake. Fishing for rainbow and native cutthroat trout is excellent, but only fly fishing is permitted.

A major study is under way on the bobcats and coyotes in this region. Other residents include blacktail deer, elk, mountain lions, black bears, beavers, porcupines, minks, river otters, and many species of small mammals. Barred, great horned, saw-whet, pygmy, great gray, and the controversial spotted owls also live in this region. The Waldo Lake Wilderness contains some wolverines, fishers, and pine martens. Waldo Lake is one of the purest in the world. Its indigo-blue water is close to the purity of distilled water.

Birdwatchers can watch for bald and golden eagles, kingfishers, grouse, quail, bandtail pigeons, water ouzels, woodpeckers, ospreys, hawks, and a multitude of songbirds.

The lush forest of mixed conifers and hardwoods has a thick understory of ferns and shrubs, including vine maples, rhododendrons, and maidenhair and spreading wood ferns. Sunlight filters through the trees and brightens the forest floor, but at times the forest is so thick that the byway travels through a tunnel of leaves. There is a swimming hole near milepost 3.7.

The byway follows the river canyon past several more swimming holes hidden along the river and through about 19 miles of second-growth forest. The trees here were replanted in 1945. The northern section of the byway passes through mature forest interspersed with younger plantations. Trees on this part of the forest include noble, subalpine, grand, and Pacific silver firs; Douglas-firs; western hemlocks; western redcedars; and Englemann spruces. Hardwoods include cottonwoods, bigleaf maples, red alders, Pacific dogwoods, chinkapin and Oregon white oaks, and madrones.

Kiahane Campground, 20 miles from Westfir, sits near the river in a grove of giant, 500-year-old Douglas-firs. This shady, quiet campground has 21 sites among the ferns and moss-covered stumps and logs.

Seven miles farther, Constitution Grove commemorates the Bicentennial of the signing of the U.S. Constitution. A short, easy footpath leads past the towering Douglas-fir trees, which reach heights of up to 180 feet. Each bears a plaque with the name of one of the founding fathers.

The trailhead for Shale Ridge is located near the hairpin turn about two miles south of Box Canyon Guard Station. This footpath travels through some of the largest old-growth Douglas-firs, western redcedars, yews, and hemlocks in the national forest. Dozens of waterfalls jet off Skookum Rim to the east, and the cedar bog is home to a variety of wildlife. Most of the North Fork river canyon was built and sculpted by lava flows and glaciation. The cedar bog was formed when glacial moraines blocked the river's flow, and the waterfalls opposite pour over a rim sliced clean by glaciers.

6 ROBERT AUFDERHEIDE MEMORIAL DRIVE

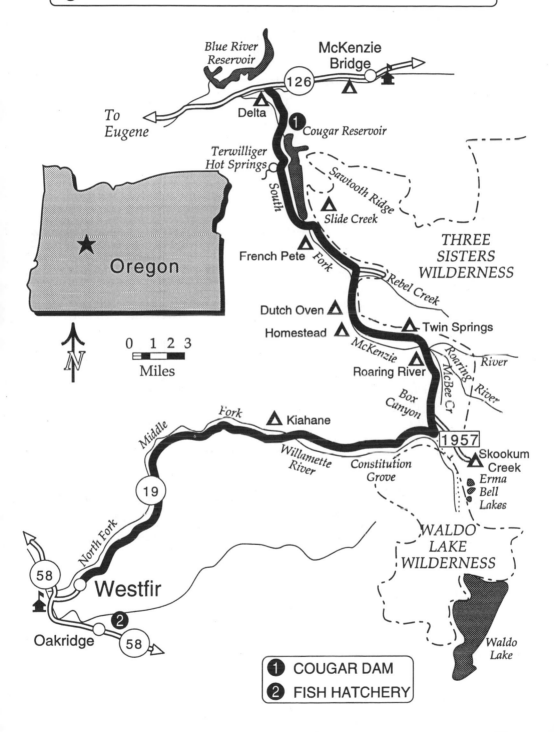

Oregon

0 1 2 3
Miles

N

To Eugene

Blue River Reservoir

McKenzie Bridge

126

Delta

Cougar Reservoir

Terwilliger Hot Springs

South Fork

Sawtooth Ridge

Slide Creek

French Pete

THREE SISTERS WILDERNESS

Rebel Creek

Dutch Oven

Homestead

Twin Springs

McKenzie

Roaring River

River

McBee Cr

Box Canyon

1957

Skookum Creek

Kiahane

Middle Fork

Willamette River

Constitution Grove

Erma Bell Lakes

WALDO LAKE WILDERNESS

19

North Fork

58

Westfir

2

Oakridge

58

Waldo Lake

❶ COUGAR DAM
❷ FISH HATCHERY

The byway climbs to Box Canyon, where volunteers staff the horse camp and information station from June through August. The shell of historic Landis cabin is just north, situated in a meadow of beautiful wildflowers. Nearby Forest Road 1957 goes to Skookum Creek Campground. Here the Erma Bell Trail traverses gentle terrain to the Erma Bell Lake Basin. The lake is full of rainbow and brook trout and is a good point from which to view the surrounding wildlands.

There is a great deal of evidence that prehistoric man, especially the Mollala, used this region. Obsidian, jasper, and chert tool remnants can be found in scattered small hunting camps and rock shelters. Please protect America's natural heritage by leaving all artifacts on the national forest sites.

The byway descends along McBee Creek to the Roaring River and the South Fork of the McKenzie River. It is a pleasure to drive alongside these sparkling cascades, through forests perfumed with healthy, deep-woods scents. Anglers try for rainbow and cutthroat trout in the rivers.

Seven small, developed campgrounds line this portion of the route, and there are numerous places to pull off the road and set up a primitive camp alongside the streams.

Cougar Reservoir lies at the northern end of the byway, providing an opportunity for water-related recreation such as waterskiing, sailboating, fishing for rainbow trout, and swimming. There are several boat launch areas, and you can camp at one of three developed campgrounds. Cougar Dam was completed in 1963 and is the highest rock-fill structure ever built in Oregon.

A road encircles the reservoir, and Sawtooth Ridge dominates the view into the Three Sisters Wilderness to the east. Several good hiking trails lead into the wilderness from the east side of the reservoir. On the west side, Terwilliger Hot Springs is a small, undeveloped site with natural hot pools about a quarter-mile walk from the byway.

The byway continues north a few miles through cliffs of volcanic rock and ends at Oregon Route 126. Nearby Delta Campground has a lovely nature trail that winds through a cool, quiet grove of 200- to 500-year-old Douglas-firs and western redcedars. □

7 SMITH RIVER SCENIC BYWAY
Six Rivers National Forest   California

General description: A 33-mile highway through the Coast Range, with far-ranging views and towering redwoods along the way.

Special attractions: Giant redwoods, excellent salmon and steelhead fishing, hiking, tubing, rafting, abundant flora and fauna.

Location: Northwest California on the Six Rivers National Forest, northeast of Crescent City. The byway begins at the junction of U.S. Highways 101 and 199, travels northeast on 199, and ends at Collier Tunnel near the California-Oregon border.

Byway route number: U.S. Highway 199.

Travel season: Year-round. Occasional poor driving conditions in winter.

A shady footpath lined with ferns meanders under the tall redwoods in Simpson-Reed Grove, along the Smith River Scenic Byway. Bill Baines photo.

Camping: Three national forest campgrounds with drinking water, fire grates, picnic tables, and toilets. One state park with picnic tables, fire grates, drinking water, flush toilets, and showers. Additional public and private campgrounds within a short distance of the byway.

Services: All services in Crescent City. Limited services scattered along the byway, including gas, groceries, food, lodging, and phones.

Nearby attractions: Redwood National Park, Siskiyou Wilderness, Lake Earl Wildlife Area, elk preserve, tide pools, giant redwoods, and the other five rivers of the Six Rivers National Forest.

For more information: Six Rivers National Forest, 507 F St., Eureka, CA 95501, (707) 442-1701. District Ranger: Gasquet Ranger District, P.O. Box 228, Gasquet, CA 95543, (707) 457-3131. Jedediah Smith Redwoods State Park, 4241 Kings Valley Road, Crescent City, CA, 95531, (707) 464-9533.

Description: Set in the valley of the historic Smith River, the scenic byway wends inland from near the northern California coast to the Oregon border. The paved, two-lane road has frequent turnouts and passing lanes and is heavily traveled, especially during the summer.

Summer visitors can expect generally favorable weather, although early mornings in the north coast country can be foggy and damp and frequent rain is never out of the question. Summer daytime temperatures range from the 70s to the 90s. Temperatures increase as you move inland. Winter is very cool to cold, with daytime temperatures in the 20s and 30s. One hundred inches of rain is not uncommon during a winter, and occasional snow falls at the higher elevations near Collins Tunnel at the end of the byway. Chains are sometimes required for winter travel.

U.S. Highway 199 begins a few miles northeast of Crescent City and branches from U.S. Highway 101. However, a bridge is out and necessitates a detour until 1991. Until then, continue north eight more miles on U.S. Highway 101, bypassing the junction. Then travel south on California Route 197, which ends at U.S. Highway 199 along the Smith River.

In spite of the detour, you should not, however, pass up the short but truly impressive few miles on 199 to the closed bridge. The route dips and winds and rises for four miles through a cathedral-like redwood forest, part of the Jedediah Smith Redwoods State Park. Ferns, redwood sorrels, rhododendrons, and azaleas abound, and muted birdcalls echo in the quiet of this untrafficked portion of the byway. On rare, clear mornings, sun filters through towering trees; on most mornings, fog wafts among the giant trunks and obscures their tops. Turnouts provide opportune parking for photographers and sightseers. Moss-covered deadfall angles across the forest floor. One downed tree is sawed into the shape of a seat and makes a handy rest stop just outside the Simpson-Reed Grove. A nature hike on the short Simpson-Reed Discovery Trail features interpretive stations among the redwoods, vine maples, western hemlocks, and huckleberries. The varied flora and the range of daylight conditions provide unusual lighting and textures.

The Walker Road is a mile-long gravel side road that goes through the forest. There are numerous trails for the hiker. Walker Road opens out onto a clearing above the Smith River and allows a beautiful view of the valley and of the clear, clean river. A short walk down to river's edge lets summer visitors take a cool dip or enjoy a picnic in the asters above the rocky beaches.

Sightseers, botanists, birdwatchers, and photographers could easily spend a full day on this section of the byway.

After detouring back to 101 and driving south on 197, you again reach the byway, on the east side of the Smith River. The rest of the byway follows U.S. Highway 199.

Near the beginning of the byway, you will find the entrance to Jedediah Smith Redwoods State Park, the northernmost of California's 30 redwood parks. Named for famous mountain man, scout, and guide Jed Smith, the site straddles the river that also bears his name. The Smith River is the state's largest undammed river. Campsites nestle among the trees along the bank, and hot showers and running water are nearby, as are drinking water and a trailer dumping station. There are 108 campsites, and barrier-free facilities are available.

A footbridge leads to Stout Grove and walking trails. There are 17 trails on both sides of the river; trail guides are available at the park entrance. According to the guide, the park's redwood stands are "considered by many to be the finest example of primeval coast redwood landscape in the world."

Along the trails and through the groves, you can see California rose bays, bigleaf maples, poison oaks, and both five-fingered and sword ferns. Tansy ragworts, Queen Anne's lace, and asters are common. Birdwatchers can expect to see ravens, pileated woodpeckers, kingfishers, barn owls, and gray, blue, and Steller's jays, as well as ospreys and many other species of coastal birds. Decimated by disease a few years ago, raccoons are making a comeback; the cute little creatures are only one of the park's resident mammal species. Black bears are fairly common in the early spring and late fall, and mountain lion sightings are increasing. Bobcats, minks, longtail weasels, gray foxes, and the diminutive Pacific Coastal blacktail deer also inhabit the area.

An oddity in the park is a stand of dawn redwoods brought as seedlings from China by a Humboldt State University professor. These trees are quite rare and apparently thrive only in the northern park and in a single Chinese mountain valley.

The South Fork Road, about 4.5 miles up the byway from the junction of routes 197 and 199, is a nice side trip. Blackberry bushes dot the edge of the canyon bridge on the far side and make a tasty snack for those who stop to take pictures of the scenic forks of the Smith River. The views of rock walls, forests, and clear blue waters are lovely.

The byway proceeds up the Middle Fork of the Smith River and wends back and forth across the stream. Most services are available in or near Gasquet (pronounced Gasky), and in summertime roadside stands offer fresh vegetables and berries. The Gasquet Ranger District office provides information about the national forest and its hiking trails, including the South-Kelsey National Recreation Trail, the Doe Flat Trail, the Myrtle Creek Trail, and Island Lake Trail, as well as access information for the 153,000-acre Siskiyou Wilderness.

Beyond Gasquet, Panther Flat Campground has 41 sites in a quiet, secluded spot among the oak trees. Small waterfalls cascade into the Middle Fork.

The climate dries and warms as the byway gets farther from the coast. Tree species in the volcanic-granitic canyon include oaks and Douglas-firs, and erosion is evident on the steep hillsides.

Grassy Flat Campground has 19 sites near the river, and Patrick Creek Campground has 17 sites. Nearby a private lodge built of logs in 1926 offers

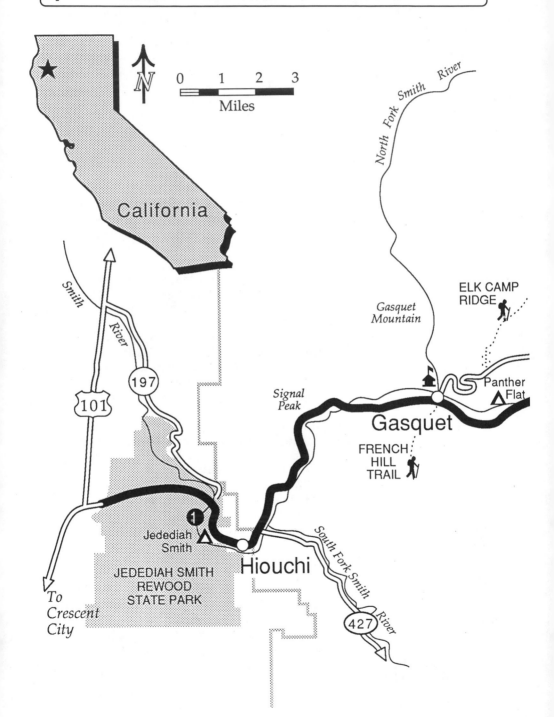

California

N

0 1 2 3
Miles

North Fork Smith River

Smith River

197

101

Gasquet Mountain

ELK CAMP RIDGE

Panther Flat

Signal Peak

Gasquet

FRENCH HILL TRAIL

Jedediah Smith

JEDEDIAH SMITH REWOOD STATE PARK

Hiouchi

South Fork Smith River

427

To Crescent City

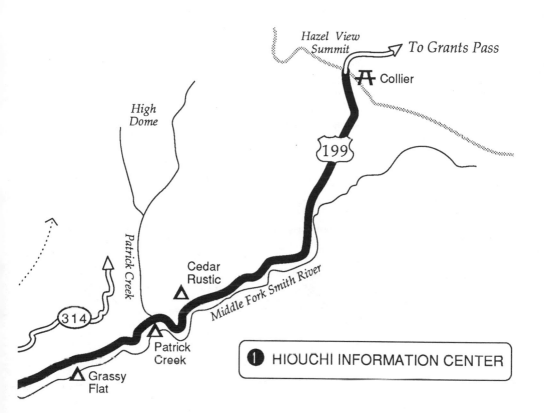

Hazel View Summit

To Grants Pass

Collier

High Dome

199

Patrick Creek

Cedar Rustic

Middle Fork Smith River

314

Patrick Creek

Grassy Flat

1 HIOUCHI INFORMATION CENTER

lodging and gourmet meals. The lodge is open from mid-March through the end of January each year.

Past Patrick Creek, the road gets a bit rough. Frequent turnouts allow views of the striking scenery, which includes the river sparkling in the rocky canyon far below. The route begins a gradual climb, and the Collier Rest Area is located two miles past the Oregon Mountain Road. Collins Tunnel, elevation 2,200 feet, marks the end of the scenic byway. Snow occasionally falls at this elevation, making for winter driving conditions.—*Bill Baines* □

8 CARSON PASS HIGHWAY
Eldorado and Toiyabe National Forests   *California*

General description: A 58-mile paved highway that crosses 8,600-foot Carson Pass in the Sierra Nevada.

Special attractions: Excellent trout fishing, abundant wildlife, developed hot springs, horseback riding, Mokelumne and Carson-Iceberg wilderness areas, sailing, sailboarding, skiing, bicycling.

Location: East-central California on the Eldorado and Toiyabe national forests, south of Lake Tahoe. The byway follows California Route 88 between Woodfords and Dew Drop.

Byway route number: California Route 88.

Travel season: Year-round. Occasional winter closures for snow and ice removal. Chains may be required.

Camping: Eleven Forest Service campgrounds with picnic tables, drinking water, fire grates, and toilets. Also numerous private resorts with lodges, cabins, and campsites.

Services: All services available along the route.

Nearby attractions: Lake Tahoe, Grover Hot Springs, ski areas, historic trans-Sierra route and monuments, Pacific Crest National Scenic Trail.

For more information: Toiyabe National Forest, 1200 Franklin Way, Sparks, NV 89431, (702) 331-6444; Eldorado National Forest, 100 Forni Road, Placerville, CA 95667, (916) 622-5061. District Rangers: Carson Ranger District, Toiyabe National Forest, 1536 S. Carson St., Carson City, NV 89701, (702) 882-2766; Amador Ranger District, Eldorado National Forest, 26820 Silver Dr., Pioneer, CA 95666, (209) 295-4251; Markleeville Guard Station and Visitor Center, Highway 89/4, P.O. Box 35, Markleeville, CA 96120, (916) 694-2911.

Description: The Carson Pass Highway rises from Nevada's Carson Valley, travels west over Carson Pass, and descends to California's Central Valley. The entire route is two-lane, paved highway with turnouts and passing lanes. The road won an award in 1965 for being the most scenic highway in the nation.

Because the terrain is high and mountainous, you can expect variable weather conditions, expecially in late spring and early autumn. From mid-June to early September, pleasant and sunny days in the 70s dominate above 5,000 feet. Evenings are much cooler, down to 45 degrees. Cold storms, though infrequent in summer, are to be expected. Winter weather ranges from sublime

Caples Lake, on Carson Pass Scenic Byway, is known for trophy-size mackinaw and brown trout fishing. Bill Baines photo.

to severe, with temperatures ranging from minus 30 up to 50 degrees. Winter driving conditions prevail, and motorists should carry chains, which are occasionally required for highway travel.

In Nevada, Route 88 begins at its junction with U.S. Highway 395 outside Minden. This small community sits on the valley floor at the foot of the Sierra Nevada in what remains basically meadows and pastureland. Small ranches, cattle, and hayfields line the road. Wildflowers—Indian paintbrushes, lupines, penstemons, and flaxes—stand out against the green meadowlands and continue to grow along the route up the mountain. Recreational glider pilots laud the Minden area for its unique thermals. The valley view from the byway toward the Sierra Nevada and Carson Canyon ranges from pleasing most mornings to spectacular in autumn and in stormy weather.

The West Fork of the Carson River flows alongside the road as it climbs from Carson and Diamond valleys through Carson Canyon and the Toiyabe National Forest into Hope Valley. "Toiyabe" originated with the Shoshone word for "Black Mountains," an apt description of the dark, pinyon- and juniper-covered range in present-day central Nevada.

A 1987 burn mars the canyon mouth on both sides, but a reforestation project was completed in 1988. The entrance is otherwise rugged and impressive. Ascending from the valley floor, Great Basin flora tapers off. Aspen groves, stands of Jeffrey pines and clumps of manzanitas line the route. The view east and south as the road climbs varies with time of day and season, but it is never commonplace.

The scenic byway begins in Woodfords, California. A granite and bronze monument in Woodfords commemorates an important early Pony Express station at Cary's Barn. Gas, groceries, and limited other services are available

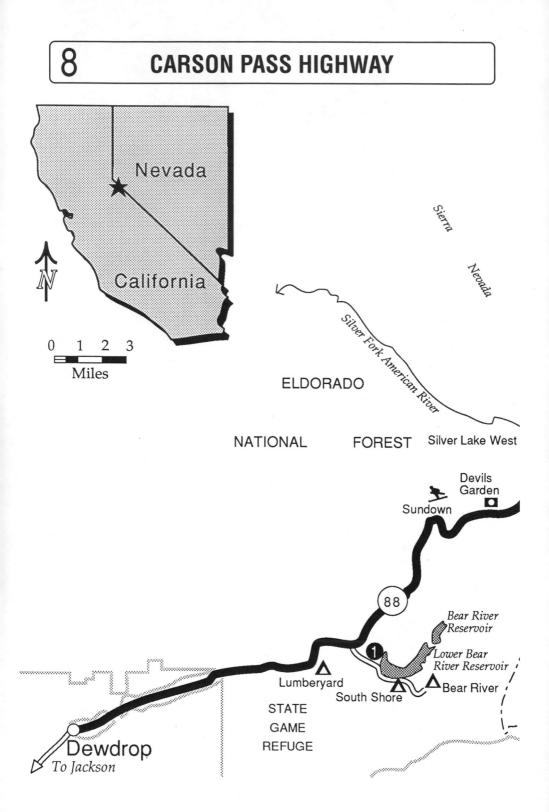

8 CARSON PASS HIGHWAY

Nevada

California

N

0 1 2 3
Miles

Sierra Nevada

Silver Fork American River

ELDORADO

NATIONAL FOREST Silver Lake West

Devils Garden

Sundown

88

Bear River Reservoir

1

Lower Bear River Reservoir

Lumberyard

South Shore

Bear River

STATE
GAME
REFUGE

Dewdrop
To Jackson

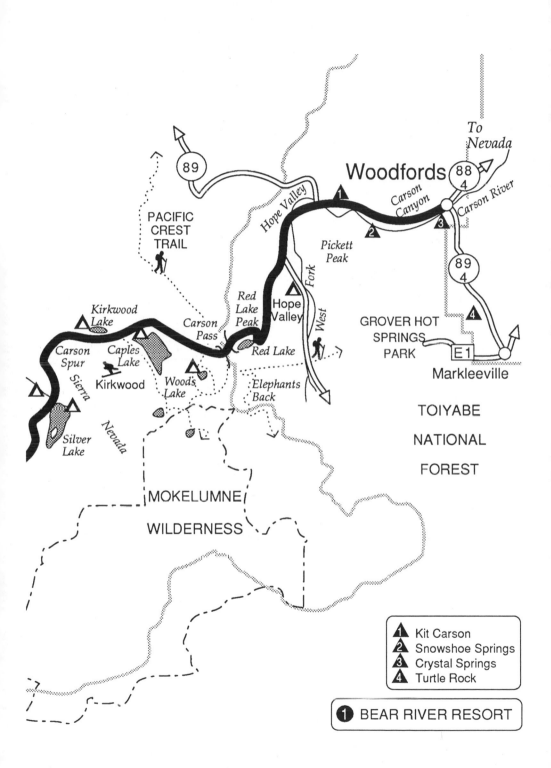

in Woodfords. A side trip from here on California Routes 89/4 leads to Markleeville and the famous Grover Hot Springs, as well as campgrounds, lakes, and access to Carson-Iceberg Wilderness and sites of historic interest.

Carson Canyon includes perhaps the most pleasant, if not spectacular, stretch of byway campgrounds. Just past Woodfords lies Crystal Springs Campground, the first of many that line the byway. Half a mile off Route 88, it sits in Jeffrey and sugar pines beneath the granitic canyon wall. The West Fork flows nearby, and picnicking and camping are possible at the campground's 20 sites.

Five miles west on the byway, Snowshoe Springs Campground has 13 sites scattered through the ashes and aspens of the West Fork bottomland, while nearby Kit Carson Campground has 12 sites situated in a very pleasant grove of aspens and lodgepole pines.

Scattered through the West Fork drainage are currant and gooseberry bushes, as well as occasional elderberries. Mountain chickadees, evening grosbeaks, and pine siskins are enjoyable to watch. Rainbow trout are stocked to provide sport for the angler and dinner for the camper.

A bit farther is a small store-restaurant-gas complex and then an all-season resort with cafe, lodging, and cross-country ski and bicycle rentals. Arrangements for rafting the East Fork of the Carson River can be made here. The season for rafting, on class II and III water, is from about late April through early July.

Hope Valley was reputedly named after the state of mind of early-day winter travelers as they looked toward Carson Pass. Here a side trip on California Route 89 wends 26 scenic miles over Luther Pass. to Lake Tahoe, one of the world's most magnificent mountain lakes. Tahoe is famous for its clarity, beautiful setting, and nearby world-class ski areas.

Hope Valley lies above Carson Canyon and features a flat, panoramic view of meadows, mountains, and lodgepole and aspen forest. Hope Valley Campground has 20 sites one mile from the highway, next to the West Fork of the Carson River. As the West Fork meanders along the valley floor, it cuts through a meadow dotted with asters, lupines, and Indian paintbrushes. Fly fishermen wade the stream, casting Pale Evening Duns, Adamses, and Mosquitoes at the evening hatch. An occasional bunch of mule deer might be seen feeding at the meadow's edge. In the autumn, aspens turn electric yellow in distant watersheds.

Past the valley and just below the pass lies Red Lake, the first in a number of lakes along the byway and one of many in the general area. Its name is derived from the color of adjacent volcanic rock. The turnout above the lake affords an excellent view of it, nearby Elephant's Back (9,635 feet) and Red Lake (10,061 feet) peaks, as well as parts of Hope Valley and points beyond.

Carson Pass, at 8,600 feet, opens up just past the turnout. Kit Carson scouted the pass while blazing trail for Lieutenant John C. Fremont in February 1844, and the crossing became one of the most significant routes over the Sierra Nevada into California. Fremont's subsequent winter passage to Sutter's Fort was both difficult and dangerous. A bronze plaque on a granite slab at the side of the byway commemorates Carson.

Eldorado National Forest maintains an information station at the pass parking area, open through the summer months. Also located there are trailheads to the Mokelumne Wilderness and the Pacific Crest National Scenic Trail. Next to the Carson monument stands a monument to Snowshoe Thompson (John Tostensen), a late nineteenth-century figure who carried mail throughout the

Sierra Nevada during winter. Tostensen is often credited with establishing recreational ski races in the region.

The Sierra formed over millions of years. Volcanic flows over a granitic base were uplifted, and faulting and glacial action scoured the mountains into the shapes seen today.

A few miles west of Carson Pass are Wood's Lake Campground and the Caples Lake Recreation Area. Wood's Lake has picnic facilities and 14 sites next to the small lake. Caples Lake has 35 sites and a boat launch. There is also a marina with lodging, restaurant, store, and lounge, open from first thaw through October. Caples Lake offers some trophy mackinaw and brown trout fishing, as well as good rainbow, cutthroat, cutbow, and eastern brook trout. It is good for both boating and sailboarding.

Beyond the spillway west of Caples Lake is another trailhead into the Mokelumne Wilderness. It gives access to local alpine lakes and to campsites for backpackers and hikers.

If you leave your car to hike or camp, you may occasionally sight a small group of deer feeding in one of the small, park-like mountain meadows. Drainages of aspens edged with blue spruces often hold blue grouse. Birdwatchers can expect to see Clark's nutcrackers, red or white breasted nuthatches, red crossbills, pileated woodpeckers, and Cassin's finches, as well as beautiful western tanagers.

The Kirkwood Inn was built in 1864 as the home of the pioneering Kirkwood and Taylor families. One of the first resorts to operate in the Sierra Nevada, the sturdy, hand-hewn log structure sits right on the byway and offers breakfast, lunch, and dinner. Nearby is a small gas station, cross-country ski area, stables, and alpine ski area with lodging, restaurants, and ski services.

Farther down the mountain, beyond the Carson Spur at 7,990 feet, is the Oyster Creek Rest Area and Silver Lake Campground. Silver Lake has 62 sites and drinking water. Slightly farther west is the Pacific Gas and Electric campground Silver Creek West, with 34 sites and drinking water. Both campgrounds are close to Silver Lake, as are several private lake resorts. Many of the resorts and other services along the scenic byway originated in the nineteenth century, and some have been operated continuously, often by the same family.

Signs and monuments mark the Old Emigrant Trail to Placerville and the Mormon Emigrant Trail. In addition to its historic role as a western passage, the byway route played an important role in the mining, logging, and cattle industries.

After the Devil's Garden turnout, South Shore and Bear River campgrounds have a total of 30 sites on pretty Lower Bear River Reservoir. Nearby Lumberyard Campground has eight sites. The terrain here is blanketed mostly in thick forests of sugar and ponderosa pines and white and red firs. Beyond, the drive through the Sierra foothills is pretty and features small towns and little shops. The byway ends in Dew Drop.—*Bill Baines* □

General description: A 100-mile paved and gravel road through the Sierra Nevada that ascends to 7,000 feet and is the vantage point for far-ranging views.

Special attractions: Mammoth Pool Reservoir, excellent views, giant sequoias at Nelder Grove, outstanding geologic displays of glaciation.

Location: East-central California on the Sierra National Forest, northeast of Fresno. The open loop begins at the national forest boundary south of North Fork, follows the Minarets Road (Forest Road 4S81) east and north to the Beasore (pronounced Baysore) Loop Road (Forest Road 5S07), goes northeast on the Beasore Loop Road (6S10X), then southwest on the Sky Ranch Road (6S10), and ends at California Route 41 just north of Oakhurst. Both Nelder Dome and Fresno Dome are accessible from Sky Ranch Road.

Byway route numbers: Forest Roads 4S81, 5S07, 6S10.

Travel season: The byway is generally open from mid-May through mid-November and is closed by winter snows the rest of the year.

Camping: Fourteen national forest campgrounds with picnic tables, fire grates, and vault toilets. A few campgrounds have drinking water. No hookups.

Services: All services in North Fork and Oakhurst. Food at Minarets Pack Station. Lodging, gas, and groceries at Mammoth Pool Resort and at Beasore Meadows.

Nearby attractions: Yosemite National Park; Bass Lake; Ansel Adams, Kaiser, and John Muir wilderness areas; San Joaquin and North Fork San Joaquin rivers (recommended for Wild and Scenic River status).

For more information: Sierra National Forest, 1600 Tollhouse Ave., Clovis, CA 93611-0532, (209) 487-5155. District Rangers: Minarets Ranger District, P.O. Box 10, North Fork, CA 93463, (209) 877-2218; Mariposa Ranger District, 41969 Highway 41, Oakhurst, CA 93644, (209) 683-4665.

Description: The Sierra Vista Scenic Byway is a 92-mile open loop through the Sierra Nevada. The byway begins and ends at elevations of about 3,000 feet but climbs to 7,000 feet in between. The route is 75 percent paved and can be traveled by all vehicles. Travel speeds vary from 15 to 35 miles an hour.

Spring and fall offer the mildest weather conditions. Days are cool to warm, and evenings are colder. Summers are hot with pleasantly cool evenings. Summer thunderstorms are not uncommon at higher elevations in the Sierra Nevada. Fire danger is extreme throughout the area during summer months.

The preferable direction to travel this byway is counterclockwise. This way you can enjoy the best possible views and end near Oakhurst, which has more lodging opportunities than other communities in the vicinity.

At each end of the byway, you will pass through woodlands dominated by digger pines (locally called bull pines) and several species of oaks. Some slopes are covered with brush species such as manzanita, ceanothus, bush poppy, and red bud. As you travel higher in elevation, mixed conifer forest develops. It is characterized by ponderosa pines, sugar pines, white firs, incense cedars, and black oaks, with an understory of bear clover, manzanitas, and gooseberries. Above 6,000 feet in elevation, red firs and lodgepole pines are the predominant species. At timberline, trees such as western white pines and hemlocks give way to the perennial bunch grasses, sedges, and wildflowers of the alpine Sierra Nevada.

Recreation available along the byway includes fishing, camping, hiking, backpacking, mountain biking, snowmobiling, boating, swimming, and waterskiing.

The byway begins five miles southeast of North Fork, where the road begins to climb. An overlook provides a spectacular view of Redinger Lake and its surrounding valley. By the time the route crosses Ross Creek at 4,320 feet elevation, the surroundings are thick with ponderosa pines, incense cedars, and black oaks, interspersed with manzanitas.

On the byway, Fish Creek Campground has seven sites in a dense forest of dogwoods, black oaks, and pines. Five miles north, Rock Creek Campground has 18 sites and drinking water. Rock Creek is one of the best fishing streams along the route.

Perhaps the most dramatic views are from 5,393-foot Mile High Vista. From here you can see Ansel Adams, John Muir, and Kaiser wilderness areas; the Mammoth Pool Reservoir; the Minarets; and numerous other significant peaks and mountains. Etched metal plates identify the prominent landmarks. Soda Springs Campground, with 18 sites, is about eight miles north on the West Fork of Chiquito Creek, another good fishing spot.

The next attraction is a four-mile side trip to Mammoth Pool Reservoir. En route are Placer Campground, with seven sites and drinking water; Sweetwater Campground, with 10 sites; and Mammoth Pool Campground, with 47 sites and drinking water.

Mammoth Pool Reservoir is about five miles long and half a mile wide. It is noted for being a very good fishery, with rainbow, eastern brook, and German brown trout. Fishing season runs from mid-April to May 1 and from June 16 through late autumn. The six-week break in late spring allows migrating deer to swim across the reservoir. Recreationists enjoy boating and waterskiing in the chilly waters. A resort offers a range of tourist facilities.

French Trail, one of many hiking trails in the area, runs past Mammoth Pool Reservoir from near Fish Creek Campground. The trail was surveyed in 1880 and built by John S. French, a mining promoter from San Francisco who developed mines in the Mammoth Mountain area. The trail runs up the spectacular San Joaquin River Canyon, offering breathtaking views of sheer glaciated canyon walls and towering domes. The canyon is essentially inaccessible except via the French Trail. Lower sections of the trail are best hiked in the spring or fall to avoid the summer heat.

Back on the byway, you will pass close by Jackass Rock, at 7,112 feet elevation, and, just beyond, the odd-shaped Arch Rock. Squaw Dome looms to the right; you are now in the midst of the very mountains you viewed from Mile High Vista.

A mile farther, the byway turns west onto Beasore Road (5S07). The route is dirt and gravel. Minarets Pack Station offers food, horseback riding, and pack trips into the Ansel Adams Wilderness. The road passes near Jackass Meadow and the geological formation known as The Balls, which rise spectacularly above the tall trees, looking like smooth scoops of butterscotch ice cream.

Five miles farther is Upper Chiquito Campground, with 20 sites available.

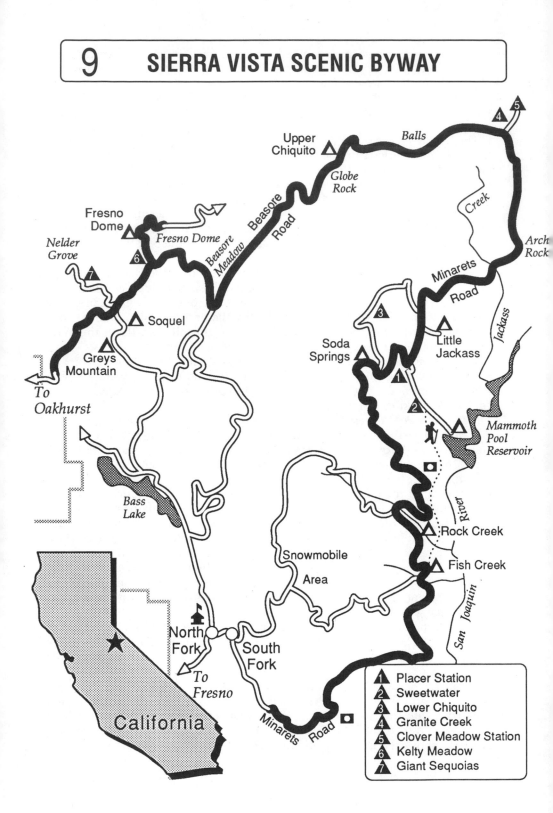

9 SIERRA VISTA SCENIC BYWAY

Upper Chiquito

Balls

Globe Rock

Creek

Beasore Road

Arch Rock

Fresno Dome

Nelder Grove

Fresno Dome

Beasore Meadow

Minarets Road

Jackass

6

7

Soquel

3

Little Jackass

Soda Springs

Greys Mountain

1

Mammoth Pool Reservoir

2

To Oakhurst

Bass Lake

River

Rock Creek

Fish Creek

Snowmobile Area

San Joaquin

North Fork

South Fork

To Fresno

California

Minarets Road

1	Placer Station
2	Sweetwater
3	Lower Chiquito
4	Granite Creek
5	Clover Meadow Station
6	Kelty Meadow
7	Giant Sequoias

Globe Rock balances precariously atop boulders in Long Meadow, on the Sierra Vista Scenic Byway. Alfred H. Golub photo.

One and a half miles beyond that is Globe Rock, an intriguing geological formation that has interpretive signing.

Several other campgrounds are accessible from the byway, including Little Jackass (five sites), Lower Chiquito (seven sites), Clover (seven sites), and Granite Creek (20 sites).

One mile past Globe Rock, the road is again paved. Five miles farther is a store that is open in summer, providing gas, groceries, and lodging. The general area of Beasore Meadows has a flourishing mosquito population in early spring, so an ample supply of repellant is desirable.

At Cold Springs Summit, at 7,308 feet the highest point on the byway, the route turns north onto the graded dirt Beasore Loop Road (6S10X). At this point, you can elect to leave the scenic byway and continue on the paved Beasore Road 13 miles to Bass Lake. The Beasore Loop Road joins the Sky Ranch Road near Kelty Meadow Campground, which has 10 sites. A side trip to the north leads past Fresno Dome Campground, with nine sites, and on to Fresno Dome, where an easy walking trail leads to the top of the dome and an outstanding view of the Sierra National Forest.

Wildlife on the national forest occurs in colorful variety. High alpine elevations provide habitat for marmots, pine martens, pikas, bears, chickadees, and juncos. As the forest canopy becomes more dense, deer, mountain lions, bobcats, coyotes, porcupines, raccoons, gray squirrels, chipmunks, spotted owls, Steller's jays, and warblers are more common. Down in the oak woodland and chaparral, quail, scrub jays, skunks, rattlesnakes, gopher snakes, gray foxes, deer, and coyotes are commonly seen. Over the rugged San Joaquin River Canyon, golden eagles, red-tailed hawks, and occasional peregrine falcons can be seen riding the thermals.

The byway ends near Oakhurst and allows access to Nelder Grove, a two-

The view from Mile High Curve on the Sierra Vista Scenic Byway includes Mammoth Pool, and the Ansel Adams, John Muir, and Kaiser wilderness areas. Alfred H. Golub photo.

mile side trip. Nelder Grove, with its incomparable giant sequoias, is home to Bull Buck tree and other giant redwoods. Bull Buck is one of the largest and oldest trees in the world. Nelder Grove is a 1,540-acre tract containing 101 mature giant sequoias intermingled with a forest of second-growth pines, firs, incense cedars, and dogwoods. There is no written mention of the grove before the 1850s, but archaeological studies have revealed that the Southern Sierra Miwok Indians camped there for several thousand years before the white man's arrival. Nelder Grove contrasts sharply with sequoia groves in the nearby national parks since there are no paved roads and no crowds blocking views of the big trees. The forest is also unusually dense. A one-mile, self-guided interpretive walk leads through the majestic sequoias, and there is ample camping at the bases of the redwoods in 13 sites at Nelder Grove Campground.

After the Nelder Grove diversion, you can return to the byway, where Sky Ranch Road leads past Gooseberry Flat to California Route 41 at Batterson Station, the end of the byway. Batterson is a few miles north of Oakhurst, a charming, comfortable gateway community to Yosemite.

Sierra Vista Scenic Byway can be traveled comfortably in about five hours without stops. But visitors may wish to make a full vacation in the area; there are sufficient activities to amuse you for a week or more.—*Colleen L. Rhodes* □

General description: A 27-mile paved and gravel road alongside pretty streams in the scenic East Pioneer and West Pioneer mountains.

Special attractions: Outstanding trout fishing in numerous streams and beaver ponds, crystal-digging area for rockhounds, proposed East Pioneer Wilderness Area, abundant wildlife, silver-mining ghost town, developed hot springs.

Location: Southwest Montana on the Beaverhead National Forest, southwest of Butte. The byway travels Forest Road 484 from Wise River south to Polaris.

Byway route number: Forest Road 484.

Travel season: Open from about mid-May until Thanksgiving and then closed by winter snows between Elkhorn Hot Springs and Sheep Creek.

Camping: Six national forest campgrounds with drinking water, picnic tables, and vault toilets. Suitable for tents, truck campers, and trailers. No hookups.

Services: All services in Wise River, but availability is limited. Phone, lodging, and restaurant at Elkhorn Hot Springs. Gas, food, phone, and lodging at Grasshopper Inn near Polaris.

Nearby attractions: Big Hole River blue-ribbon trout fishery, Bannock ghost town, Big Hole Battlefield National Monument.

For more information: Beaverhead National Forest, 420 Barrett St., Dillon, MT 59725, (406) 683-3900. District Rangers: Wise River Ranger District, P.O. Box 86, Wise River, MT 59762 (406) 832-3178; Dillon Ranger District, 420 Barrett St., Dillon, MT 59725, (406) 683-3900.

Description: Set between the granite peaks of the East Pioneer and West Pioneer mountain ranges, the Pioneer Mountain's Scenic Byway gently ascends a 7,800-foot divide between the Wise River and Grasshopper Creek drainages. The two-lane road is paved except the sixteen mile segment on the south end which is gravel surface. There are frequent turnouts, traffic is light, and the highway is well-maintained. The scenery, traveling in either direction, is exceptional.

Summer visitors can expect variable mountain weather conditions, ranging from very hot to windstorms or severe frosts. Most common are pleasantly warm days in the 70s and cool nights in the 40s or 50s. Winter recreation includes cross-country skiing, alpine skiing, and snowmobiling on closed roads. Weather conditions in winter may be severe.

The town of Wise River is located on the Big Hole River. The main industry is cattle ranching, along with some logging and mining. Fishing fanatics congregate here seasonally to try their skill on the Big Hole blue-ribbon trout stream. Wise River, a small community, offers all services to travelers.

South of Wise River, the lower slopes are sage brush with willow bottomlands along the river, providing habitat for beavers, moose, coyotes, and mule deer. Lodgepole pine and Douglas-fir forests cover the adjacent mountainsides. Historically, this northern section of the Pioneer Mountain's Scenic Byway was used by miners and ranchers. Settlers' journals chronicle hunting and fishing in the late 1800s; both popular activities continue today. A scattering of prehistoric sites shows early man also used the Wise River-Polaris area.

10 PIONEER MOUNTAIN'S SCENIC BYWAY

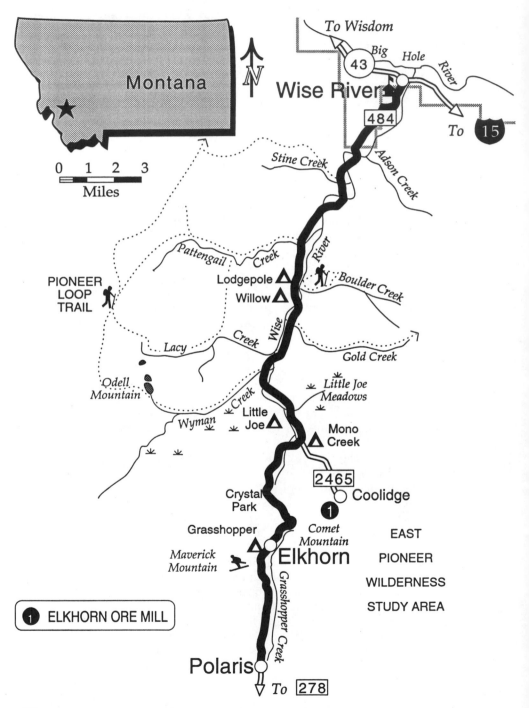

Montana

0 1 2 3
Miles

To Wisdom

43 Big Hole River

Wise River

484

To 15

Stine Creek

Adson Creek

PIONEER LOOP TRAIL

Pattengail Creek

River

Lodgepole

Willow

Boulder Creek

Wise

Lacy

Creek

Gold Creek

Odell Mountain

Creek

Little Joe Meadows

Wyman

Little Joe

Mono Creek

2465

Crystal Park

Comet Mountain

1

Coolidge

Grasshopper

Maverick Mountain

Elkhorn

EAST

PIONEER

WILDERNESS

STUDY AREA

1 ELKHORN ORE MILL

Grasshopper Creek

Polaris

To 278

52

Adson Creek, five miles south of Wise River, has many undeveloped camp-sites along the sparkling creek. Fishing is good, meadowlarks sing, and firs and aspens provide shady picnic spots. Marmots, mule deer, and cattle inhabit the area.

About seven miles from Wise River, just south of Stine Creek, look for mountain goats near the steep, rocky outcrop west of the road. They are most commonly seen there in spring and winter.

Mountain- and forest-dwelling wildlife is abundant along the entire byway, including moose, elk, mule deer, black bears, and golden eagles. Watch for them in the open meadows and along timbered edges of the forest. Best viewing times are early morning and late afternoon through evening. If the sky is clear and the moon bright, watch for a cow moose and her calf strolling along a willow-lined stream in the moonlight, or spot a bull elk grazing in a clearing.

Stine Creek Trailhead provides access to the Pioneer Loop Trail. This strenuous 35-mile hiking route is a National Recreation Trail that penetrates deep into the West Pioneer peaks.

Backpackers and hikers can choose from a wide array of other trails in the area. Day hikes along the byway are abundant, and intermediate and strong hikers can enjoy ascending Gold Creek to the high lakes and panoramic views or hiking to Odell Lake and Odell Mountain, set in spectacular alpine country. Several easy to moderate trails suitable for family hikes are Pattengail Creek, Little Joe Creek, and Boulder-Fourth of July creeks loop. Halfway Meadows and Harrison Park trails meander through elk calving grounds.

Hikers may spot colorful specks on the rock walls of the David Creek drainage. These are rock-climbers, testing their skills on the highly fractured rock faces. The Pioneers are primarily composed of granite, approximately 70 million years old, from the Pioneer batholith. Sedimentary rock is from the Precambrian Belt series, with some gneiss and schist.

Farther south, Pattengail Creek's beaver ponds and sparkling waters provide an ideal fishing and exploring spot for youngsters. Watch for moose in the meadows of spring-blooming lupines and Indian paintbrushes. Lacy, Wyman, and Steel creeks also offer outstanding fishing opportunities and trails for easy day hikes. There are abundant brook trout at Anderson Meadows, on Wyman Creek. Generally speaking, fishing for grayling, rainbow, brook, and cutthroat trout is best in the larger west-slope tributary streams.

Camping along the Wise River-Polaris Road is quite enjoyable. Campground elevations range from 6,000 to 7,000 feet, and annoying insects are scarce after June. Lodgepole, Boulder, and Willow campgrounds lie midway between Wise River and Polaris. They have six sites nestled amid fir and pine trees on the banks of the Wise River.

Lacy Creek is two miles south of Willow Campground. A one-lane dirt road along the creek weaves through the open forest for four miles, offering plenty of opportunities to pull over and fish, explore, or set up camp. Lacy, Odell, Wyman, Skull, and Steel creeks, all in this vicinity, offer solitude and good fishing, particularly in the many feeder streams and beaver ponds.

The gentle ascent of the Wise River drainage brings you to the upper reaches of the byway region. Broad meadows of grasses and wildflowers underscore snowcapped 11,000-foot summits. The proposed East Pioneer Wilderness is a jewel in the heart of the range. Streams and trails meander

Moose, elk, mule deer, black bears, and other large game animals such as bighorn sheep inhabit the Wise River—Polaris area. Christopher Cauble photo.

Peaks in the East and West Pioneer ranges tower over the river along the Pioneer Mountain's Scenic Byway.

invitingly across the high open parks adjacent to the road.

Little Joe and Mono Creek campgrounds are near the divide. Little Joe has four sites along the Wise River, and secluded Mono Creek Campground has five sites three-quarters of a mile from the highway in an open pine forest.

Look for a thin ridge east of the byway, just north of the Mono Creek Campground turnoff. This is the old railroad bed for the Montana Southern Railway, the last narrow-gauge railroad built in the United States. In 1927, Pattengail Dam broke and washed out the tracks, which were never rebuilt. The railroad served the Elkhorn Mine, one of the largest ore-mill structures in the United States. You are welcome to explore the old mine and adjoining ghost town of Coolidge, but don't enter the buildings. They are in severe disrepair and potentially dangerous.

To reach Coolidge, follow the signs past Mono Creek Campground. School children will be delighted to see the tumbledown schoolhouse straddling the creek, with water rushing through the classroom.

Atop the Wise River-Grasshopper Creek divide, rockhounds can dig for quartz crystals at Crystal Park. There are abundant finger-sized clear crystals. Less common are amethyst scepters, lovely purple or violet crystals. The Crystal Park area has acres of full-grown trees that were blown down in a violent windstorm. The young trees growing up around them are the result of natural revegetation.

South of Crystal Park, the byway follows Grasshopper Creek. This southern portion of the road was developed in the early 1900s to provide access to Elkhorn Hot Springs. Today visitors still enjoy the naturally heated hot waters in the two outdoor pools. An enclosed spa, bar, restaurant, horses, and primitive cabins are also available.

Grasshopper Campground lies one mile south of Elkhorn Hot Springs. It has a group picnic area and 24 sites in the spruce and pine forest along Grasshopper Creek.

The descent along Grasshopper Creek brings you back among the open sage foothills. Grasshopper Inn and Polaris signify the southern end of the scenic byway. The byway terminates at Beaverhead County Highway 278, 6.5 miles south of Polaris. □

11 BEARTOOTH HIGHWAY
Custer, Gallatin, and Shoshone National Forests
Montana and Wyoming

General description: A 60-mile route across alpine plateaus and lakes, with spectacular mountain views.

Special attractions: Yellowstone National Park, outstanding views, alpine vegetation, Absaroka-Beartooth Wilderness, trout fishing, hiking, camping.

Location: The Montana-Wyoming border country adjacent to the eastern edge of Yellowstone National Park, on the Gallatin, Shoshone, and Custer national forests. The byway begins at the national forest boundary just west of Red Lodge, Montana, and travels U.S. Highway 212 west to the Northeast Gate of Yellowstone National Park. The eastern portion of the byway drops 5,000 feet down a steep mountain slope via a series of switchbacks. The drop-offs adjacent to the highway are impressive; this section of road is not for the fainthearted.

Byway route number: U.S. Highway 212.

Travel season: Memorial Day weekend through about mid-October, then closed by winter snows.

Camping: Ten national forest campgrounds with picnic tables, fire grates, toilets, drinking water. No hookups.

Services: All services in Cooke City and Red Lodge, Montana. Lodging, gasoline, and small store at Top of the World, (summer season only).

Nearby attractions: Sunlight Basin, Bighorn Canyon National Recreation Area, Pryor Mountains National Wild Horse Range, North Absaroka Wilderness.

For more information: Custer National Forest, 2602 First Ave. N., P.O. Box 2556, Billings, MT 59103, (406) 657-6361; Gallatin National Forest, Federal Building, 10 E. Babcock St., P.O. Box 130, Bozeman, MT 59715, (406) 587-6701; Shoshone National Forest, 225 W. Yellowstone Ave., P.O. Box 2140, Cody, WY 82414, (307) 527-6241. District Rangers: Beartooth Ranger District, Route 2, Box 3420, Red Lodge, MT 59068, (406) 446-2103; Clarks Fork Ranger District, P.O. Box 1023, Powell, WY 82435, (307) 754-2407; Gardiner Ranger District, P.O. Box 5, Gardiner, MT 59030, (406) 848-7375.

Description: The Beartooth Highway is one of the most spectacular routes on this continent. Charles Kuralt, on television's "Open Road," once called it "the most beautiful drive in America." Opened in 1936, the route roughly

Pilot and Index peaks are prominent features of the North Absaroka Wilderness, adjacent to the Beartooth Highway.

follows the old Sheridan Trail, laid out in 1882.

The road crests at an elevation of 10,946 feet and overlooks hundreds of square miles of alpine lakes and forests, rugged mountain peaks, and prairies on the far horizon. The two-lane highway is paved and has frequent turnouts for scenic and recreational opportunities. Traffic is generally light and travels at a slow pace, both for scenic and safety reasons.

Expect variable high-altitude mountain weather. Summer temperatures range from the 70s on clear sunny days to below freezing during sudden snowstorms. Most common are sunny mornings, cloudy afternoons, and clear evenings. Late August brings regular afternoon thunderstorms.

The Beartooth Highway is awesome driven from either direction. To avoid glare, you may want to drive east to west in the morning but west to east in the afternoon. Driving from east to west entails a long, steep climb, but it avoids riding your brakes down that same stretch of highway.

Red Lodge lies near the eastern end of the scenic byway. This small mountain resort community is tucked into Rock Creek Valley at 5,555 feet elevation. There are festivals and celebrations to enjoy, interpretive nature trails, and cross-country and alpine skiing opportunities. A number of competitions, such as the Peaks to Prairie Triathalon and the Beartooth Run, attract athletes and spectators. The downtown is pleasant, with nice shops.

A side trip on Forest Road 71 follows Rock Creek to campgrounds, picnic areas, and hiking trails. The valley, surrounded by steep mountains, is lovely.

To reach the beginning of the byway, travel eight miles southwest of Red Lodge on U.S. Highway 212 to the national forest boundary. Sheridan and Ratine campgrounds have seven sites each, off the byway along Rock Creek. Parkside, Limberpine, Greenough Lake, and M-K are just off the byway on Forest Road 421.

57

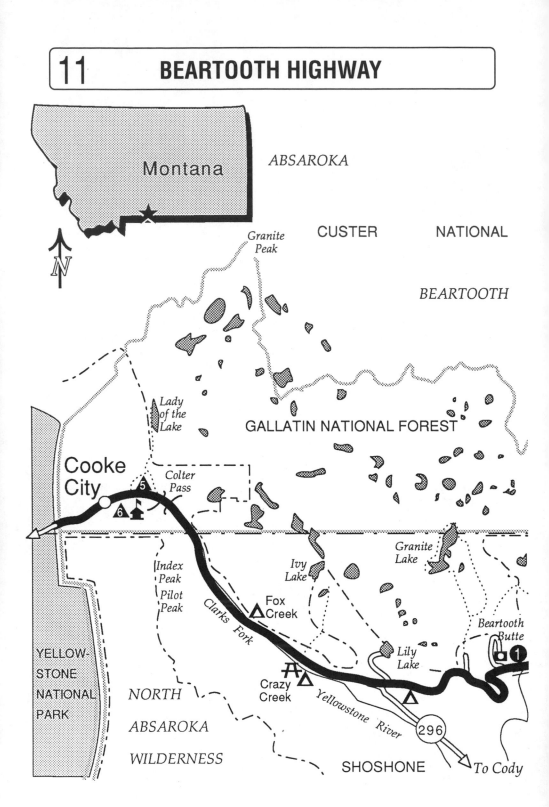

ABSAROKA

CUSTER   NATIONAL

BEARTOOTH

Montana

*Granite
Peak*

*Lady
of the
Lake*

GALLATIN NATIONAL FOREST

Cooke
City

*Colter
Pass*

5

6

*Granite
Lake*

*Index
Peak*

*Pilot
Peak*

*Ivy
Lake*

Clarks Fork

Fox
Creek

*Lily
Lake*

*Beartooth
Butte*

1

YELLOW-
STONE
NATIONAL
PARK

NORTH

ABSAROKA

WILDERNESS

Crazy
Creek

Yellowstone River

296

SHOSHONE

To Cody

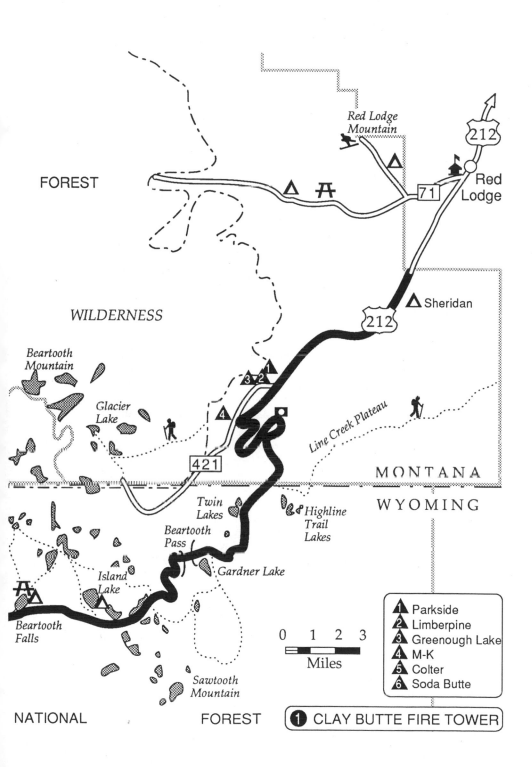

FOREST

Red Lodge
Mountain

*Red Lodge
Mountain*

212

71

Red
Lodge

212 Sheridan

WILDERNESS

*Beartooth
Mountain*

3 2 1

*Glacier
Lake*

4

Line Creek Plateau

421

MONTANA

WYOMING

*Twin
Lakes*

*Beartooth
Pass*

*Highline
Trail
Lakes*

Gardner Lake

*Island
Lake*

*Beartooth
Falls*

*Sawtooth
Mountain*

NATIONAL   FOREST

0 1 2 3

Miles

1 Parkside
2 Limberpine
3 Greenough Lake
4 M-K
5 Colter
6 Soda Butte

1 CLAY BUTTE FIRE TOWER

The route ascends the steep mountain slope via a series of hair-raising switchbacks. Rock Creek Vista provides an opportunity to stop and enjoy the view. Sage-covered fields lead back to Red Lodge, Rock Creek pours out of Glacier Lake high in its cirque, and Hell Roaring Creek sparkles and dances down the mountainside. Miners and pack strings once traveled to Cooke City via the Sliderock Trail, which is visible along the south wall of the valley. Mining played an important role in the early settlement of the Beartooth area.

Scars of the 1948 Hell Roaring and Glacier Lake fires are still evident midway up the canyon. Watch for bighorn sheep, which inhabit the area east of Rock Creek Vista.

From the byway, you can see the Twin Lakes Headwall on the east summit of Beartooth Pass. The permanent snowfield is host to the summer Red Lodge International Ski Race Camp, for individuals aspiring to become Olympic-class slalom skiers. On the west summit, the public can ski at the Gardiner Headwall.

The byway ascends more than 5,000 feet to the high plateaus. Twin Lakes, two blue gems, are just a foreshadowing of the beautiful alpine lakes to come. Hiking trails head north and south from the byway, inviting foot travel through the wildflower-covered alpine meadows. Fishing for brook, golden, cutthroat, and rainbow trout is generally excellent in the stocked lakes. There are no natural fisheries in these glacial cirque lakes. Get the appropriate licenses before fishing: the byway crosses from Montana into Wyoming and then goes back into Montana. Licenses for both states are available in Red Lodge, Top of the World, and Cooke City.

The Beartooth Loop National Recreation Trail begins at Gardner Lake and crosses 10 miles of alpine landscape similar to that found in arctic regions. Growing conditions are severe, and plants have evolved unique adaptive abilities, such as remaining small and low to the ground or having hairy or waxy surfaces. It can take a plant as long as 15 years to produce a single blossom.

Across the valley to the north, a black, jutting fang tucked in a notch low on the horizon is locally called the Bear's Tooth. The Beartooth Mountains are part of the Rocky Mountains, pushed up more than 10,000 feet above sea level 75 million years ago. The softer sedimentary rocks of the ancient seabed eroded away, and older granites and metamorphic rocks were exposed along with intrusive magma dikes. Much of the exposed rock is among the oldest known to man. Volcanoes added lava, ash, and debris, particularly to the western end of the Beartooth Range and into the Absaroka Range. Glaciers occupied the valleys and sculpted the terrain seen today. Remnants of the once-mighty glaciers still remain in the Beartooth.

Beartooth Pass opens views to the west and south into mountain goat country. The grandeur is unsurpassed: snowcapped peaks, glaciers, alpine lakes, colorful flowers, scattered stands of gnarled trees, and rolling plateaus. The pristine air is invigorating; the impact of the Beartooth is unforgettable.

Snowfields usually last through mid-July, and summer visitors can cross-country ski. The byway continues to Top of the World Store. Little Bear Creek babbles across the tundra, and wildflowers bloom in profusion among the emerald-green grasses.

Island Lake Campground has 20 sites and a boat launch. A few miles west, Beartooth Lake lies at the base of Beartooth Butte. The campground has 21 sites and a boat launch. Anglers try for mackinaw, rainbow, cutthroat, and brook trout. Hikers stride off for backcountry lakes and views, and archaeologists head for the butte, looking for fossils of trilobites, corals, crinoids, and brachiopods.

Beartooth Butte has a unique geology. The ocean-deposited sedimentary layers that were completely worn off the rest of the Beartooth Plateau remain on Beartooth Butte. The bright red rock near the top of the butte was the mouth of an ancient stream and contains many fossils.

Across from the butte, Beartooth Falls can be reached via a half-mile trail along the creek. The pretty cascade drops about 100 feet. You can spot it from a pullout where the byway traverses the steep side of a ravine. The highway guardrails are a welcome feature, as the route borders some astonishing drop-offs.

A short distance farther west, the byway leaves the alpine vegetation. Clay Butte Fire Tower is a good three-mile side trip. The visitor information center at the lookout is open in summer. The panoramic view from the top includes the North Absaroka Wilderness and Yellowstone National Park to the west, the Clarks Fork Valley and the Absaroka Mountains to the southwest, and the Big Horn Mountains to the east. Granite Peak, Montana's highest at 12,799 feet, juts up to the northwest, surrounded by the Absaroka-Beartooth Wilderness. The wilderness encompasses 943,377 acres of stunning alpine beauty.

The byway descends through an evergreen forest of lodgepole pines, Engelmann spruces, and alpine firs, mixed with stands of aspens. Views extend south and west into the North Absaroka Wilderness, where Pilot and Index peaks are prominent features. Lake Creek and other streams and waterfalls plunge down mountain slopes and over cliffs.

The Beartooth Highway reaches a junction with Wyoming Route 296, also called Chief Joseph Scenic Highway. A side trip on this road into Sunlight Basin is well worthwhile. The remote valley is simply beautiful, and there are camping, hiking, and fishing opportunities. Evidence of a raging 1988 forest fire blackens portions of the north-facing slopes, and the limestone palisades are of similar composition as Beartooth Butte.

The byway descends to the Clarks Fork Yellowstone River, climbs over historic Colter Pass, and travels through burn scars from the 1988 fires. The river weaves channels through glacial moraine and debris and flows over boulders and fallen trees. The north side of the byway, shows regrowth already beginning after the fires, and mountain bluebirds flit through the understory of flowers and shrubs. Other residents of the byway region include moose, grizzly and black bears, bighorn sheep, mountain goats, marmots, and pikas. Water ouzels bob along stream banks, while falcons, hawks, and eagles soar high above.

Crazy Creek Campground has 16 sites in the forest, and, farther west, Fox Creek Campground has 27 sites.

Cooke City is a small mountain resort community with a rich and colorful history. There are two national forest campgrounds nearby, with a total of 44 sites. Good hiking trails lead through the adjacent rolling, forested backcountry, and fishing is excellent at the many nearby lakes.

The byway descends through Silver Gate and terminates at Northeast Gate in Yellowstone National Park. Yellowstone is the world's first national park, and it features an incredible array of mountains, lakes, geothermal features, wildlife, and natural beauty. □

General description: A 28-mile paved road through a forest near Yellowstone National Park, with views of waterfalls and the Grand Tetons.
Special attractions: Two waterfalls, excellent fishing, river floating, scenic canyons, birdwatching, and wildlife viewing.
Location: Eastern Idaho on the Targhee National Forest, northeast of St. Anthony. The byway travels Idaho Route 47 between Ashton and Harriman Ranch State Park on U.S. Highway 20.
Byway route numbers: Idaho Route 47.
Travel season: The entire byway is generally open from mid-May until late October, and then it is closed by winter snows between Bear Gulch and the junction of Route 47 and Highway 20.
Camping: Two national forest campgrounds with picnic tables, fire grates, and toilets. Water available only at Warm River Campground.
Services: All services in Ashton and Island Park. Limited services in Last Chance.
Nearby attractions: Yellowstone National Park, Grand Teton National Park, Red Rock Lakes National Wildlife Refuge, Warm River Springs, Harriman Ranch State Park and Wildlife Refuge, Island Park Recreation Area, Wyoming Centennial Scenic Byway.
For more information: Targhee National Forest, P.O. Box 208, St. Anthony, ID 83445, (208) 624-3151; District Ranger: Ashton Ranger District, P.O. Box 858, Ashton, ID 83420, (208) 652-7442.

Description: The Mesa Falls Scenic Byway travels through a variety of terrain that includes rolling agricultural lands, forested hills, and a steep river canyon with two beautiful waterfalls. The narrow two-lane road is paved and has scenic turnouts along its winding course. Elevations range from 5,300 to 6,100 feet. Traffic is fairly light, and scenic views of the Tetons, the Island Park Caldera, and the Centennial Range are splendid.

Summer visitors can expect variable weather conditions, ranging from heat waves to thunderstorms to severe frosts. Pleasantly warm days in the 70s and cool nights in the 40s or 50s are most common. Spring and autumn visitors should expect crisp days and freezing temperatures most nights. The road is closed by snow about the end of October, and it reopens when snows melt, around the middle of May. Winter recreation on the closed road includes cross-country skiing and snowmobiling. Weather conditions in winter can be severe.

Begin the loop in the agricultural community of Ashton, and then travel east and north through about nine miles of farmland. Potato, malt barley, alfalfa, and oat fields spread out on all sides, and to the east the giant Tetons soar to above 14,000 feet.

Six miles from Ashton, the Cave Falls Road (Forest Road 582) takes off, promising a wonderful side trip. This partially paved and gravel road will take you to remote Cave Falls and the southwest corner of the Bechler Meadow area of Yellowstone National Park. The area has abundant waterfalls, hiking trails, and camping and fishing opportunities. Be certain you

A visitor enjoys a view of the cascades and Upper Mesa Falls.

have the correct fishing licenses: Idaho, Wyoming, or national park. Also keep in mind that this is prime grizzly bear habitat.

Back on the byway, travel north through Warm River to the first national forest campground, situated near the confluence of Warm River and Robinson Creek. Choose a sunny or cottonwood-shaded site right on the river-bank, and enjoy watching the rainbow trout. This natural fishery exists because the Warm River emerges from a constant 50-degree spring. You may feed and watch the trout, but no fishing is permitted at the fish feeding site. Look for the old narrow-gauge railroad bed running through the campground. The Union-Pacific Railroad once ran a passenger service into Yellowstone, and the bed is now a pleasant hiking, mountain biking, and snowmobiling trail.

The Henry's Fork Canyon drops off to the west, and the byway descends through aspen and lodgepole pine forest. The Henry's Fork is a world-famous fishery, and anglers will find many places to scramble down to the river to try their luck.

Continue north past an old alpine ski area to Lower Mesa Scenic Area, which offers a fine view of Lower Mesa Falls. Built by the Civilian Conservation Corps, the stone overlook and paved walking trails offer a pleasant view of forested hills and river canyon. The small campground has no drinking water available. Huckleberries are abundant and delicious.

Upper Mesa Falls Scenic Area is located one mile north, and a short paved road brings you to an old log lodge planned for use as interpretive center after renovation. Follow the newly constructed winding asphalt path down the hill to the boardwalk trail which offers viewing opportunities for everyone. The accessible trails were constructed to protect vegetation n the hillside from foot traffic while still allowing intimate experiences for visitors with the canyon, river, and waterfall. Rainbows dance over the cascading

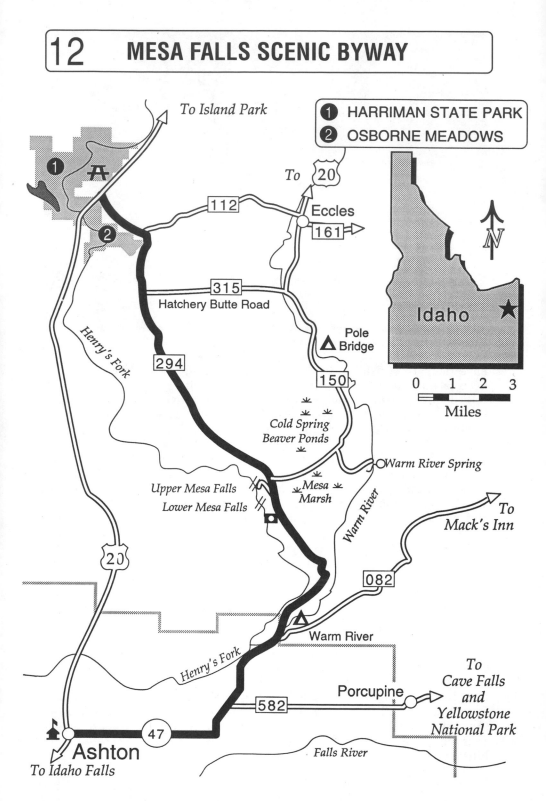

12 MESA FALLS SCENIC BYWAY

To Island Park

1 HARRIMAN STATE PARK
2 OSBORNE MEADOWS

To [20]

Eccles
[161]

[112]

[315]
Hatchery Butte Road

Henry's Fork

[294]

Pole
Bridge

[150]

Idaho

0 1 2 3
Miles

Cold Spring
Beaver Ponds

Warm River Spring

Upper Mesa Falls
Lower Mesa Falls

Mesa
Marsh

Warm River

To
Mack's Inn

[082]

Henry's Fork

Warm River

To
Cave Falls
and
Yellowstone
National Park

Porcupine

[582]

[47]

Ashton
To Idaho Falls

[20]

Falls River

64

water, and cliff walls of columnar basalt are decorated with the bright greens of berry bushes and large Douglas-fir trees. Fully accessible sanitation facilities are available at Upper Mesa Falls.

Upper and Lower Mesa Falls are the last free-flowing major waterfalls in the Columbia River watershed. Upper Mesa Falls drops 100 feet, while Lower Mesa Falls drops 70 feet. The amount of water going over is very impressive.

Mesa Marsh is less than a mile north of Grandview. This is very good bird-watching territory, and enthusiasts can expect to see trumpeter swans; Canada geese; bald eagles; a variety of ducks, such as bufflehead, mallard, and teal; yellow-headed and red-winged blackbirds; and sandhill cranes. Beavers and moose frequent the area, as do elk, mule deer, pronghorns, and occasional black and grizzly bears. The area is unmarked to protect the site from too much human activity.

Forest Road 150 begins one mile north of the Upper Mesa Falls turnoff. This graveled side road offers many possibilities. Follow the signs to Warm River Springs, a pretty and interesting spot seven miles from the scenic byway. A short walk leads to the spring, which bubbles out of an otherwise dry hillside and forms the Warm River. Several hiking trails are in the area, there are toilets and a grassy picnic area, and a Forest Service cabin is available for rental by the public.

Another option is to continue north on Forest Road 150 to Pole Bridge Campground, good fishing opportunities, and pretty forest scenes with views into Yellowstone. The road eventually emerges onto U.S. Highway 20 near Island Park.

The remaining 14 miles of scenic byway travel through some of the active timber-sale areas on the Targhee National Forest. Clearcuts and reforestation are evident, and an interpretive fire display is interesting. Fireweed sports its crimson blossoms in disturbed areas, together with lupines, goldenrods, yampas, asters, and Indian paintbrushes.

The byway ascends the lip of an ancient caldera as it climbs away from Warm River. The rim of the caldera includes Big Bend Ridge, Thurman Ridge, and the eastern ridges adjacent to Yellowstone National Park. This is the largest volcanic caldera in the United States.

Osborne Meadows is a large, open area on an oxbow curve of the Henry's Fork. Wildflowers are abundant and beautiful. Watch for deer, elk, and moose, particularly in the mornings and evenings.

Mesa Falls Scenic Loop ends at U.S. Highway 20, directly across from Harriman Ranch State Park in Harriman Wildlife Sanctuary. The park is day-use only, with picnicking, hiking, fishing, and interpretive programs. The sanctuary protects a wide variety of songbirds, waterfowl, fish, and mammals. □

General description: A 161-mile route in mountainous western Wyoming, along rivers and past the magnificent Teton Range.

Special attractions: Grand Teton National Park; National Elk Refuge; Bridger, Teton, Gros Ventre, and Washakie wilderness areas; varied terrain; outstanding views.

Location: West-central Wyoming on the Shoshone and Bridger-Teton national forests, west of Thermopolis. The byway travels a horseshoe-shaped route on U.S. Highway 287 from Dubois west to Moran Junction and then south and east on U.S. Highway 191 to Pinedale.

Byway route numbers: U.S. Highways 287 and 191.

Travel season: Year-round. Winter driving conditions may be hazardous.

Camping: Five national forest campgrounds with picnic tables, toilets, fire grates, and drinking water. Numerous campgrounds in Grand Teton National Park. One Bureau of Land Management campground with picnic tables, toilets, trailer dumping station, fire grates, drinking water.

Services: All services in Dubois, Jackson, and Pinedale. Limited services at numerous locations along the byway.

Nearby attractions: Yellowstone National Park, Snake River, hot springs, fishing, alpine and cross-country skiing, hiking, mountain biking, camping, Fremont Lake.

For more information: Bridger-Teton National Forest, P.O. Box 1888, Jackson, WY 83001, (307) 733-2752; Shoshone National Forest, P.O. Box 2140, Cody, WY 82414, (307) 527-6241. District Rangers: Dubois Ranger District, P.O. Box 106, Dubois, WY 82513, (307) 455-2466; Buffalo Ranger District, Highway 287, P.O. Box 278, Moran, WY 83013, (307) 543-2386; Jackson Ranger District, 140 E. Broadway, P.O. Box 1689, Jackson, WY 83001, (307) 733-4755; Pinedale Ranger District, 210 W. Pine St., P.O. Box 220, Pinedale, WY 82941, (307) 367-4326.

Description: The Wyoming Centennial Scenic Byway follows the routes set by several rivers through the spectacular mountains of western Wyoming. The two-lane highway is paved and well-maintained, and it has frequent turnouts from which to view the scenery or gain access to recreation. Traffic can be constant, especially in the park and around Jackson, but it is rarely congested.

Elevations on the byway range from 6,200 to more than 9,600 feet. Summer visitors can expect variable mountain weather. Most common are days in the 70s and evenings down to the 40s, with afternoon thunderstorms. Occasional summer sleet and snow are not unheard of. Spring and fall are cooler, with temperatures ranging from below freezing to days in the 50s and 60s. Winter is cold, with snow on the ground from December until April.

The most scenic direction to travel this byway is counterclockwise, beginning in Dubois. This allows the fullest views of the spectacular Tetons. However, you will not be disappointed driving this route in the opposite direction; the area is beautiful.

Dubois, at 6,900 feet elevation, is adjacent to Horse Creek and the Wind

13 WYOMING CENTENNIAL SCENIC BYWAY

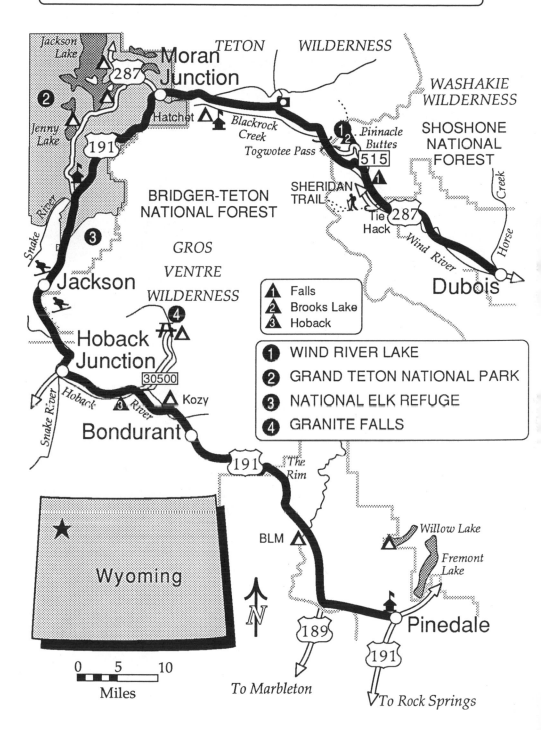

Jackson Lake

TETON   *WILDERNESS*

Moran Junction

287

WASHAKIE WILDERNESS

SHOSHONE NATIONAL FOREST

Hatchet

Blackrock Creek

Togwotee Pass

1 **2** *Pinnacle Buttes*

515

2

Jenny Lake

191

BRIDGER-TETON NATIONAL FOREST

SHERIDAN TRAIL

1

Creek

Snake River

3

GROS VENTRE WILDERNESS

Tie Hack

287

Wind River

Horse Creek

Jackson

Dubois

Hoback Junction

4

▲**1**	Falls
▲**2**	Brooks Lake
▲**3**	Hoback

30500

Kozy

Hoback River

3

Bondurant

1	WIND RIVER LAKE
2	GRAND TETON NATIONAL PARK
3	NATIONAL ELK REFUGE
4	GRANITE FALLS

Snake River

191

The Rim

BLM ▲

Willow Lake

Fremont Lake

★

Wyoming

N

189

191

Pinedale

0   5   10
Miles

To Marbleton

To Rock Springs

67

The Tetons grace the horizon along the Wyoming Centennial Scenic Byway.

River, at the base of the Wind River Range. The byway climbs northwest up the tiny, winding headwaters of the Wind River and through the colorful reds and rusts of the Eocene Wind River formation, arid fields of sage, and an interesting badlands landscape. Ranches dot the long valley, and clearcuts wear the bright green of new growth. A few miles inside the Shoshone National Forest, about 17 miles west of Dubois, is a monument to the tie hacks of the railroad era. The display is both understandable and interesting, and the views of the surrounding landscape are good.

Falls Campground is a peaceful area with 46 sites among the trees. A lovely waterfall soothes campers here. A few miles north on Forest Road 515, Brooks Lake sits in a basin. Anglers can enjoy both the views of the mountains and the cutthroat and brook trout fishing. The campground has 14 sites, the resort lodge is listed on the National Register of Historic Places, and the Brooks Lake Trail crosses Bear Cub Pass into the Teton Wilderness. A different trail leads to Upper and Lower Jade lakes, an easy hike through old-growth Engelmann spruce forest.

Pinnacle Buttes and then Breccia Cliffs dominate the northern horizon. Pinnacle Buttes are primarily layers of volcanic rocks and ash. The route climbs through gorgeous fields of subalpine wildflowers to reach the Continental Divide.

Togwotee (TOE-get-ee) was a Northern Shoshone medicine man. Togwotee Pass, at an elevation of 9,544 feet on the Continental Divide, marks the boundary between the Shoshone and Bridger-Teton national forests. Bridger-Teton is the second-largest national forest in the contiguous 48 states, encompassing slightly more than 3.4 million acres. The view from the pass includes Two Ocean Mountain, with its terraced west-side cliffs. Hikers can prolong their enjoyment by walking four to five miles back to Brooks Lake. The trail passes under Brooks and Sublette mountains over moderately easy terrain.

68

The forest is composed primarily of lodgepole, limber, and whitebark pines, Douglas-firs, subalpine firs, and Engelmann spruces. Aspens and Colorado blue spruces grow in the wetter areas. Forest inhabitants include moose, bighorn sheep, mule deer, elk, coyotes, and grizzly and black bears.

The byway descends alongside Blackrock Creek through lush green meadows. An overlook lets you pull off the road and savor the first views of the Tetons in the distance. A footpath climbs about 1,500 vertical feet in two miles to Angle Mountain, and hikers can see Mount Hancock in Yellowstone, the Tetons, and the Gros Ventre and Bridger wilderness areas. Nearby, Togwotee Lodge hosts a year-round Forest Service ranger naturalist. There are numerous trails for hiking, cross-country skiing, and snowmobiling.

The byway descends into the Buffalo Valley, and views of the Tetons are riveting. Blackrock Ranger Station has information about the national forest and the byway, and nearby Hatchet Campground has nine sites in the trees adjacent to the highway. The byway crosses into Grand Teton National Park and turns south onto U.S. Highway 191 at Moran Junction.

Grand Teton National Park has numerous recreational offerings: fishing, hiking, mountain climbing, horseback-riding, ranger-led naturalist programs and hikes, boating, and more. There are visitor centers, lodges, restaurants, shops, and other services available.

The byway travels past Jackson and Jenny lakes, down the Snake River and Jackson Hole. Hole, a term used by early trappers, means valley. The summit of the Grand Teton, at 13,770 feet, towers over the 6,000- to 7,000-foot valley floor. There are numerous turnouts, and camera buffs and sightseers will be ecstatic.

The Tetons are granitic, sculpted by glaciers. They are the youngest of Wyoming's mountains, and they are still rising. An enormous fault raised the Teton Range and dropped Jackson Hole. Then Ice Age glaciers covered the Tetons and filled Jackson Hole with more than 2,000 feet of ice. Jackson Lake was created by glacial melt, and small glaciers still remain in pockets of the Tetons.

East of the byway, the Jackson National Fish Hatchery is open for tours. The National Elk Refuge is a quiet place, good for summer drives and peaceful contemplation. In winter there are thousands of elk, along with tundra swans and trumpeter swans.

The town of Jackson is a tourist's paradise. A rodeo, shops, art galleries, restaurants and bars, lodging, and theater all enhance the Wild West theme of the community. Visitors enter the central park through arches of elk antlers, and recreation and fun is the norm. There are two downhill ski areas and ample opportunities for cross-country skiing, summer hikes, rafting, and bicycling.

The byway continues south on 191, past the distinctive haystacks along Flat Creek and the Snake River to Hoback Junction. Here the byway turns east, staying on U.S. Highway 191. The route climbs up the Hoback River canyon, through winter range for deer, elk, and bighorn sheep. Hoback Campground has 16 sites under the Douglas-firs along the road. More sites are available across the river, but they are accessible only to the adventuresome since the bridge is washed out.

The folding and faulting of the Gros Ventre and the Wind River ranges is exposed here by the Hoback River, which sliced through the layers of rock

Anglers find many opportunities to fish in the streams and rivers near the Wyoming Centennial Scenic Byway. Christopher Cauble photo.

and revealed the geologic evolution of the area. Red, maroon, pink, gray, tan, and yellow sedimentary layers of Paleozoic, Mesozoic, and Jurassic eras are just some of the exposed geologic story.

The byway climbs up the canyon, and you can take a very good side trip by turning north onto Forest Road 30500 to Granite Hot Springs. The route follows a gravel road up Granite Creek to a campground, developed hot springs, waterfall, and hiking trails into the Gros Ventre Wilderness. This may well be the prettiest side road in the Bridger-Teton National Forest.

A few miles east of the Granite turnoff, Kozy Campground has eight sites in an open park along the river. Picturesque log fences in the area are typical of fencing in the arid West, where soils are too rocky to justify digging post holes.

The scenic byway continues east, and vistas open up after Cliff Creek. Pronghorn and sandhill cranes inhabit the ranchland, and the Gros Ventre Range provides scenic viewing. The small structure next to the Bondurant Elementary School is the original schoolhouse. Willows and beaver ponds adorn the waterway next to the byway.

The highway climbs through scenic aspen groves to The Rim, an abrupt break between the Hoback Basin and the Green River watershed. Then it leaves the national forest. The descent passes a BLM campground in the open sagebrush fields at Warren Bridge.

The byway ends in rural Pinedale. A ranger station has information on the national forest and the byway. The community has a Mountain Man Rendezvous the second weekend in July, traveler services, and lots of access to the magnificent recreational opportunities in the Wind River Range. □

14 BIGHORN SCENIC BYWAYS
Bighorn National Forest   Wyoming

General description: The byways are three distinctive highways that cross 111 miles of the gorges and high country of the scenic Big Horn Mountains.
Special attractions: Shell Falls, colorful autumn foliage, Antelope Butte and Meadowlark Lake (High Point) ski areas, Medicine Wheel National Historic Landmark, Cloud Peak Wilderness, alpine vegetation, extensive views.
Location: North-central Wyoming on the Bighorn National Forest, west and southwest of Sheridan. The scenic byway on U.S. Highway 16 travels 44.3 miles on national forest lands between Buffalo and Ten Sleep. The scenic byway on U.S. Highway 14 travels 40 miles on national forest lands between Dayton and Shell. The scenic byway portion of U.S. Highway 14A is 26.8 miles on national forest lands between Burgess Junction and the national forest boundary near Medicine Wheel National Historic Landmark east of Lovell.
Byway route numbers: U.S. Highways 16, 14, and 14A.
Travel season: Year-round on U.S. Highways 16 and 14, with occasional temporary winter closures for emergency snow removal. U.S. Highway 14A is open from about Mother's Day in May through mid-November, then closed by winter snows.

Camping: Thirteen national forest campgrounds with picnic tables, toilets, fire grates, and drinking water. No hookups.

Services: Limited services at Burgess Junction, Meadowlark Lake, and other locations along the byways. All services in nearby Sheridan, Buffalo, Ten Sleep, Worland, Greybull, Shell, Dayton, and Lovell.

Nearby attractions: Bighorn Canyon National Recreation Area, Custer Battlefield, Fort Phil Kearney, Story Fish Hatchery, Wagon Box Fight and Fetterman Massacre areas, Bradford-Brinton Memorial, Trails End Museum, Medicine Lodge Archaeological Site.

For more information: Bighorn National Forest, 1969 S. Sheridan Ave., Sheridan, WY 82801, (307) 672-0751. District Rangers: Buffalo Ranger District, 300 Spruce St., Buffalo, WY 82834, (307) 684-7981; Ten Sleep Ranger District, 2009 Bighorn Ave., Worland, WY 82401, (307) 347-8291; Paintrock Ranger District, P.O. Box 831, Greybull, WY 82426, (307) 765-4435; Medicine Wheel Ranger District, P.O. Box 367, Lovell, WY 82431, (307) 548-6514; Tongue Ranger District, 1969 S. Sheridan Ave., Sheridan, WY 82801, (307) 672-0751.

Description: The Bighorn Scenic Byways are three separate roads that cross the Big Horn Mountains. The routes are all two-lane, paved highways with frequent turnouts for scenic and recreational opportunities. Traffic is light, and the roads are a pleasure to travel. Many travelers come from the eastern United States, and the Big Horn Mountains are the first oasis of mountainous relief after a long haul over the flat Great Plains. The alpine splendor of the range will meet any traveler's expectations.

Elevations on the byway range from about 4,800 feet to more than 9,600 feet. Summer visitors can expect variable mountain weather. Generally, daytime temperatures are in the 60s and 70s, while nights dip to the 40s. Afternoon thundershowers are common. Spring and autumn are cooler, with temperatures ranging from below freezing to the 50s and 60s. Winter snowcover generally lasts from about December through March.

One segment of the Bighorn Scenic Byways system travels U.S. Highway 16. Beginning in Buffalo, drive west about seven miles on Highway 16 to the Bighorn National Forest boundary, the beginning of the byway. This is prime elk wintering and calving grounds. Views into the Cloud Peak Wilderness are breathtaking as the route ascends 3,000 feet into the Big Horns. There are numerous picnic areas along the way.

The first campground is Middle Fork, with nine sites in the trees at 7,400 feet elevation. Nearby Circle Park Campground has 10 sites, Tie Hack Campground has nine sites, and South Fork Campground has 18 sites.

Wildflowers such as lupines, arrowleaf balsamroots, and asters line the byway route, and deer are often seen grazing along the edge of large, grassy slopes that lead the eye up to lodgepole pine forests and snowcapped peaks. An overlook atop Loaf Mountain provides a satisfying panoramic view, with the Cloud Peak Wilderness drawing the most attention.

Crazy Woman Campground has six sites, not recommended for travel trailers. Close by, Canyon Campground has four sites, and Lost Cabin Campground has 20. The probability of spotting moose in this area is very good.

The byway ascends 9,677-foot Powder River Pass, the highest point on the route. Vistas west and east include the Big Horn Basin, Powder River Basin, 13,000-foot mountain parks and peaks, extensive talus slopes, and fragile alpine tundra vegetation. You will want to linger here.

The byway descends through open rangeland to Meadowlark National Recreation Area, a lovely area centered around Meadowlark Lake. There is a ski area, resort, lodging, and services. Five nearby campgrounds have more than 100 sites available. Boating is popular in summer; cross-country skiing and snowmobiling take over in winter.

West of Meadowlark's green forests and mountain vistas, the byway enters a dramatically different area. Tensleep Canyon has steep, red- and buff-colored limestone cliffs, and the byway descends steeply with sharp turns. Tensleep Creek glitters below, and the arid slopes are covered with sage. There is good fishing for rainbow trout in the creek. Cottonwood trees offer shade and shelter for songbirds.

At the bottom of the canyon, Tensleep and Leigh Creek campgrounds have five and 11 sites, respectively, at an elevation of 5,400 feet. You can visit and picnic at the Tensleep Fish Hatchery. The byway ends at the national forest boundary. U.S. Highway 16 continues another seven miles to Tensleep, a quiet community with traveler services.

Another segment of the Bighorn Scenic Byways travels U.S. Highway 14 between Dayton and Shell. The byway begins about six miles southwest of Dayton at the national forest boundary and offers instant gratification to sightseers. Geologic formations are signed as the route ascends steep switchbacks into the mountains; they include Chugwater, Tensleep, Amsden, Madison, Bighorn, and Gros Ventre.

Several overlooks partway up the switchbacks allow views of Buffalo Tongue Mountain with its massive slide and the Fallen City rockslide area. The exposed, steeply inclined surfaces make it easy to understand the geology here. Fallen City has slabs of limestone jumbled on a thin layer of sand; a good earthquake will undoubtedly cause it to slide even farther down the mountain. Buffalo Tongue Mountain, sometimes called Horseshoe Mountain by the less imaginative, is the namesake of a river and national forest district. You may be treated to the sight of a hang glider soaring the western slopes of the Big Horns. On a clear day, look east over the Sheridan Valley to Devils Tower, 100 miles away.

The route climbs into grassy parks with patches of lodgepole pines. Wildflowers put on a magnificent show from spring through autumn, and photographers will want to stop again and again for pictures. A side trip on Forest Roads 16 and 26 loops around, with access to Black Mountain Lookout, a historic sawmill and flume site, fishing for brown and brook trout in the South Tongue River, and camping opportunities. One section of the side trip can be very slick when wet. Woodrock had a sawmill, tie flume, and splash dam for railroad ties. The ties shot down to Dayton in the wooden flume.

Sibley Lake is a peaceful spot, with 10 campsites in the lodgepole pines and Douglas-firs, picnicking, nonmotorized boating, and fishing for the stocked rainbow trout. Nearby Prune Creek Campground, elevation 7,700 feet, has 21 sites. There are 26 miles of cross-country ski trails in this area. Wildlife enthusiasts should watch for deer, elk, and moose.

The Big Horns are home to 265 species of birds. Songbirds include vireos, warblers, finches, and meadowlarks. Waterfowl, owls, hummingbirds, grouse, eagles, hawks, and gulls can also be found.

U.S. Highway 14 turns south at Burgess Junction, about 20 miles from the

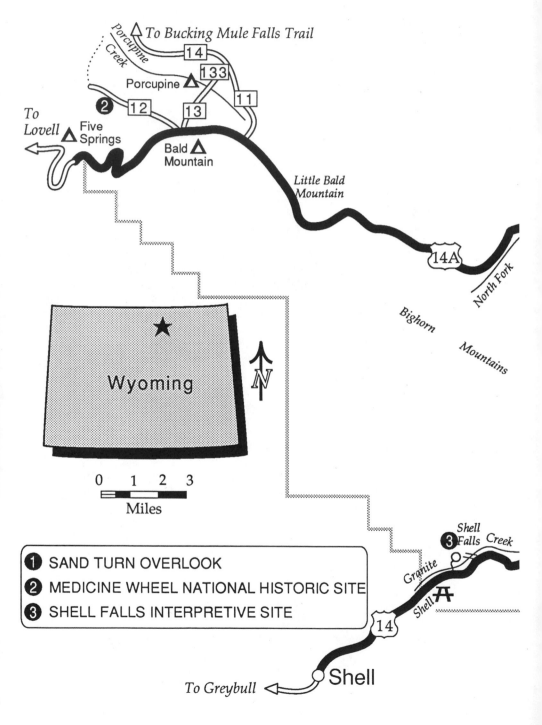

To Bucking Mule Falls Trail

Porcupine Creek

Porcupine

To Lovell

Five Springs

Bald Mountain

Little Bald Mountain

14A

North Fork

Bighorn Mountains

★

Wyoming

N

0   1   2   3
Miles

Shell Falls Creek

Granite

Shell

14

Shell

To Greybull

1 SAND TURN OVERLOOK
2 MEDICINE WHEEL NATIONAL HISTORIC SITE
3 SHELL FALLS INTERPRETIVE SITE

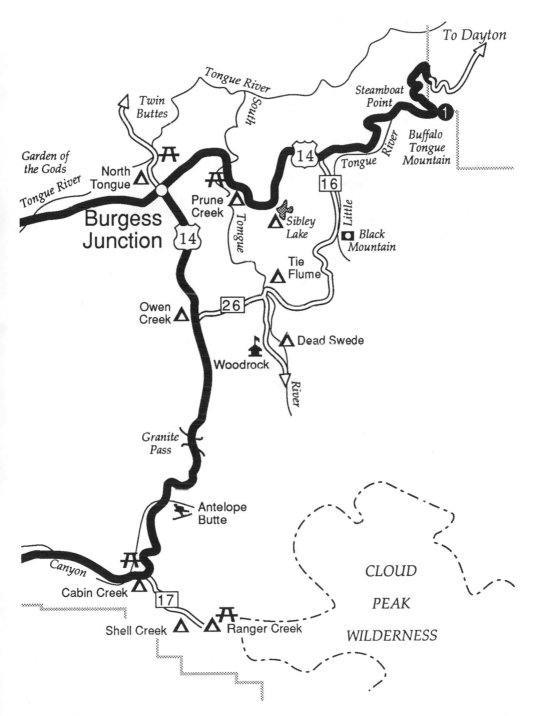

To Dayton

Twin Buttes

Tongue River

Tongue River South

Steamboat Point

Buffalo Tongue Mountain

Garden of the Gods

Tongue River

North Tongue

Burgess Junction

Prune Creek

14

16

Tongue River

Little Tongue River

Sibley Lake

Black Mountain

Tongue

14

Owen Creek

26

Tie Flume

Dead Swede

Woodrock

River

Granite Pass

Antelope Butte

Canyon

Cabin Creek

17

Shell Creek

Ranger Creek

CLOUD

PEAK

WILDERNESS

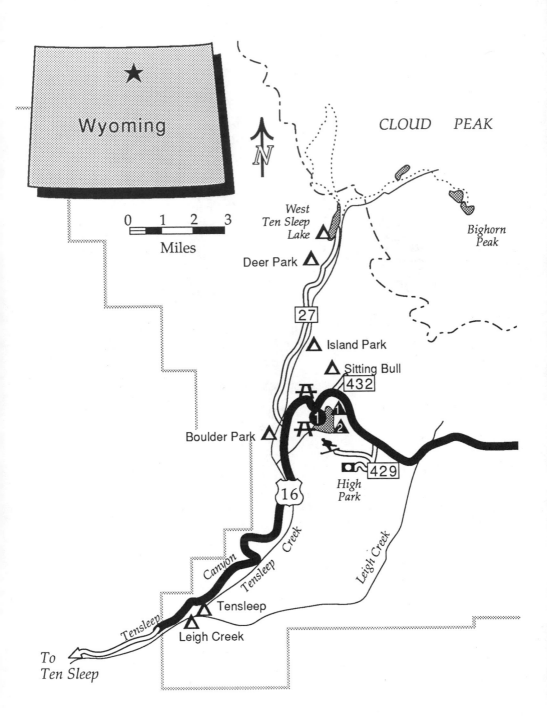

Wyoming

CLOUD PEAK

0 1 2 3
Miles

West
Ten Sleep
Lake

Deer Park

Bighorn
Peak

27

Island Park

Sitting Bull

432

1

1
2

Boulder Park

429

High
Park

16

Canyon

Tensleep Creek

Leigh Creek

Tensleep

Tensleep

Leigh Creek

To
Ten Sleep

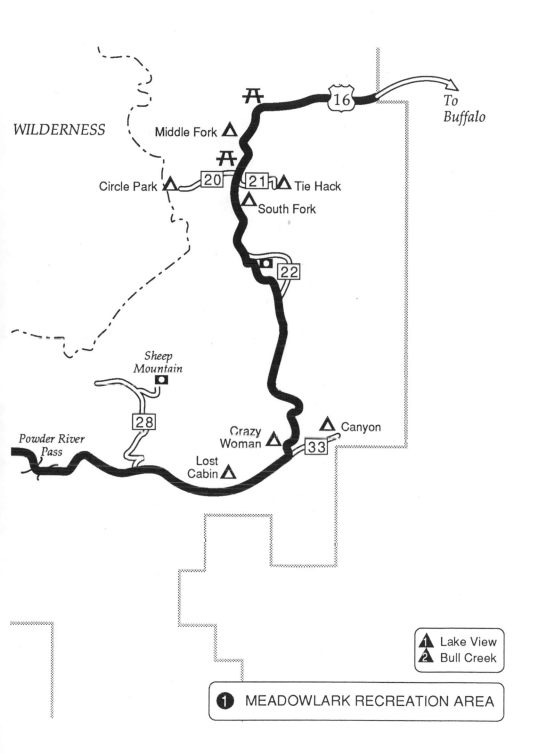

WILDERNESS

Middle Fork

16

To Buffalo

Circle Park 20 21 Tie Hack

South Fork

22

Sheep Mountain

28

Powder River Pass

Crazy Woman

Canyon

33

Lost Cabin

1 Lake View
2 Bull Creek

1 MEADOWLARK RECREATION AREA

Panoramic, extensive views of alpine vegetation and snowcapped mountains grace the Bighorn Scenic Byways routes.

byway's beginning at the national forest boundary. A visitors center is scheduled to open here in 1995. Be alert here: recreational motorists can be unpredictable at the junction. The Twin Buttes rise to the north, there are traveler services available, and the wildflowers in the open parks along the byway are gorgeous. Lupines, arnicas, and shooting stars cover the fields in June. The byway continues south on 14 through grassy meadows with stands of conifers. Views extend into the Cloud Peak Wilderness to the south, and occasional marmots may pop up to watch the cars roll by.

Owen Creek Campground, in the heart of moose and elk country, has seven sites at 8,400 feet elevation. A few miles east of the byway, Tie Flume Campground has 25 sites and Dead Swede Campground 23 sites. Watch for beaver and their dams and houses while ascending 8,950-foot Granite Pass.

A few miles west of the pass is Antelope Butte Ski Area and then Cabin Creek Campground, with four sites. The arid slopes along Granite Creek support sagebrush and drought-hardy forbs. The route descends into Shell Canyon, a deep limestone and granite gorge carved into Precambrian rocks by Shell Creek.

A staffed information center and interpretive trails are open in summer at Shell Falls, midway down the canyon. The falls is very pretty, and the exhibits are interesting.

The byway descends and follows cottonwood-lined Shell Creek to the small community of Shell. This area is rich in fossils and Native American artifacts. Early white settlers were primarily miners, loggers, and ranchers.

The third segment of the Bighorn Scenic Byways begins at Burgess Junction and follows U.S. Highway 14A west to the national forest boundary. Blue-ribbon cutthroat and rainbow trout fishing can be found in the North Fork Tongue River. Bull moose and elk cows and calves inhabit the area west of Burgess Junction. North Tongue Campground has 11 sites at elevation 7,900 feet. The large limestone pillars north of the byway are locally referred to as Garden of the Gods.

Dolomite cliffs on both sides of the byway contain fossils of hard-shelled marine organisms of 530 million years ago. The byway has a fine observation point near Little Bald Mountain where you can see north into Montana and west to the Rockies.

A side trip on Forest Roads 11 and 14 leads north on a one-lane gravel road to Porcupine Falls and Bucking Mule Falls National Recreation Trail.

Along Highway 14A, Bald Mountain Campground lies at 9,200 feet elevation and has 15 sites. Just north, Porcupine Campground has 12 sites. Half a mile west of Bald Mountain Campground, you can drive to the Medicine Wheel National Historic Landmark on Forest Road 12. The road is narrow, and one section passes by some steep drop-offs. The Medicine Wheel was built by Indians, but its exact origin is unknown. Today it is used by Native Americans for religious and spiritual ceremonies. The views of the Big Horns and vicinity from this spot are unbelievable and worth the trip.

The byway descends steep grades and ends at the national forest boundary. Views are extensive to the west over the Big Horn Basin. □

15 SPEARFISH CANYON HIGHWAY
Black Hills National Forest South Dakota

General description: A 20-mile highway through a steep-walled, limestone canyon in the Black Hills.

Special attractions: Trout fishing, picnicking, waterfalls, skiing, colorful autumn foliage.

Location: West-central South Dakota near the Wyoming border, on the Black Hills National Forest. The byway travels U.S. Highway 14A from Interstate 90 at Spearfish south to Cheyenne Crossing.

Byway route number: U.S. Highway 14A.

Travel season: Year-round.

Camping: There is no overnight camping in the canyon, but there are several campgrounds in or near Spearfish. Three national forest campgrounds, open Memorial Day through Labor Day, are within four miles of the canyon highway, with drinking water, picnic tables, barbeque grates, and vault toilets. No hookups.

Services: All services in Spearfish. Restaurant and cabins at Rimrock Lodge. Visitor center and restaurant in Savoy. Cabins at Spearfish Canyon Lodge. All services in Cheyenne Crossing, although availability is limited.

Nearby attractions: Historic Deadwood, Mount Rushmore National Memorial, gold mine, trout hatchery, Devils Tower National Monument, Bighorn Scenic Byways, Bear Butte State Park, Black Hills Passion Play.

For more information: Black Hills National Forest, Rural Route 2 Box 200, Custer, SD 57730 (605) 673-2251. District Ranger: Spearfish Ranger District, 320 Ryan Road, Spearfish, SD 57783 (605) 642-4622.

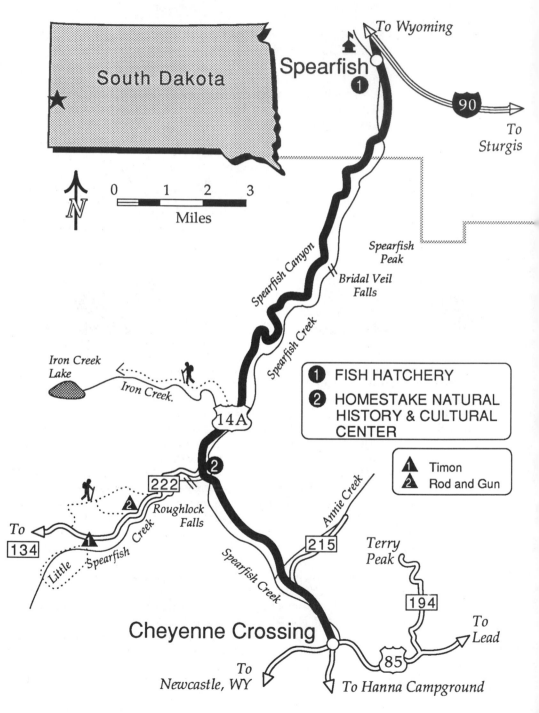

15   SPEARFISH CANYON HIGHWAY

To Wyoming

South Dakota

Spearfish ❶

90

To Sturgis

N

0   1   2   3
Miles

Spearfish Canyon

Spearfish Peak

Bridal Veil Falls

Spearfish Creek

Iron Creek Lake

Iron Creek.

14A

❶ FISH HATCHERY

❷ HOMESTAKE NATURAL HISTORY & CULTURAL CENTER

▲❶ Timon
▲❷ Rod and Gun

❷

222

Roughlock Falls

Little Spearfish Creek

To 134

Annie Creek

215

Terry Peak

194

To Lead

Spearfish Creek

Cheyenne Crossing

85

To Newcastle, WY

To Hanna Campground

Description: Spearfish Canyon Highway winds alongside Spearfish Creek through a high-walled limestone canyon. The wide, paved road ascends gently, and numerous turnouts provide space for you to stop and admire the scenery.

The Black Hills climate is generally mild for the snowbelt region. Summer temperatures in the canyon range from 50 to 90 degrees, and the sky is usually clear. Daily afternoon thunderstorms are common in July and August. Autumn temperatures average 50 degrees in the daytime, with freezing temperatures at night. Snow is possible from December to April, especially in the upper canyon. Spring begins around mid-April, when the snow melts and wildflowers emerge.

In Spearfish, where the byway begins, you will find all services, as well as the Black Hills Passion Play in summer, a fish hatchery, and a pleasant city park. The byway leaves town and winds south through the canyon. The buff-colored rocks soar as high as 1,200 feet overhead, while deciduous trees such as oaks, birches, cottonwoods, willows, ashes, and aspens provide a brilliant green canopy to shade the canyon floor. White spruces and ponderosa pines ascend the canyon walls and create a lovely mosaic of dark greens against the light-colored limestone. The canyon is renowned for its showy display of golden leaves in autumn.

About seven miles south of the canyon entrance, Bridal Veil Falls cascades down the lower canyon walls. It is easily seen from the highway. In winter, it becomes a frozen icefall.

Watch for whitetail and mule deer in the canyon. Overhead, bald eagles and a variety of hawks may circle lazily above the rim, riding the warm thermal air that rises out of the canyon. Porcupines cling to trees, marmots hide in rock piles, and chipmunks and other small rodents scurry about the ground.

Most of the canyon bottom is owned by Homestake Mining Company, which has mined gold in the area for more than 100 years. Remnants of abandoned mining shacks and towns dot the area, and you can see the water flume that still brings drinking water into the town of Spearfish. Look overhead to the east for the covered aquaduct, visible as it crosses openings in the canyon.

Fishing is very good in Spearfish and Little Spearfish creeks, for brown, brook, and rainbow trout. Some sections are catch and release only. The canyon highway is also a popular bicycle route, with its gentle grade and wide shoulders.

Numerous side canyons provide good day hikes for families. About five miles south of Bridal Veil Falls, you can follow an old roadbed that winds along Iron Creek, which has lovely little cascades, pools, and hanging rock gardens in the first mile. Roughlock Falls, farther along the byway, is situated a very short walk from a pleasant picnic area that has tables, barbeque grates, and vault toilets. Rim Rock Trail ascends the north side of Little Spearfish Canyon and crosses the open forest and grasses of the rims. Little Spearfish Trail also brings hikers onto the limestone plateau, after following the creek through a forest of ponderosa pines. Deer, elk, and wild turkeys can often be seen up on the plateau. Forest Road 215 is a single-lane dirt road that ascends Annie Creek. Drive up it a mile or two, and then hike the old roads to get some nice views of the canyon. Watch for poison ivy throughout the entire canyon area.

Four-wheelers and snowmobilers will find several access roads leading from

Spearfish Creek, mist, and clouds add to the beauty of Spearfish Canyon Highway.

the canyon to the limestone plateaus above. Forest Roads 222 and 215 lead to the miles of unimproved roads through mining and timbering sites that crisscross the upper plateaus.

Rod and Gun and Timon campgrounds are a few miles up Little Spearfish Creek Canyon. Both lie at about 5,300 feet elevation, and each has seven sites scattered along the creek under an open forest canopy. Hanna Campground is farther south along East Spearfish Creek. Hanna has 13 sites along the creek under tall spruce trees and in the adjacent meadow. Portions of the movie "Dances with Wolves" were filmed at the Rod and Gun Campground.

At the south end of Spearfish Canyon Highway is tiny Cheyenne Crossing, an old stage stop on the run between Cheyenne and Deadwood. From 1878 to 1885, stagecoaches carried gold bullion, supplies, and passengers between the two communities.

A good side trip lies a few miles west of Cheyenne Crossing. Take U.S. Highway 85 and then go north on Forest Road 194 to the old lookout atop Terry Peak for a 360-degree view of the Black Hills and surrounding area. Look west to the Bearlodge Mountains in Wyoming, south to Inyan Kara Mountain, southeast to Custer Peak, and north to Bear Butte. □

General description: A 29-mile route across the scenic Medicine Bow Mountains.

Special attractions: High peaks, alpine lakes, Snowy Range Ski Area, wildflowers, colorful autumn foliage, trout fishing, hiking, camping.

Location: Southeastern Wyoming on the Medicine Bow National Forest, west of Laramie. The route begins at the national forest boundary just west of Centennial and travels Wyoming Route 130 to the national forest boundary just west of Brush Creek Visitors Information Center.

Byway route number: Wyoming Route 130.

Travel season: Memorial Day weekend until early November, and then closed by winter snows.

Camping: Twelve national forest campgrounds with picnic tables, fire grates, toilets, and drinking water. No hookups.

Services: Limited lodging, meals, store, gasoline, and phone in Centennial. Two guest ranches located on the byway. All services in nearby Laramie and Saratoga.

Nearby attractions: Savage Run Wilderness, Saratoga Hot Springs, Curt Gowdy State Park, Bamforth and Hutton Lake National Wildlife Refuges, museums and a planetarium in Laramie, Wyoming-Colorado Scenic Railroad Snowy Range route, Vedauwoo rocks, Grand Encampment Museum in Encampment, Lincoln Monument, Wyoming Territorial Park.

For more information: Medicine Bow National Forest, 2468 Jackson St., Laramie, WY 82070-6535, (307) 745-8971. District Ranger: Laramie Ranger District, 2468 Jackson St., Laramie, WY, 82070-6535, (307) 745-8971; Brush Creek Ranger District, 212 S. First St., P.O. Box 249, Saratoga, WY 82331, (307) 326-5258.

Description: The scenic byway crosses the Medicine Bow Mountains, a region of beautiful alpine vegetation, high lakes, dramatic peaks, and far-ranging views. Locally the highest peaks of the Medicine Bows are called the Snowy Range, because the white, Precambrian quartzite on the crest of the peaks looks like snow even in late summer. The two-lane highway is paved and has numerous turnouts for scenic and recreational opportunities. Traffic is generally light, and the wide shoulders are good for bicycling.

Elevations range from 7,900 feet to more than 10,800 feet. You should expect variable mountain weather. Summer temperatures range from below freezing to highs in the 80s. Most common are sunny days in the 60s and 70s and nights down to the 40s. Afternoon thunderstorms are a regular occurrence.

The scenery is exceptional when traveling in either direction. Beginning in Laramie, drive 30 miles west on Wyoming Route 130 through ranchland in Big Hollow Basin. The Medicine Bow Mountains look like low, forested hills, with the Snowy Range rising out the top. The peaks of Colorado's Mount Zirkel Wilderness are visible to the south.

The community of Centennial lies near the start of the byway at the Medicine Bow National Forest boundary. Centennial is a delightful stop. A tiny but very good museum is housed in the old railroad station; it is open

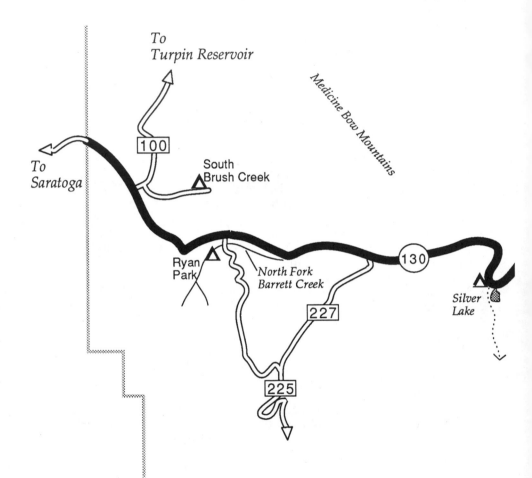

To
Turpin Reservoir

Medicine Bow Mountains

100

South
Brush Creek

To
Saratoga

Ryan
Park

North Fork
Barrett Creek

130

Silver
Lake

227

225

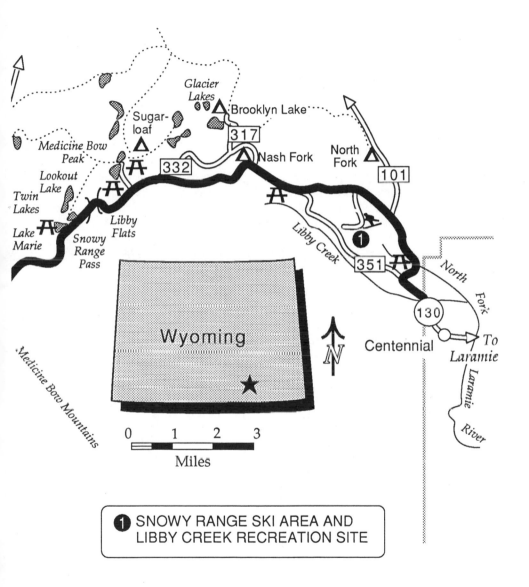

Glacier Lakes

Brooklyn Lake

Sugar-loaf

△ 317

Medicine Bow Peak

North Fork

△ 101

Lookout Lake

332

Nash Fork

Twin Lakes

Lake Marie

Libby Flats

Snowy Range Pass

Libby Creek

351

North Fork

1

Wyoming

130

Centennial

To Laramie

Medicine Bow Mountains

Laramie River

N

0   1   2   3

Miles

1 SNOWY RANGE SKI AREA AND LIBBY CREEK RECREATION SITE

weekends from July through Labor Day. Centennial also has three restaurants with fine dining and live entertainment.

The mountain mahoganies in the Medicine Bow Mountains were prized by Indians for making bows, and the region was the site of ceremonial gatherings. White trappers, prospectors, and explorers such as John C. Fremont and Kit Carson passed through the area. Some had high hopes of finding gold here, but the only enduring activity was and still is recreation.

The scenic highway was opened in July 1926 to a drizzly fanfare. Two tons of watermelons were served to 600 to 700 revelers who braved a two-hour downpour and drove up the slippery dirt road to the ceremonies.

The byway begins an immediate ascent. Within a mile of the National Forest boundary, the road forks. Forest Road 351 is the southern fork, and it leads past Libby Creek Recreation Area, and Barber Lake Picnic Area. Later it rejoins Route 130. Libby Creek has four small campgrounds under the trees. There are a total of 38 campsites, and there is good fishing for brook trout in the nearby creek.

Snowy Range Lodge, just past Libby Creek campgrounds, is on the National Register of Historic Places. This beautiful log structure is being restored.

To stay on the byway, bypass Forest Road 351 and continue to the north on Route 130. The road climbs through aspens and lodgepole pines, crisscrossing the North Fork Little Laramie River. A turn north on Forest Road 101 leads 1.5 miles through willows, marshes, and logging areas to North Fork Campground, which has 60 sites. There are popular snowmobile and cross-country ski trails in this area. A mile past 101 on the byway, Snowy Range Ski Area has alpine skiing, a day-use lodge, meals, ski school, and equipment rentals.

The byway keeps climbing, traveling above 10,000 feet elevation through a spectacular alpine landscape. Stands of Engelmann spruce and subalpine fir enclose the open parks. In very exposed areas, the subalpine fir twist and gnarl into the krummholz shapes so characteristic of mountaintops. Wildflowers such as moss campion, sky pilot, pussytoe, and cinquefoil adorn the grassy meadows.

A side trip on Forest Roads 317 and 332 leads to Nash Fork Campground, with 27 sites, and Brooklyn Lake Campground, with 17 sites and boating opportunities. Just north of Brooklyn Lake, the Glacier Lakes basin is the site of intensive study centering on acid rain and pollution. Researchers have monitored and analyzed the air, soil, and water here since the late 1960s.

The byway travels west across the mountains. A turn north leads to Sugarloaf Recreation Area. The campground has 16 sites, and the picnic areas overlook the rock-strewn tundra and alpine lakes and mountains. Hikers can climb Medicine Bow Peak from Lewis Lake, a moderately strenuous but rewarding climb up a small saddle and then up the talus slopes of the peak for a 360-degree view. Other trails, requiring a less vigorous effort, wander among the lovely lakes and fields of this alpine region.

The Medicine Bow Mountains include 1.7 billion-year-old metamorphosed sedimentary rocks. Look for the distinctive white quartzite on the crest, gneiss, schist, dolomite, marble, and round balls of fossilized algae. The western slopes have greenish-gray sandstones and clays.

The byway climbs 10,847-foot Snowy Range Pass. Libby Flats has a short interpretive trail through the subalpine vegetation. You can stand on the

A hiker returns from climbing Medicine Bow Peak, along the Snowy Range Highway.

picturesque stone observation platform and see for miles. On a clear day, look for Longs Peak in Rocky Mountain National Park to the south.

Several inviting picnic areas line the byway. Lake Marie, with Medicine Bow Peak as a backdrop, is one of the highlights of the drive. A paved path along the shore is suitable for wheelchair use and connects the east and west parking lots. There is also a trailhead to Medicine Bow Peak and Libby Lake in the Sugarloaf area.

West of the pass, Silver Lake Campground's 19 sites are sheltered by large Engelmann spruce and subalpine fir. The route descends, and a side trip on Forest Roads 227 and 225 loops through the aspen, which are especially beautiful in autumn.

Ryan Park Campground, at about 8,000 feet elevation, has 49 sites in the aspen and lodgepole pine off the byway. A few miles west, South Brush Creek campground has 20 sites about two miles off the byway, on Forest Road 200.

Travel 2.6 miles up Forest Road 100 to Lincoln Park Campground with 8 sites where Mollison, Lincoln, and South Brush Creek converge.

The byway continues to descend and ends at the national forest boundary. The highway continues west through sagebrush and willow-lined creeks toward Encampment and Saratoga. □

General description: A 39-mile route through a sheer-walled limestone canyon into the high country overlooking the turquoise waters of Bear Lake.

Special attractions: Bear Lake, nature trails, Jardine Juniper, limestone cliffs, Mount Naomi Wilderness, colorful autumn foliage, camping, Beaver Mountain Ski Area.

Location: Northeast Utah on the Wasatch-Cache National Forest, northeast of Logan. The byway follows U.S. Highway 89 between Logan and the national forest boundary near Garden City.

Byway route number: U.S. Highway 89.

Travel season: Year-round. Winter driving conditions may be hazardous, especially at higher elevations.

Camping: Ten national forest campgrounds with picnic tables, toilets, drinking water, and fire grates.

Services: All services in Logan and Garden City.

Nearby attractions: Wellsville Mountain Wilderness, Minnetonka Cave, Great Salt Lake, ski areas.

For more information: Wasatch-Cache National Forest, 8230 Federal Building, 125 S. State St., Salt Lake City, UT 84138, (801) 524-5030. District Ranger: Logan Ranger District, 860 N. 1200 E., Logan, UT 84321, (801) 753-2772.

Description: The Logan Canyon Highway gains more than 3,000 feet in elevation during its gradual ascent of the canyon. The prominent limestone cliffs of the China Wall are exposed on both sides of the route. The two-lane road is paved and has frequent scenic turnouts. Traffic is generally light, though weekends and holidays can be busy.

Summer temperatures range from the 50s at night to the 80s in the daytime. Spring and autumn range from below freezing at night to daytime temperatures in the 50s and 60s. Winters drop into the teens at night, with days around 30 degrees. An unusual, localized weather pattern gives Peter Sinks, near the top of the canyon, the dubious distinction of being the coldest spot in Utah; an unofficial record of 65 degrees below zero was recorded in 1888, and an official 49 degrees below zero in 1979.

The byway begins in Logan, a thriving city that is home to Utah State University. The ranger station there has national forest and byway information. Travel northeast on U.S. Highway 89 to the mouth of Logan Canyon. There Lady Bird Rest Stop has restrooms, a trailer dumping station, and a nice view of the city. Hydro Park and First Dam have picnic tables scattered across the lawn adjacent to Logan River and fishing opportunities.

Most of the route follows the Logan River, which nurtures thick riparian vegetation in the canyon bottom. Willows, water birches, burdocks, grasses, and teasels are common. The steep slopes above have a mixture of bushes and conifers growing next to the nearly vertical limestone cliffs. Bigtooth maples, Douglas-firs, arrowleaf balsamroots, sagebrush, and violets dominate the slopes. The subtle hues of autumn foliage in the canyon are lovely.

Logan Canal, about a mile past the national forest boundary, is a popular put-in spot for tubing enthusiasts seeking an escape from the summer heat.

Logan Canyon Highway ascends alongside the Logan River, crosses a small pass, and overlooks turquoise-blue Bear Lake.

Another mile on the byway brings you to Second Dam, a popular fishing spot for rainbow trout. The river contains rainbow, native cutthroat, brook, and brown trout, and Rocky Mountain whitefish. The world's second largest brown trout was caught in the Logan River; it weighed a whopping 36 pounds.

Zanavoo Lodge is a historic log building that has lodging and a restaurant. Just beyond it, Bridger Campground has 11 sites tucked into the shrubs and trees along the riverbank. Spring Hollow Campground is one mile beyond, with 16 sites and several good hiking trails. The Red Bridge Trail, a popular jogging and bicycling route, runs 2.5 miles back down the canyon. The three-mile Crimson Trail climbs steeply up to the limestone cliffs above, while the Riverside Nature Trail wanders an easy mile along the river to Guinavah Campground.

About midway along the Riverside Nature Trail, look across the canyon to see the Wind Caves, a triple arch formed by wind and water erosion. A footpath leads up to it from the byway.

Malibu-Guinavah Campground has 48 sites in a shady grove of willows and box elders. It also has group areas and a huge stone amphitheater. On summer evenings, the Forest Service sponsors programs on natural and regional history at the amphitheater.

Farther north along the byway, several picnic areas are located next to the river, and Preston Valley Campground has eight sites. The nearby roadside geology exhibit explains an unusual rock on the ground next to the sign. In this fucoidal quartz, you can see worm burrows and seaweed imprints, cemented 400 million years ago into the sand of an ancient beach.

A side trip on Forest Road 047 leads past Tea Pot Rock and the Lion's Head rock formations. There are several active beaver ponds along this road, and it is fun to watch the industrious animals at work.

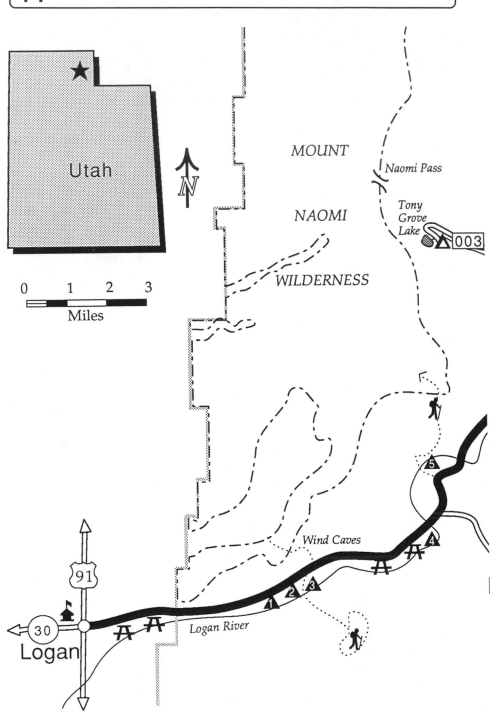

Utah

N

0 1 2 3
Miles

MOUNT

Naomi Pass

Tony
Grove
Lake

003

NAOMI

WILDERNESS

5

Wind Caves

4

91

A A

30

Logan

Logan River

1 2 3

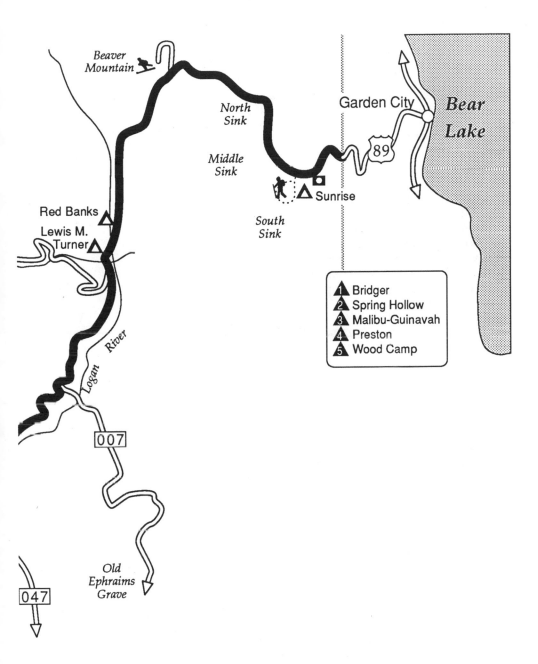

Beaver
Mountain

North
Sink

Garden City

*Bear
Lake*

89

Middle
Sink

△ Sunrise

Red Banks △

Lewis M.
Turner △

South
Sink

1 Bridger
2 Spring Hollow
3 Malibu-Guinavah
4 Preston
5 Wood Camp

Logan River

007

Old
Ephraims
Grave

047

The Jardine Juniper Trail begins near Wood Camp Campground, which has 11 sites and no drinking water. The trail is fun to hike; it passes through an avalanche chute, across glacial moraines, and through aspens, Douglas-firs, and junipers. It climbs 2,000 feet in five miles to the Jardine Juniper, one of the oldest living trees of its species, and thought to be approximately 1,500 years old.

About halfway up the canyon, Forest Road 007 offers a seven-mile bumpy side trip to Old Ephraim's Grave. Ephraim, one of the biggest grizzly bears ever seen in the area, preyed on cattle and sheep until he was shot in 1923. Boy Scouts erected a marker and composed a poem about the bear.

Tony Grove Lake, elevation 8,500 feet, lies at the end of seven-mile Forest Road 003, which climbs 2,300 feet to reach it. The cirque lake is a visual delight, and anglers enjoy the productive rainbow trout fishery. Tony Grove Lake is frozen about six months of the year. The 39-site campground sits in an aspen grove. Numerous horse and hiking trails traverse the area, and many lead into nearby Mount Naomi Wilderness.

Moose are frequently seen by the lake. Other byway residents include mule deer, muskrats, beavers, porcupines, elk, and longtail weasels. A wide variety of warblers, sparrows, chickadees, swallows, and woodpeckers fill the canyon with sound. Great blue herons and mallard ducks can also be found.

Lewis M. Turner Campground has 10 sites on Forest Road 003, and Red Banks Campground has 12 sites on the river. Franklin Basin is a popular winter sports area along the byway. Just off the route, Beaver Mountain Ski Area provides alpine skiing runs, and the Logan Ranger District grooms cross-country ski trails. A lodge, shop, and restaurant operate in the winter. Nearby the Sinks are popular with backcountry recreationists in both winter and summer.

The highest point on the byway is 7,800-foot Bear Lake Summit. Limber Pine Nature Trail leads about a mile through a cool forest of Engelmann spruces, Douglas-firs, and subalpine firs. The sinks, or depressions in the ground, were formed by water seeping through cracks in the dolomite bedrock, which eventually eroded it enough that whole sections of the land sank down.

Logan Canyon is located in the Wasatch Range, composed of upthrusted limestone and dolomite. You can see the sedimentary layers bent eastward at the canyon mouth. At its widest and highest, Logan Canyon is about five miles across and one mile deep.

Sunrise Campground has 27 sites and nice views from its high-elevation location. About half a mile farther, Bear Lake Overlook provides a breathtakingly beautiful view. Bear Lake is the extraordinary aquamarine color that people paint swimming pools. Rising to the east of the lake are the gentle slopes of the Trump Range, and it is possible to see Utah, Idaho, and Wyoming. Bear Lake is 20 miles long and was isolated from the Bear River by earthquake activity. Eight thousand years of isolation have resulted in a unique water chemistry, as well as the evolution of four species of fish found nowhere else in the world. There are also rare plants and animals.

The byway descends rapidly to Garden City and the lake, where there are resorts, services, marinas, and other recreational opportunities, including the chance to refresh your palate with a famous Bear Lake raspberry shake. □

General description: A 66.5-mile route that ascends 3,000 feet into the Uinta Mountains and curves alongside Flaming Gorge Reservoir, offering spectacular views and unique opportunities to see dozens of geologic formations.

Special attractions: Flaming Gorge National Recreation Area, outstanding views, Sheep Creek Canyon Geological Area, Utah Field House of Natural History Museum and Dinosaur Garden.

Location: Northeast Utah on the Ashley National Forest. The byway begins in Vernal, travels north on U.S. Highway 191, turns west onto Utah Route 44, and ends in Manila.

Byway route numbers: U.S. Highway 191 and Utah Route 44.

Travel season: Year-round. Winter driving conditions may be hazardous at higher elevations.

Camping: Eight national forest campgrounds with picnic tables, fire grates, toilets, and drinking water. There are numerous additional campgrounds in the adjacent Flaming Gorge National Recreation Area.

Services: All services in Vernal and Manila. All services with limited availability at Red Canyon Lodge and nearby Flaming Gorge Lodge.

Nearby attractions: Dinosaur National Monument, High Uintas Wilderness, Flaming Gorge Dam, the Green River.

For more information: Ashley National Forest, 355 N. Vernal Ave., Vernal, UT 84078, (801) 789-1181. District Rangers: Vernal Ranger District, 355 N. Vernal Ave., Vernal, UT 84078, (801) 789-1181; Flaming Gorge Ranger District, P.O. Box 278, Manila, UT 84046, (801) 784-3445.

Description: Ashley National Forest Scenic Byway travels U.S. Highway 191 and Utah Route 44 into the Uinta Mountains and then parallels the upper canyon of Flaming Gorge Reservoir. The highway was designed to lie lightly on the land, and it rolls and curves gently with the terrain. The two-lane road is paved and has frequent turnouts for scenic and recreational opportunities. Traffic is light to moderate; weekends and holidays are quite busy.

Summer visitors can expect temperatures ranging from nighttime lows in the 40s to daytimes in the 90s. Spring and fall are more moderate, with days in the 50s through 70s and nights below freezing. Winters can be snowy, and temperatures range from below zero to the 40s. Most rain falls from July through October in the form of sudden, severe afternoon thunderstorms.

Vernal has a number of self-guided loop tours outlined in brochures. National forest and byway information can be obtained from the ranger station. Undoubtedly the most interesting place in Vernal is the Utah Field House of Natural History, with its museum and Dinosaur Garden. The wildlife and geology exhibits are easy to understand and enjoy, and big slabs of sandstone contain petroglyphs carved by prehistoric man more than a thousand years ago. The showpiece exhibit lies outside the museum walls in the Dinosaur Garden. There, amidst living trees and shrubs, in a swamp and next to a small lake, are 14 life-sized models of dinosaurs. A 90-foot-long diplodocus stares at visitors. A woolly mammoth is 14 feet high at the shoulder, and a tyrannosaurus stands 18 feet tall. Visitors learn that the four-to six-ton stegosaurus had a 2.5-ounce brain, the size of a kitten's.

The museum goes hand-in-hand with a visit to nearby Dinosaur National Monument, which has one of the world's greatest concentrations of dinosaur bones. Excavations have unearthed the petrified bones of crocodiles, turtles, and 14 species of dinosaurs. The monument has a wealth of wild backcountry in its rugged canyon wilderness.

The byway travels north from Vernal through pinyons and junipers. Steinaker Reservoir and State Park have picnicking, boating, fishing, and swimming. Four miles farther is the turnoff for Red Fleet Reservoir, which offers camping, picnicking, boating, hiking, and fishing.

From the byway, you can see an open-pit phosphate mine, where five miles of deep gashes were scraped into the earth. Windy Point offers views back to the Ashley Valley and beyond to the Book Cliffs.

A few miles past the national forest boundary, a side trip on Forest Roads 018 and 020 leads to East Park Reservoir, where there is camping and fishing. The byway continues north on 44/191, rolling through pleasant stands of aspens and conifers. Watch for logging trucks and loose cattle on the open range.

The route ascends several canyons through pinyon and ponderosa pines and quaking aspens. About 20 miles north of Vernal is Bassett Spring Trail, a moderately difficult four-mile route popular with cross-country skiers and mountain bikers.

The byway reaches its highest elevation of 8,428 feet at the county line. This is the eastern edge of the Uinta Mountains. The overlook has interpretive signs regarding the mining, and vistas include lodgepole pine forest, clearcuts, and evidence of a big fire. A later pullout interprets the geology of the area.

The Uinta Mountains are actually a giant dome, formed when the earth's crust heaved upward. There are 20 different geologic eras exposed by the cutting action of erosion, including the billion-year-old Precambrian core.

Red Springs Campground has 13 sites in an aspen grove, and across the road Lodgepole has 35 sites. The byway descends past Cart Creek Gorge Overlook and into the Flaming Gorge National Recreation Area. The reservoir's waters are deep green and blue, and the multi-colored cliffs glow in burnished earth tones. The colors are especially rich in late afternoon.

At Greendale Junction, the byway turns west and follows Utah Route 44. A side trip north on U.S. Highway 191 brings you to resorts, campgrounds, services, Flaming Gorge Reservoir, marinas, and the dam.

Utah Route 44 goes through ponderosa pines and aspens. The Canyon Rim Trail is a five-mile-long footpath that begins at Greendale Overlook and meanders through Skull, Green Lakes, and Canyon Rim campgrounds.

Forest Road 95 leads to Red Canyon Visitor Center, open May through September. En route are Green Lakes, Canyon Rim, Gooseneck, and Red Canyon campgrounds, with a total of 51 sites. Red Canyon Lodge has food, lodging, gasoline, phone, boat rentals, and store.

The Red Canyon Visitor Center has a spectacular vantage point over Flaming Gorge Reservoir. The jade-green water sparkles 1,700 feet below, and sheer cliffs line the waterway. The reservoir impounds 91 miles of the Green River. Anglers fish for mackinaw, brown, rainbow, and cutthroat trout, kokanee salmon, and smallmouth bass.

Wildlife along the byway includes elk, moose, mule deer, bald and golden

18 FLAMING GORGE–UNITA'S SCENIC BYWAY

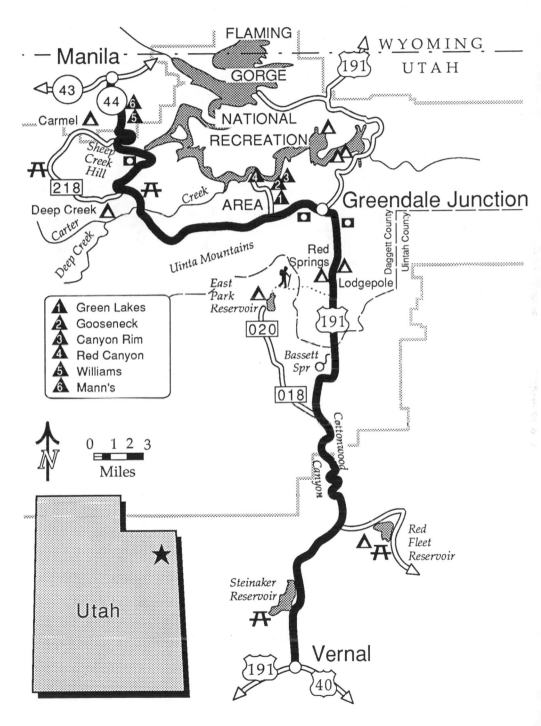

Legend:
1. Green Lakes
2. Gooseneck
3. Canyon Rim
4. Red Canyon
5. Williams
6. Mann's

Manila

Carmel

Sheep Creek Hill

Deep Creek

Carter

Deep Creek

218

FLAMING GORGE NATIONAL RECREATION AREA

Creek

Uinta Mountains

Greendale Junction

Daggett County / Uintah County

Red Springs

Lodgepole

East Park Reservoir

020

191

Bassett Spr

018

Cottonwood Canyon

WYOMING
UTAH

191

N

0 1 2 3
Miles

Utah

Red Fleet Reservoir

Steinaker Reservoir

Vernal

191   40

A scenic overlook on the Ashley National Forest Scenic Byway provides views of Flaming Gorge Reservoir's deep greens and blues. Multicolored cliffs glow in burnished earth tones.

eagles, ospreys, and red-tailed hawks. Bighorn sheep and peregrine falcons have been reintroduced to the area.

The byway goes through timber cuts, stumps, and logging debris for about 10 miles. Deep Creek Campground has 17 sites in the ponderosas and aspens. The route descends past the red canyon walls of Carter Creek Canyon and meets Forest Road 218, which follows a 13-mile horseshoe-shaped route into the Sheep Creek Canyon Geological Area and back out to the byway.

This area is well worth a visit, and you could easily spend a full day walking around, picnicking, and enjoying the varying hues of the canyon walls as the sun's rays change direction. It is a photographer's paradise. Travelers with limited time will enjoy a quick drive through the geologic area.

Sheep Creek Canyon is split by the Uinta Crest Fault, an immense fracture that exposes the convoluted and uplifted strata of the Uinta Mountains. Self-guided tour brochures, available at ranger stations, will help clarify what you see. The geology includes 18 formations, from the 600-million-year-old Uinta Mountain Group, through the appearance of the first forms of life, through the age of dinosaurs, to the Mancos Shale, a mere 80 million years old.

The Sheep Creek Canyon Road is partially gravel and partially paved. The route is narrow and winding, and it passes through aspens and ponderosa pines down a steep-walled canyon to a creek bottom filled with lush grasses and the striking black skeletons of burned cottonwood trees. Carmel Campground has 15 sites along Sheep Creek. The Sheep Creek Canyon Road emerges on the byway about seven miles below its first junction with the highway.

In that seven miles, the byway descends a steep cliff via hairpin turns. The views of Flaming Gorge Reservoir are outstanding, and a scenic overlook is well-situated for the best view. Visitors who drove the Sheep Creek Canyon Road should consider traveling back up the byway five miles for the view from the overlook.

Mann's and Willow campgrounds each have dispersed primitive sites located along a creek in the cottonwoods. The byway emerges from the canyon, and views open to include broad fields, mountains, and the community of Manila, the end of the scenic byway. □

19 BOULDER MOUNTAIN HIGHWAY
Dixie National Forest   Utah

General description: A 30-mile paved highway that ascends and descends Boulder Mountain, providing magnificent views into Capitol Reef National Park and beyond.

Special attractions: Slickrock canyons, subalpine meadows, far-reaching views east over the Waterpocket Fold and San Raphael Swell, cooler elevations, colorful autumn foliage.

Location: Southern Utah on the Dixie National Forest, southwest of Capitol Reef National Park. The byway travels Utah Route 12 between Boulder and Grover.

Byway route number: Utah Route 12.

Travel season: Year-round. The road may be closed for as long as a day for snow removal after major winter storms.

Camping: Three national forest campgrounds and two group areas with drinking water, picnic tables, fire grates, and vault toilets. No hookups.

Services: All services in Escalante and Torrey, but availability is limited. Gas, phone, and store in Boulder. Many businesses are closed on Sundays.

Nearby attractions: Bryce Canyon National Park, Capitol Reef National Park, backcountry slickrock canyons, Kodachrome Basin State Park, Escalante Petrified Forest, Calf Creek Falls Recreation Area, Boulder Top subalpine meadows.

For more information: Dixie National Forest, P.O. Box 580, Cedar City, UT 84720, (801) 586-2421. District Rangers: Teasdale Ranger District, P.O. Box 99, Teasdale, UT 84773, (801) 425-3702; Escalante Ranger District, P.O. Box 246, Escalante, UT 84726, (801) 826-5400.

Description: The Boulder Mountain Highway climbs rapidly out of desert slickrock country and ascends 2,500 feet along the side of Boulder Mountain before winding back down. Views into the geologic splendors of southern Utah are magnificent. The two-lane road is paved, and it has two paved overlooks and frequent scenic turnouts. Traffic is light and the highway well-maintained. Lower speeds are recommended because of the many curves and occasional steep grades. The byway travels along some very steep drop-offs that require additional caution. Scenery is exceptional, traveling in either direction, particularly if you are traveling in the late afternoon when the long rays of the sun enliven the desert's deep hues.

June is generally dry and warm, with pleasant temperatures between 40 and 80 degrees. In July and August, expect hotter temperatures and afternoon thunderstorms. September and October are generally dry again, with nighttime temperatures that dip to freezing. Light snow is common from November until April, and wind is a constant variable year-round.

The tiny community of Boulder, at the southern end of the byway, was extremely isolated until the highway was paved in 1981. Now you can easily visit the important Anasazi Indian Village Historical Site here. Rangers and a museum help to interpret the lives of the prehistoric Indians who dwelt here nearly a thousand years ago.

In cooler seasons, you may opt to camp at the lower elevation of nearby Deer Creek BLM campground, about six miles southeast of Boulder. A side trip from Boulder travels the Burr Trail, a very scenic and remote dirt road that leads 66 miles to Lake Powell.

The byway travels north from Boulder, abruptly exiting the slickrock sandstone desert. The countryside is primarily agricultural, dotted with sage and then stands of ponderosa pines. The ascent of the mountain begins about five miles from Boulder and quickly brings you up into aspen glades and open fields, with glimpses eastward over the desert. Chriss Lake, an easy two-mile hike from the byway, is popular with anglers and campers.

Views from Point Lookout will take your breath away. Below are the burnished reds and oranges of the Circle Cliffs and the Waterpocket Fold, while the Henry Mountains and Navaho Mountain adorn the skyline. This paved overlook has interpretive signs to help identify the various geologic features.

19 BOULDER MOUNTAIN HIGHWAY

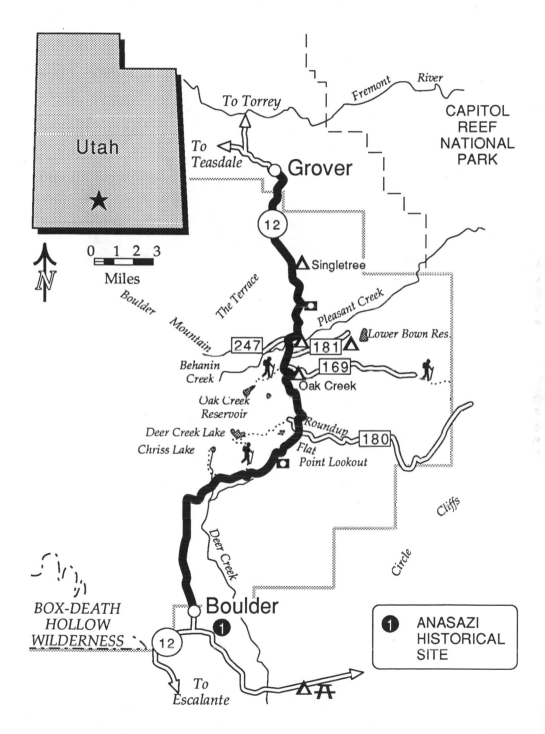

Utah

0 1 2 3
Miles

N

To Torrey

To Teasdale

Grover

CAPITOL
REEF
NATIONAL
PARK

Fremont River

12

Singletree

The Terrace

Pleasant Creek

Boulder Mountain

247

181

Lower Bown Res

169

Behanin Creek

Oak Creek

Oak Creek Reservoir

Roundup

180

Deer Creek Lake

Chriss Lake

Flat Point Lookout

Cliffs

Circle

Deer Creek

Boulder

1

BOX-DEATH HOLLOW WILDERNESS

12

To Escalante

1 ANASAZI HISTORICAL SITE

Views extend into the exposed geologic splendors of Capitol Reef National Park from the Boulder Mountain Highway. Joe Colwell photo.

Boulder Mountain geology is very interesting. The mountain is composed of the same sedimentary rock formations as the Colorado Plateau. After the region was uplifted along the Waterpocket Fold and the Aquarius Plateau, a lava flow covered the area that is now Boulder Mountain. In the ensuing millenium, the softer sedimentary rocks of the Colorado Plateau eroded into the fascinating forms and canyons seen from the overlook, while the hard, lava-capped Boulder Mountain area resisted erosion. The top of Boulder Mountain is quite flat and dotted with lakes. It is easy to pick out the lava cap on the mountain on any of the short day hikes along the route by noting where the softer sedimentary rocks begin to crumble and erode away from the protective hard lava.

Roundup Flat is a few miles north of the overlook. This is the highest point on the byway, at 9,400 feet. Here the route rolls gently through open fields of wildflowers and groves of aspen trees. The latter are especially beautiful when they turn gold in autumn. A side road for mountain bikes and four-wheelers leads east to Dry Bench, Capitol Reef National Park, and slickrock canyons. No motor vehicles are allowed into the park on this trail.

West of the highway, footpaths out of Sunflower Flat offer easy access to the Great Western Trail and the top of Boulder Mountain. Hike a few miles and drop your fishing line into Deer Creek Lake, or hike farther and join up with one of the many trails atop Boulder.

Oak Creek Campground lies at 8,800 feet elevation. This small campground has eight sites, hiking trails, and fishing opportunities. Oak Creek Reservoir has very good fishing after July 1. It can be reached via a rough 4 X 4 road and then a quarter-mile footpath. The dirt road leading east to slickrock country is recommended for high-clearance vehicles only.

Two miles north, Pleasant Creek Campground has 18 sites, as well as fishing and hiking opportunities. Meeks Draw and Behanin Creek trails lead hikers to the top of Boulder Mountain with its 50,000 acres of relatively flat subalpine meadows and forest. There are lots of good fishing lakes atop Boulder.

Lower Bown Reservoir dominates the scenery to the east, and the dirt road to it is passable by car. This lake offers some of the best fishing on the mountain. Past the reservoir, a primitive road leads mountain bikers and hikers into Capitol Reef National Park. This is an especially popular route in spring and autumn, when temperatures are cooler.

Singletree Campground, about six miles north of Pleasant Creek, has 26 sites, as well as group areas. Walk along the creek about half a mile to a pretty little waterfall, and enjoy the expansive view eastward.

The byway then descends through ponderosa pines to Grover, nestled under the red rock cliffs between Thousand Lake Mountain and Boulder Mountain. □

20 SAN JUAN SKYWAY
San Juan and Uncompahgre National Forests   Colorado

General description: A 236-mile loop drive through the scenic San Juan Mountains and across high plateaus.

Special attractions: Million Dollar Highway, Old West and mining towns, spectacular views of the Rocky Mountains, historic narrow-gauge passenger railroad, alpine and cross-country skiing, five wilderness areas, Mesa Verde National Park, Anasazi Heritage Center, bicycling, fishing, boating, natural hot springs, hiking, camping.

Location: Southwest Colorado on the San Juan and Uncompahgre national forests. The loop goes from Durango north to Ridgway on U.S. Highway 550, turns west onto Colorado Route 62 to Placerville, follows Colorado Route 145 southwest to Cortez, and takes U.S. Highway 160 back to Durango.

Byway route numbers: U.S. Highway 550, Colorado Routes 62 and 145, and U.S. Highway 160.

Travel season: Year-round. Winter driving conditions may be hazardous. Some sections of the byway cling to steep cliffs with astounding drop-offs. This route is not for the fainthearted.

Camping: Several national forest campgrounds with picnic tables, fire grates, and toilets. Some have drinking water. No hookups. One national park campground with picnic tables, fire grates, bathhouse, laundry facilities, amphitheater, and general store. Some hookups.

Services: All services in Durango, Silverton, Ouray, Ridgway, Telluride, Dolores, Cortez, and Mancos.

Nearby attractions: Black Canyon of the Gunnison National Monument, Monument Valley, Bureau of Land Management Alpine Loop, Chimney Rock Archaeological Area.

For more information: San Juan National Forest, 701 Camino del Rio, Suite 301, Durango, CO 81301, (303) 247-4874; Uncompahgre National Forest,

2250 Highway 50, Delta, CO 81416, (303) 874-7691. San Juan National Forest District Offices: Dolores Ranger District, 100 N. Sixth, Dolores, CO 81323, (303) 882-7296; Mancos Ranger District, 41595 Highway 160, Mancos, CO 81328, (303) 533-7716; Pagosa Ranger District, Second and Pagosa, Pagosa Springs, CO 81147, (303) 264-2268; Pine Ranger District, 367 S. Pearl, Bayfield, CO 81122, (303) 884-2512.

Description: The San Juan Skyway crosses four high mountain passes, weaves alongside sparkling streams, drops down into the high desert country of prehistoric and modern Indians, and visits a national park. The two-lane road is paved and has frequent turnouts for scenic and recreational enjoyment. Traffic is moderate, and speeds vary considerably from highway cruising to slow, careful navigation of switchbacks and steep grades.

Expect variable mountain weather. Elevations range from around 5,000 feet to more than 11,000 feet, and the temperature difference can be startling. Summer days might be over 90 degrees, or a sudden storm may bring sleet. Snow is common in the upper elevations from October to June. Freezing nights can occur anytime, and afternoon thundershowers are common in the summer. The lower elevations are often very hot, with pleasantly balmy nights.

The byway is a loop that can be entered at several points. The scenery is spectacular and diverse when viewed from any direction.

Durango is a popular starting point. This community has adopted a western theme, with summer rodeos and live theater. The interesting and historic downtown district is chock full of shops and restaurants. The Durango & Silverton Narrow Gauge Railroad depot is downtown, and the coal-fired, steam-operated locomotives take passengers on a day-long scenic trip alongside the Animas River through the San Juan Mountains to Silverton and back. Riding the D&SNG can be a real highlight of any visit to southwest Colorado. The Animas River has stretches of wild whitewater—especially in spring—and deep, still jade-green pools.

The byway travels north on U.S. Highway 550 through the pastoral Animas River Valley. Cuestas, mesas, and plateaus of red and beige sandstone adjoin the valley. Trimble Hot Springs is a National Historic Site open to the public. A few miles farther, you may see the D&SNG stopped under the old, wood-sided water tower in Hermosa. The train needs 1,500 to 3,500 gallons of water just to steam up the passes and reach Silverton, 90 miles away.

One mile north of the San Juan National Forest boundary is the turnoff to Haviland Lake and Chris Park campgrounds, at 8,100 elevation. Chris Park has three group sites. Haviland Lake has 47 sites in the ponderosa pines on a hillside overlooking the lake, which has good fishing for trout. Drinking water is available.

The byway continues to climb. Purgatory-Durango Ski Area has summer and winter activities. In summer, there is live theater, a chamber music festival, an alpine slide, and chairlift rides. In winter, of course, activity centers around skiing the powder snow.

Filling the horizon ahead is Engineer Mountain, composed of sedimentary redbeds and an igneous intrusion that forms the cliffs. Engineer is a "nunatak,"

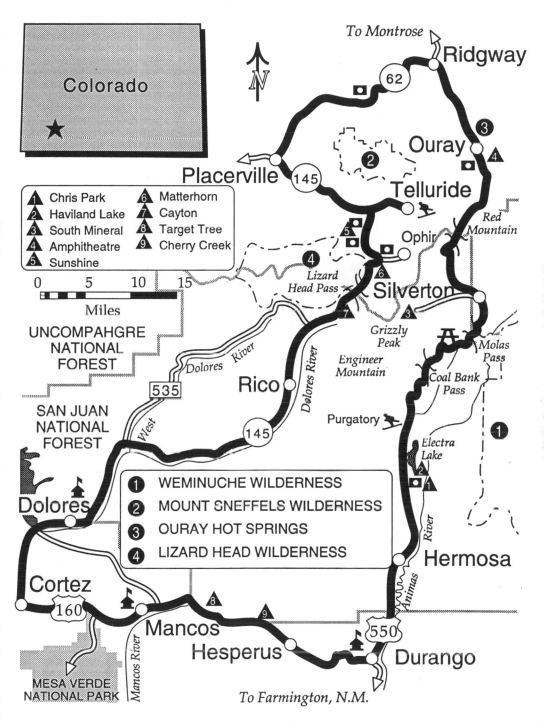

20   SAN JUAN SKYWAY

Colorado

To Montrose

Ridgway

62

Ouray ③

④

Placerville

145

Telluride

② Red Mountain

Chris Park | ⑥ Matterhorn
Haviland Lake | ⑦ Cayton
South Mineral | ⑧ Target Tree
Amphitheatre | ⑨ Cherry Creek
Sunshine

① Chris Park
② Haviland Lake
③ South Mineral
④ Amphitheatre
⑤ Sunshine

Ophir

⑤

0   5   10   15

Miles

④ Lizard Head Pass

⑥ Silverton

UNCOMPAHGRE NATIONAL FOREST

Grizzly Peak

③

Molas Pass

535

Dolores River

Dolores River

Engineer Mountain

Coal Bank Pass

SAN JUAN NATIONAL FOREST

West

Rico

⑦

145

Purgatory

①

Electra Lake

② ①

Hermosa

① WEMINUCHE WILDERNESS
② MOUNT SNEFFELS WILDERNESS
③ OURAY HOT SPRINGS
④ LIZARD HEAD WILDERNESS

Dolores

Cortez

160

⑧

Mancos

⑨

550

Animas River

Mancos River

Hesperus

Durango

MESA VERDE NATIONAL PARK

To Farmington, N.M.

a peak that stuck up through the immense glaciers that covered the area in the Pleistocene era. The San Juan Mountains are largely sedimentary, overlain by a volcanic cap. The immense heat of the volcanic magma baked, hardened, and reddened the adjacent sandstone and limestone into pottery-like hardness. Minerals were crystallized by the heat, and then glaciers scoured the whole region. Most mining today—for silver, gold, lead, zinc, copper, and uranium—is done at those contact points of volcanic and sedimentary rock.

The byway climbs 10,640-foot Coal Bank Pass, offering views down the Animas Valley, over the ski area, and east to the impressive West Needles Mountains and Weminuche Wilderness, the state's largest at a half-million acres. Hikers who want to climb Engineer Mountain will find a trailhead here. As the byway descends the pass, waterfalls adorn the slopes, and the Animas River cuts deeply into its canyon. A yellow-green stripe of transplanted lodgepole pines outlines the 1879 Lime Creek Burn.

Molas Pass is a beautiful subalpine region at almost 11,000 feet in elevation, dotted with tarns full of lily pads. The nearby lakes are peaceful, and views extend to the vertical walls of the Grenadier Range and the colorful red mountains north of Silverton. Many of the mountains to the east are higher than 14,000 feet. Molas Pass has the clearest air in the United States, and views can extend 170 miles.

The route weaves down the divide to Silverton, which provides a lot of entertainment for a small community. The D&SNG railroad steams in and out of the depot, shops line the streets, and mountains rise in all directions. Jeep trails lead to old silver and gold mines and mills. Mining is still a dominant economic activity in Silverton and in the San Juans in general.

The scenic byway heads north from Silverton on 550/789, the Million Dollar Highway. This 24-mile section of road cuts a tortuous path along the face of the mountains. Thousand-foot drop-offs and blind curves are the norm; slow speeds and steady nerves are essential.

North of Silverton, incredible reds, oranges, and yellows streak the mountain slopes, evidence of iron-oxide deposits. The route follows colorful Mineral Creek past mining relics, crosses into the Uncompahgre National Forest and ascends 11,018-foot Red Mountain Pass. Mill Creek spills over and cascades down from Columbia Lake, and other views from the pass are equally breathtaking. The afternoon sun on Red Mountain reflects clearly in the little pond just north of the pass, and in autumn aspens glow brightly against the colorful mountains. This is a photographer's and sightseer's paradise.

The byway hangs on the side of Uncompahgre Gorge and descends toward Ouray. Just above town is an overlook and the turnoff to the Amphitheatre Campground and Picnic Area. There are 30 sites, and drinking water is available. The steep, narrow route travels one mile through oaks and spruces into the Amphitheatre area. This road is not recommended for large vehicles.

Ouray nestles in a picturesque basin surounded by high peaks. Attractions include a tour of one of the world's largest operating gold mines, picnicking at and enjoying Box Canyon Falls, strolling through town, and soaking in the natural hot springs pool.

North of Ouray, the countryside includes agricultural lands, with lower, less dramatic relief. The byway turns west in Ridgway onto Colorado Route 62. Mount Sneffels dominates the background, while green fields of hay brighten the foreground. The byway crosses Dallas Divide and then turns south

San Juan Skyway elevations range from 5,000 feet to more than 11,000 feet, as the byway traverses beautiful mountains and high deserts.

onto Colorado Route 145 to follow the San Miguel River. Deep-red bluffs and aspens and cottonwoods abut the river.

Telluride sits three miles off the main byway in a steep drainage surrounded by mountains. This charming community has a festival for every and any reason, celebrating things as diverse as wild mushroom season, bluegrass music, chamber music, hang gliding, and films. The alpine skiing here is legendary, and some runs end right in town. A historic galloping-goose railcar is displayed, the museum covers the area's rich and varied mining heydey, and downtown shops offer a smorgasbord of items.

Back on the scenic byway, travel south again on Route 145, which goes below and east of prominent Sunshine Mountain. Sunshine Campground has 15 sites in an aspen grove, with an interesting bog nearby. Matterhorn Campground has 23 sites among Engelmann spruces, aspens, and willows, as well as pretty views of San Bernardo Mountain. Both campgrounds have drinking water available.

The grassy parks atop Lizard Head Pass open a view of 13,113-foot Lizard Head Mountain and the adjacent wilderness. Wildflowers include columbines, Indian paintbrushes, asters, and other subalpine varieties. The byway route looks into four wilderness areas: the Weminuche, the Big Blue, the Mount Sneffels, and the Lizard Head. Backcountry hiking opportunities are varied, often strenuous, and always splendid.

Cayton Campground has 27 sites and drinking water at an elevation of 9,400 feet along the headwaters of the Dolores River. Anglers enjoy fishing for rainbow, brook, and brown trout in the Dolores. The byway descends alongside the river past Rico and the historic coke ovens just outside town and into lower relief and the red sandstone country again. Spear-like stalks of mullein line the roadside, and aspens, oaks, and ponderosa pines dominate the slopes. Autumn colors here are a delight.

There is a ranger station in Dolores, as well as access to nearby McPhee Reservoir for boating, picnicking, and camping. Two miles south of town, take a side trip to the Anasazi Heritage Center. This hands-on learning center and museum will open your eyes to the prehistoric Indian culture that inhabited this region more than a thousand years ago. Route 145 leads into Cortez, a fairly large community with a strong Indian culture. The town is just north of the Ute Mountain Indian Reservation. Native American arts and crafts flourish, and all traveler services are provided. The wide valleys offer views typical of the high southwest desert.

Turn east onto U.S. Highway 160, toward the La Plata Mountains. Mesa Verde National Park can be a four-hour or four-day visit. This World Heritage Cultural Site is one of the largest archaeological preserves in the United States. You can climb down into cliff dwellings, enjoy nature walks, camp, and watch wildlife. Mesa Verde has lodging, meals, a gift shop, and ranger-led natural history programs. The campground has 490 sites, a store, laundry, showers, and refreshment center.

Back on the byway, continue east on 160. The route rolls across agricultural land, drops into Mancos, crosses Hesperus Hill, and descends, completing the loop in Durango. □

21 KAIBAB PLATEAU—NORTH RIM PARKWAY
Kaibab National Forest   Arizona

General description: A 44-mile paved highway across a forested high plateau, ending at the north rim of the Grand Canyon.

Special attractions: Grand Canyon National Park, abundant wildlife, cool elevations, hiking trails.

Location: Northern Arizona on the Kaibab National Forest, north of Flagstaff. The byway begins at the intersection of U.S. Highway 89A and Arizona Route 67 and ends in North Rim.

Byway route number: Arizona Route 67.

Travel season: The byway is open from about mid-May through mid-November or early December, and then it is closed by winter snows. Vehicle weight restrictions may apply through June; check locally for road conditions. No services available in the national park after the middle of October. Jacob Lake services available year-round.

Camping: Two national forest campgrounds with drinking water, fire grates, toilets, and picnic tables. One national park campground with showers, water, tables, restrooms, laundry, store, horses, and gas.

Services: All services on a limited basis at Jacob Lake and North Rim. Lodging, restaurant, and gift shop at Kaibab Lodge.

Nearby attractions: Vermillion Cliffs, Glen Canyon Dam, Pipe Spring National Monument, Lee's Ferry.

For more information: Kaibab National Forest, 800 S. Sixth St., Williams,

AZ 86046, (602) 635-2681. District Ranger: North Kaibab Ranger District, P.O. Box 248, Fredonia, AZ 86022, (602) 643-7395; Kaibab Plateau Visitor Center, Jacob Lake, AZ 86022, (602) 643-7298. Grand Canyon National Park, Grand Canyon, AZ 86023, (602) 638-7888.

Description: The byway travels through dense forests of pines, firs, and aspens atop the high-elevation Kaibab Plateau. Construction and improvements on this two-lane, paved highway will be completed about 1999, but delays during periods of construction are minimal. Daytime traffic can be constant, and there are numerous side roads and pullouts to divert you.

The byway opens about the middle of May, when winter snows have melted. Temperatures at these elevations of 8,000 to 9,000 feet can be quite cool, even in summer. Expect 40s to 70s, with afternoon thunderstorms in July, August, and September. Winter recreationists should expect variable and sometimes severe weather, with temperatures that range from 30 degrees to below zero.

The byway begins in Jacob Lake, a tiny service community set in a ponderosa pine forest. A Forest Service visitor center is open May through October. It provides books about the area and information on the national forest and its recreational opportunities. Jacob Lake was named for Jacob Hamblin, a Mormon pioneer known as "the Buckskin Apostle." Hamblin was proficient in several Native American languages, and he negotiated with the Indians prior to the Mormon settlers' arrival.

Jacob Lake national forest campground is very pleasant and shady. It offers naturalist-led amphitheater programs in the evening. The campground, at 7,920 feet elevation, has 55 sites, a half-mile self-guided nature trail, and barrier-free facilities. There are a number of pleasant five- to 10-mile hiking or bicycling loops in the vicinity.

From Jacob Lake, travel south on Arizona Route 67 through a five-mile-long corridor of ponderosa pines and bright aspen trees. The white trunks of the aspens stand in startling contrast to the deeper hues of the pines. Autumn colors along this byway are beautiful. The entire byway is paralleled by the Kaibab Plateau Trail, a portion of the non-motorized-travel-only Arizona Trail that eventually will span the state from north to south. The Kaibab Plateau Trail is being planned and constructed by volunteers, the private sector, and the Forest Service.

The byway follows a livestock trail used by Mormon settlers and early visitors to the Grand Canyon. The trip from the nearest railhead at Marysville, Utah, took five jolting days of stagecoach travel before tourists reached the North Rim. Pioneers, sheepherders, and cattlemen carved initials and messages in the aspen trunks, which explains the graffiti along the road.

The plateau rises gradually, and the forest changes to a mixed conifer type that includes Douglas-firs, spruce, and white firs. Wildlife on the Kaibab Plateau is plentiful, and you are likely to see mule deer, wild turkeys, coyotes, and many species of squirrels. The rare Kaibab squirrel is unique to the area and is distinguished by its tufted ears and white tail. Look for the lively little creature up in the ponderosa pine trees.

The Kaibab mule deer is another interesting resident. President Theodore Roosevelt was so enamored of the area and its hunting opportunities that in 1906 it was designated the Grand Canyon Game Preserve. The population of predators, especially mountain lions, was systematically wiped out, and

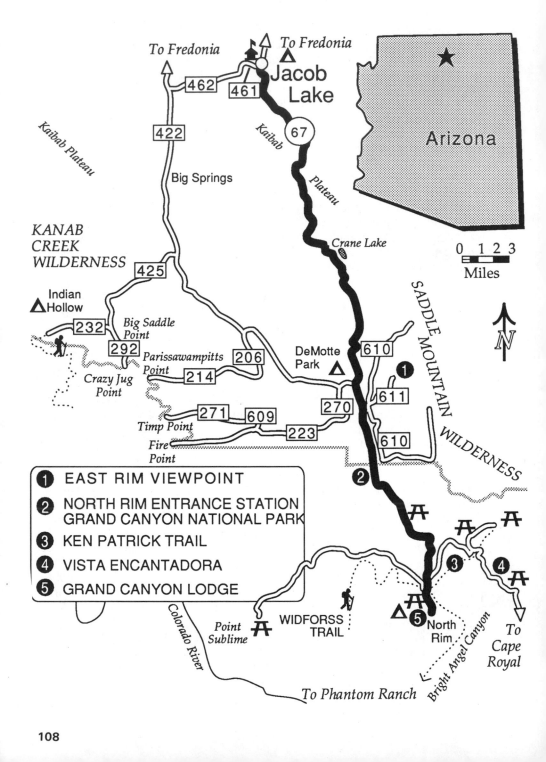

21 KAIBAB PLATEAU—NORTH RIM PARKWAY

To Fredonia

To Fredonia

Jacob Lake

462

461

422

Kaibab

67

Kaibab Plateau

Big Springs

Crane Lake

Arizona

0 1 2 3
Miles

N

KANAB CREEK WILDERNESS

425

Indian Hollow

232

Big Saddle Point

292

Parissawampitts Point

206

DeMotte Park

610

SADDLE MOUNTAIN

214

Crazy Jug Point

271

609

270

611

WILDERNESS

Timp Point

223

610

Fire Point

1 EAST RIM VIEWPOINT

2 NORTH RIM ENTRANCE STATION GRAND CANYON NATIONAL PARK

3 KEN PATRICK TRAIL

4 VISTA ENCANTADORA

5 GRAND CANYON LODGE

2

3

4

5

North Rim

Colorado River

Point Sublime

WIDFORSS TRAIL

Bright Angel Canyon

To Cape Royal

To Phantom Ranch

Unique views into Grand Canyon National Park await visitors at Fire Point, a side trip from the Kaibab Plateau-North Rim Parkway.

the deer population soared, and then, predictably, starved to death. Since that time, game managers and sportsmen have realized the importance and delicate balance of our earth's predator-prey-forage ecological relationships. Today hunters are able to bag record-class trophy deer here.

The forest type changes again around Crane Lake and includes Engelmann spruces, blue spruces, and subalpine firs. The large, grassy meadows along the road to DeMotte Park are good places to watch for wildlife, particularly in early morning and late evening. The Kaibab Plateau is home to more than 50 species of mammals, several species of reptiles, and more than 90 species of birds. Listen for the many songbirds and owls, and watch for hummingbirds, hawks, and endangered peregrine falcons. Wildflowers are abundant and include the unique and sensitive Kaibab paintbrush.

DeMotte Park is about 26 miles south of Jacob Lake. Here you will find a lodge, restaurant, horses, gasoline, groceries, and gift shop. DeMotte Park Campground lies at 8,760 feet elevation and has 22 sites.

There are several good side trips from here on gravel roads. Forest Road 422 leads through blown down timber to Dry Park, Big Springs, and eventually Jacob Lake via Forest Roads 462 and 461. Big Springs gushes forth as a waterfall; it was a popular rendezvous point on the plateau for early explorers. Forest Road 422 also gives access to many branch dirt roads, several of which lead to spectacular Grand Canyon overlooks, among them Timp Point, North Timp Point, Crazy Jug Point, and Fire Point. You will likely have these overlooks entirely to yourselves, and the solitude and grandeur are well worth the dusty, bumpy drive. Be certain you have plenty of gas, bring a picnic lunch or sleeping gear, and take out the camera; the Grand Canyon spreads out below, and you can see Tapeats Amphitheater, Fishtail Mesa, Steamboat Mountain, Great Thumb Mesa, and tributaries of the Colorado River. Thunder

Colorado River. Thunder River pours out from a barren cliff wall visible from Timp Point, and strong hikers at Indian Hollow can drop down on a good trail to Thunder River and its shady, cool canyon. Hiking permits are available at Grand Canyon National Park offices.

These viewpoints offer the first tangible indication of the enormity of the Kaibab Plateau. Atop the plateau, the road travels through relatively flat, forested terrain. But to emerge suddenly at the rim of the Grand Canyon and see the mile-deep swath cut through the earth lends some perspective to the plateau. The geologic history of our earth becomes accessible, understandable, and intriguing.

You can also choose a side trip to the east of the highway and drive Forest Roads 611 and 610 to East Rim and Dog Point overlooks, which show an entirely different part of the Grand Canyon. The panorama includes House Rock Valley, the Vermillion Cliffs, and Marble Canyon. Hiking trails from this area lead directly into the 40,610-acre Saddle Mountain Wilderness, a rugged and steep area that parallels the Colorado River's Marble Canyon. A herd of bison roams the upper parts of House Rock Valley.

Driving south again on the byway, you cross into Grand Canyon National Park. There are several picnic areas and hiking trails along the route. The Widforss Trail is a 10-mile round-trip walk along the rim of the Grand Canyon over very easy terrain. Wildlife is plentiful, as are the views into the canyon. The Ken Patrick Trail and the Uncle Jim Trail are east of the byway and also wind through the forest along the rim. The park offers eight day hikes ranging from a half-mile to 12 miles in length.

Two side trips are worth noting here: Point Imperial and Cape Royal. Point Imperial is 11 miles from Grand Canyon Lodge and is the highest place in the park at an elevation of 8,803 feet. Views extend over the canyon to the Painted Desert and beyond. There are walking trails, toilets, and picnic tables available. Cape Royal is 23 miles from the lodge and has a half-mile walking trail to Angel's Window. Interpretive signs explain the area's natural history. Pinyon pines, junipers, and cacti grow here at this lower elevation of 7,865 feet.

Return to the byway on the same road, and stop at the Anasazi Indian ruin across from Walhalla Overlook. There is evidence of human habitation on the Kaibab Plateau as far back as 7,000 B.C., but the majority of prehistoric artifacts were left by the Anasazi, who lived here from about A.D. 500 to 1200 and then disappeared.

The last few miles of the byway lead to North Rim. The historic Grand Canyon Lodge perches on the edge of the canyon, and Bright Angel Point is a short half-mile walk away. Ranger-led programs and hikes are offered daily, and they cover subjects as diverse as geology, politics, and natural history.

North Rim Campground is set in a shady pine forest. There are 82 sites, hot showers, a laundromat, country store, gasoline, and trailer dumping station available.

Grand Canyon Lodge has a restaurant, cafeteria, gift shop, and lodging in cabins or a motel. The lodge is constructed of native limestone blocks and timber, and its rustic and informal atmosphere is very pleasing.

A park brochure sums up the Grand Canyon as follows: "...no word is really adequate to describe this amazing creation of nature. The scene continually changes as light plays off the rocks and clouds, creating shadows and contrasts. The world seems larger here with sunrises, sunsets, and storms taking on an added dimension to match the landscape. The permutations are unceasing, and the moods are without end. This is a land to humble the soul.'' □

22 APACHE TRAIL
Tonto National Forest   Arizona

General description: A 38-mile, narrow dirt and paved road that twists along steep canyon walls and provides spectacular views of desert, mountains, and lakes.

Special attractions: High Sonoran desert, Four Peaks and Superstition wilderness areas, outstanding views, large freshwater lakes, historic Theodore Roosevelt Dam.

Location: Central Arizona on the Tonto National Forest, east of Phoenix. The byway begins on Arizona Route 88 at the Tonto National Forest boundary near Apache Junction and ends at Theodore Roosevelt Dam.

Byway route number: Arizona Route 88.

Travel season: Year-round. Not recommended for vehicles with trailers because of a narrow, winding, unpaved 20-mile section. Parts of the byway are subject to occasional temporary closure during flash floods. Until mid-1990, a four-mile section of the byway near the dam will be closed daily between 6 a.m. and 2:30 p.m. to allow dam construction.

Camping: Two national forest campgrounds with picnic tables, toilets, fire grates. One state park with picnic tables, toilets, water, trailer dumping station, nature trails. Several other national forest campgrounds within a few miles of the byway on Theodore Roosevelt Lake.

Services: All services on a limited basis at Apache Lake Resort. Restaurant, gift shop, bar, and groceries in Tortilla Flat. Restaurant and campground at Canyon Lake Marina. All services in nearby Apache Junction and Globe.

Nearby attractions: Boyce Thompson Southwestern Arboretum, Salt River, Tonto National Monument, Lost Dutchman State Park.

For more information: Tonto National Forest, P.O. Box 5348, 2324 E. McDowell Road, Phoenix, AZ 85010, (602) 225-5200. District Rangers: Mesa Ranger District, P.O. Box 5800, 26 N. MacDonald St., Mesa, AZ 85211, (602) 835-1161; Tonto Basin Ranger District, P.O. Box 649, Roosevelt, AZ 85545, (602) 467-2236.

Description: The Apache Trail parallels a stretch of the Salt River and its blue reservoirs and winds through scenic desert country. The first 18 miles at the southwestern end of the two-lane byway are narrow and paved. The remaining 20 miles follow a narrow, washboard dirt road that winds along precipitous cliffs with blind corners and steep drop-offs. The scenery is awesome, but the drive is not for the fainthearted. Frequent overlooks provide safe places to enjoy the views.

Giant saguaros and other unique desert plants line the Apache Trail, which overlooks the reservoirs of the Salt River.

Albany Covered Bridge over the Swift River in New Hampshire, Drive 32.
Photo by George Wuerthner.

Whitefish Point Lighthouse in Michigan, Drive 30. Photo by David J. Case.

Eastern red cedar frames a cliff of Magazine Mountain, Ozark National Forest, Arkansas, Drive 36. Photo by Laurence Parent.

Basalt boulders in colorful Capitol Reef National Park, Utah, Drive 19. Photo by Laurence Parent.

Hikers among saguaro cacti in Arizona, Drive 22. Photo by Stewart M. Green.

Top: *Goodpasture Covered Bridge above the McKenzie River, Oregon, Drive 5. Photo by Steve Terrill.*

Bottom: *Chokecherry in reddish autumn hues frame the Snake River and Mount Moran, Wyoming, Drive 13. Photo by George Wuerthner.*

Top: *Canoeing on Sparks Lake with South Sister in the background, Oregon, Drive 4. Photo by Larry Geddis.*

Below: *U.S. Highway 212 crossing the Beartooth Plateau, Montana/Wyoming, Drive 11. Photo by Michael S. Sample.*

New Mexico Highway 6563 winds through Lincoln National Forest, Drive 28.
Photo by Laurence Parent.

October through April is generally very pleasant, with temperatures ranging from the low 40s at night to the mid-80s during the day. From May through September, the thermometer often registers well over 100 degrees. Intense rainstorms can occur anytime and cause flash floods. In July and August, daily afternoon thunderstorms are common.

The Apache Trail begins at the Tonto National Forest boundary about five miles northeast of Apache Junction. Lost Dutchman State Park is nearby, with 35 campsites, day-use areas, and several good nature walks laid out in the Sonoran desert.

The legend of the Lost Dutchman Mine has many versions, but all assume the existence of a mother-load gold mine somewhere in the Superstition Mountains. Prospectors still comb the mountains in search of the elusive fortune.

The Superstition Wilderness, adjacent to and south of the byway, is crisscrossed by a multitude of trails. The Second Water Trail leaves from First Water Trailhead at the end of Forest Road 78 near the national forest boundary. It is an easy three-mile walk with interesting views. You can choose to loop back to the trailhead via one of several other trails. Backpackers gain extended access to the wilderness here.

The byway heads northeast, following a route taken by prehistoric Indians and their descendents. The Apache Trail was built in 1905 to provide a supply route to Theodore Roosevelt Dam. The rock crib work shoring up the road along the cliffs was crafted by Apache Indians and continues to hold fast.

Needle Vista allows a very clear view of 4,553-foot Weaver's Needle, a distinctive volcanic plug in the Superstition Wilderness. The wilderness encompasses 159,780 acres with elevations from 2,000 feet to more than 6,000 feet. The mountains are composed primarily of volcanic tuff, ash, and lava, and vegetative types range from Sonoran desert scrub to chaparral. The unique saguaro cactus creates dramatic silhouettes against the sunsets.

Apache Gap lies at elevation 2,304 feet, and the terrain includes red and green cliffs and rounded rock formations. Jojoba and green-barked palo verde join ironwood and mesquite trees. Views expand northward into the Mazatzal Mountains and the Four Peaks Wilderness from Canyon Lake Vista Point. The highest summit in that wilderness is 7,657-foot Brown's Peak, one of the four peaks for which the area was named.

Canyon Lake Recreation Area has fishing, two boat-launching areas, picnicking, swimming, and some services. A steamboat tour leaves from the marina, which also offers boat rentals and a snack bar. Acacia Beach and Picnic Site has a swimming area, ramadas (open arbors), and picnic tables. The views across blue green Canyon Lake to the red hued cliffs and mountains are lovely. Boulder Recreation Site has barrier-free fishing access and good swimming. The dominant fish species are bass and catfish.

At Jojoba Vista Point, you can take a short walk to the top of a ridge for views of Canyon Lake and Tortilla Flat. The latter is another mile down the byway. Tortilla Campground, elevation 1,752 feet, is open from October 1 to April 30. It has 76 sites, drinking water, sewer hookups, and a trailer dumping station.

Tortilla Flat boasts a post office, restaurant, bar, limited groceries, and several gift shops. The rustic restaurant's walls are plastered with signed dollar bills and the business cards of visitors. The restaurant also carries books pertinent to the byway.

APACHE TRAIL

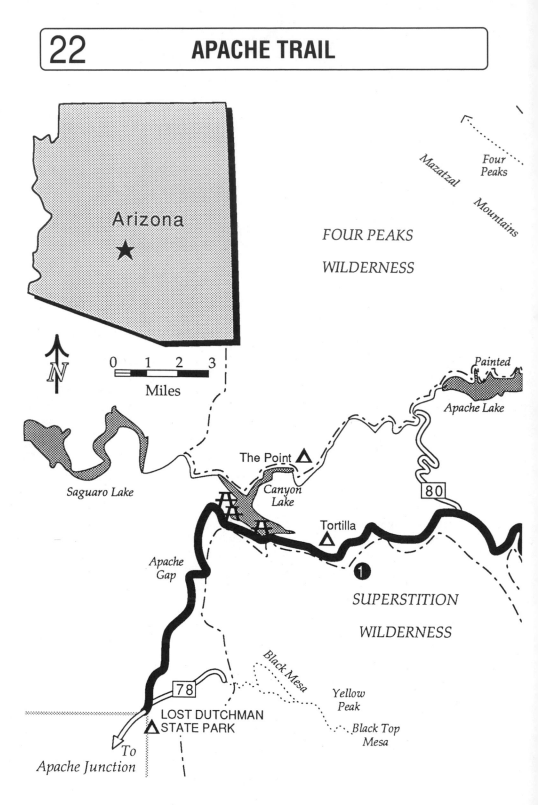

Arizona

N

0   1   2   3
Miles

Mazatzal Mountains

Four
Peaks

FOUR PEAKS

WILDERNESS

Painted

Apache Lake

The Point △

Saguaro Lake

Canyon
Lake

80

Tortilla
△

*Apache
Gap*

1

SUPERSTITION

WILDERNESS

Black Mesa

*Yellow
Peak*

78

LOST DUTCHMAN
△ STATE PARK

*Black Top
Mesa*

*To
Apache Junction*

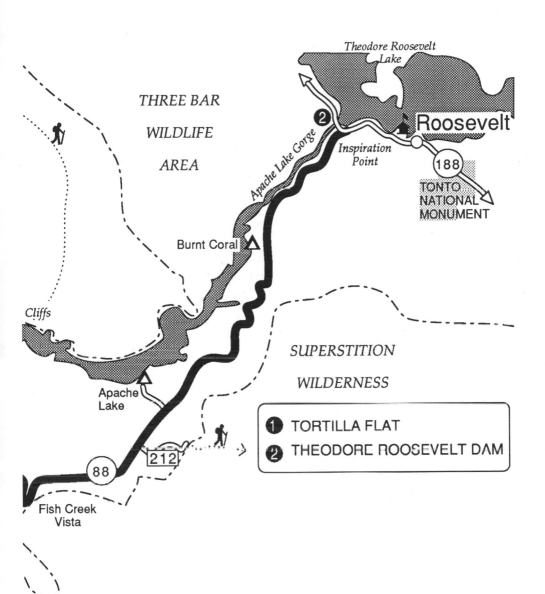

Theodore Roosevelt Lake

THREE BAR

WILDLIFE

AREA

Roosevelt

Apache Lake Gorge

② *Inspiration Point*

188

TONTO
NATIONAL
MONUMENT

Cliffs

Burnt Coral △

SUPERSTITION

WILDERNESS

Apache
Lake △

❶	TORTILLA FLAT
❷	THEODORE ROOSEVELT DAM

212

88

Fish Creek
Vista

The byway climbs east out of Tortilla Flat, and eventually the pavement gives way to dirt. There is room to pull over at several scenic overlooks. Fish Creek Vista is definitely worth a stop. Walk around the mesa a bit and enjoy the views of Phoenix and beyond, three of the Four Peaks, and Salt River canyons. If you are imaginative, you may be able to see in the rock formations such images as sitting judges, a devil's cauldron, and elephant and monkey faces.

Fish Creek Hill is one of the most amazing sections of the Apache Trail. Cliffs rise more than a thousand feet, and the road was carved right into them. The Wall of Bronze and Fish Creek Gorge provide fascinating visual contrasts, with the multi-hued rocks especially brilliant in the long rays of a late afternoon sun. The byway descends the precipitous cliffs and crosses Fish Creek, which sparkles amidst lush cottonwoods and riparian vegetation.

The route then turns north. A side trip for high-clearance vehicles on Forest Road 212 leads three miles to the Reavis Ranch Trailhead. Visitors will appreciate the 3,600-foot elevation and resulting views into the Superstition Mountains from the trailhead. The trail leads about 10 miles to the now-abandoned homestead of a hermit. Families might prefer to walk just a portion of the trail, which follows an old roadbed.

Forest Road 79 takes off from the byway and leads one mile north to 17-mile-long Apache Lake, a marina, and a national forest campground with 12 sites. Apache Lake Resort offers most services, including lodging, restaurant, lounge, marina, launch ramp, boat rental, camping with hookups, laundromat, gas, and groceries.

The byway climbs, drops, and winds north through Apache Lake Gorge. Across the lake, you can see the Four Peaks Wilderness and the Three Bar Wildlife Area. A variety of desert creatures inhabit the Apache Trail area, including javelinas, mule deer, mountain lions, bobcats, coyotes, ringtails, and skunks. Bighorn sheep were reintroduced and have dispersed, and you might see some between Fish Creek Hill and Apache Lake Gorge. Rattlesnakes and scorpions also call this area home.

Birdwatchers interested in soaring raptors may spot bald eagles, which winter here, turkey vultures, ospreys, and red-tailed hawks. Campers may hear Gambel's quail calling in the early morning.

Burnt Corral Campground lies in a lovely mesquite bosque that forms a perennially shady canopy over the 17 sites. The campground has no drinking water, but it does have vault toilets, a boat launch, and picnic tables. Watch for great blue herons fishing at water's edge near the camp.

The last few miles of the scenic byway lead to Theodore Roosevelt Dam. The byway is high above Apache Lake, and a primitive road, passable only by high-clearance vehicles, leads down to a pretty cove on the lake for picnicking or undeveloped camping. Vegetation includes saguaro, barrel, and cholla cacti. The latter is also called Teddy bear cactus because of its shape, or jumping cactus because its spines dislodge at the slightest touch and lodge firmly in the skin of the toucher.

Theodore Roosevelt Dam was built from 1906 to 1911 and is the highest masonry structure in the world. All the rocks used were quarried at the dam site and mortared with cement made in a nearby kiln. The kiln burned juniper wood that was packed in by burros. A National Historic Landmark, the dam is 750 feet long, 284 feet high, 184 feet thick at the base, and 16 feet thick at the top. The structure itself is a pleasure to look at, with its castle-like turrets across the top. The byway ends here at the dam.

Theodore Roosevelt Dam impounds the Salt River to form Theodore Roosevelt Lake. This popular body of water is 23 miles long and has boat launches, camping, picnicking, scenic overlooks, and a resort marina. The area is rich in prehistoric Indian history. Two Salado Indian cliff dwellings can be seen at Tonto National Monument. The visitor center has items made and used by the Salado, who lived in the area between A.D. 1100 and 1400. □

23 WHITE MOUNTAINS SCENIC HIGHWAY
Apache-Sitgreaves National Forest   Arizona

General description: A 123-mile series of connecting routes through and atop the White Mountains.

Special attractions: Expansive views, excellent fishing, cool elevations, resorts, skiing, camping, and hiking.

Location: East-central Arizona on the Apache-Sitgreaves National Forest, northeast of Phoenix. The byway is a series of interconnecting roads that form an open loop with spur roads: Arizona Route 73 from Whiteriver to Hon Dah, Arizona Route 260 from Hon Dah to the junction of Highways 273 and 260 near Eagar and Springerville, the entire lengths of Arizona Routes 273 and 373 and Forest Roads 87 and 249.

Byway route numbers: Arizona Routes 73, 260, 273, and 373. Forest Roads 87 and 249.

Travel season: Arizona Routes 73 and 260 are open year-round. All of Route 273 is closed by winter snows beyond Sunrise Ski Area. All of Route 249 is closed by winter snows, except about five miles near Alpine.

Camping: Five national forest campgrounds with picnic tables, fire grates, and vault toilets. All have drinking water except Benny Creek. Open June through September. No hookups. One trailer dumping station. Sixteen Fort Apache Indian Reservation campgrounds with picnic tables, fire grates, and vault toilets. Most have drinking water. Campgrounds open in summer.

Services: All services in Eagar, Springerville, Alpine, Hon Dah, and Whiteriver. Food, phone, and lodging at Sunrise.

Nearby attractions: Coronado Trail Scenic Byway, Inner Loop-Gila Cliff Dwellings Scenic Byway, Petrified Forest National Park, Lyman Lake State Park, Mount Baldy Wilderness Area, Kinishpa Ruins.

For more information: Apache-Sitgreaves National Forest, S. Mountain Ave., Highway 180, P.O. Box 640, Springerville, AZ 85938, (602) 333-4301. District Rangers: Alpine Ranger District, P.O. Box 469, Alpine, AZ 85920, (602) 339-4384; Springerville Ranger District, P.O. Box 640, Springerville, AZ 85938, (602) 333-4372.

Description: The White Mountains Scenic Byway system leads through cool green forests and across rolling fields of grasses and wildflowers to abundant clear lakes. The two-lane highways are paved, except Forest Roads 87 and 249 and Arizona Route 273 from Sunrise to Crescent Lake, which are graveled. Traffic on the byway is light.

Summer visitors can expect mild temperatures from the 50s to the 80s. Daily thunderstorms are common from July to September. Autumn and spring are cooler, with daytime temperatures in the 50s and 60s and evenings below freezing. Above 8,000 feet, snow usually remains on the ground from Thanksgiving until Easter.

The section of byway on Arizona Route 73 begins at Whiteriver and ends at Hon Dah. Whiteriver, at elevation 5,290 feet, is surrounded by colorful rimrocks and peaks in the White Mountains. Red mudstone and siltstone of ancient Pennsylvanian marine deposits, yellowish Coconino sandstone, and buff-colored Kaibab limestone are all visible in this area. Lava flows are from the White Mountain volcanic field. Nearby Big A Mountain is a resort development with food and lodging available.

The byway climbs north past numerous campgrounds and great fishing streams and lakes. A tribal permit is necessary for all recreational activities on the reservation. Permits are available in Whiteriver at the tribal Game and Fish Office, or at Hon Dah, McNary, Horseshoe Lake, and Sunrise.

The pinyons and junipers make way for deciduous oaks and shrubs, and the byway passes scattered residences with pastures and horses. A corridor of ponderosa pines leads to Hon Dah, which has a motel, campground, restaurant, and gasoline station.

The section of byway on Arizona Route 260 lies between Hon Dah and Springerville. Again there are numerous campgrounds near the route, as well as fishing in streams and lakes. Hawley Lake lies at the end of Arizona Route 473. The resort there has lodging, food, store, boat rentals, and campground.

The state's largest German brown trout was caught in 1985 at Horseshoe Lake. It weighed 16 pounds, 7 ounces. Horseshoe is stocked with rainbow, brook, and brown trout. A small store has supplies and rents boats.

Arizona Route 260 reaches a junction with Arizona Route 273, also part of the byway. That stretch of road is described later in this section.

Staying on Route 260, the byway enters the Apache-Sitgreaves National Forest and continues east toward Eagar and Springerville. The slopes of Sunrise Ski Area are visible to the south across the grassy fields. North of the byway, Forest Roads 117 and 61 lead to Greens Peak Lookout. For a side trip, drive to the base of the peak and walk up, or drive up in a high-clearance vehicle. The view from 10,115 feet is spectacular. On a clear day, the panorama can include the San Francisco Peaks far to the north. Songbirds sing nearby, and you may find yourself eye to eye with a hawk riding the updraft alongside the road. It is a beautiful and serene place.

Arizona Route 373 leads five miles south through a corridor of pines and grassy parks to Greer, a small mountain-resort community. En route are Tunnel, River, and Bunch reservoirs and Benny Creek and Rolfe Hoyer campgrounds. Benny Creek has 30 sites, and Hoyer has 100 sites, a trailer dumping station, showers, nature trail, amphitheater, and barrier-free access. The Butler Canyon Nature Trail is a delightful one-mile stroll through quaking aspens, evergreens, and riparian vegetation along the stream.

The tiny community of Greer is in an alpine-like setting and has lodges, restaurants, RV sites, and cabins available. The confluence of the East Fork and West Fork of the Little Colorado River is nearby. Fishing is very good

Mexican Hay Lake, along the White Mountains Scenic Byway, is usually covered with waterfowl.

for rainbow and brown trout, and winter recreationists enjoy cross-country skiing.

Back on Route 260, the byway continues east and descends gradually along the Little Colorado River. A side trip on Forest Road 560 leads to good fishing in the Little Colorado (watch for rattlesnakes) and camping at South Fork.

Hayfields line the road into Eagar and Springerville. Both communities offer complete traveler services. The White Mountains Historical Society has a number of historic buildings and displays adjacent to Springerville Park. The ranger station has information on the national forest and the byway.

Arizona Route 273 begins a few miles west of Eagar on 260 and makes a horseshoe-shaped circuit south through the heart of the White Mountains. The route climbs rapidly out of Round Valley, and views to the north extend for miles. Mexican Hay Lake is usually covered with ducks, including teals, buffleheads, and mallards.

Other wildlife inhabiting the byway area includes mule and whitetail deer, elk, pronghorns, porcupines, skunks, foxes, and turkeys. Bald and golden eagles soar overhead, and great horned owls hoot at night. Great blue herons and sandhill cranes raise long necks to watch passing vehicles.

Continue south past Crescent Lake, which offers boating, fishing, and boat rentals. Big Lake has several developed campgrounds with 248 sites for tents, trailers, and motor homes. A nature trail begins at the visitor center, and a small store supplies provisions and rents boats. The lake sits in a grassy basin, with wildflowers and waterfowl lining the shores.

Back at Crescent Lake, Route 260 travels northwest. Dipping Vat Spring is the site of a waterfowl development project, and you can hike about half a mile over the ridge to see the rich meadow environment. The byway travels through high meadows, grazing cattle, patches of aspens, and forest. Volcanic

To Show Low

260

Pinetop

Greens Peak

61

117

McNary

Hon Dah

Bog Tank

North Fork White River

473

Trout

Cyclone Lake

Hawley Lake

Creek

Sunrise Lake

Bear Cienega Creek

Paradise Creek

73

Diamond Creek

INDIAN

RESERVATION

Sunrise Peak

Whiteriver

Mount Baldy ④

73

Fort Apache

East Fork White River

To Carrizo

Arizona

★

N

0 1 2 3
Miles

① Benny Creek
② Rolfe C Hoyer
③ South Fork
④ Winn

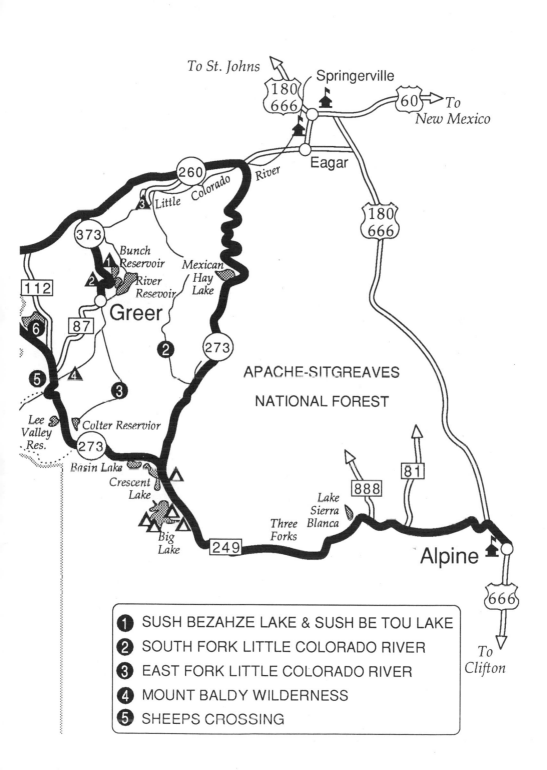

To St. Johns

Springerville

180
666

60 → To
New Mexico

Eagar

260

Little Colorado River

373

Bunch
Reservoir

112

River
Resevoir

Mexican
Hay
Lake

87

Greer

6

273

180
666

APACHE-SITGREAVES

NATIONAL FOREST

5

4

3

Lee
Valley
Res.

Colter Reservoir

273

Basin Lake

Crescent
Lake

Big
Lake

249

Three
Forks

Lake
Sierra
Blanca

888

81

Alpine

666

To
Clifton

❶ SUSH BEZAHZE LAKE & SUSH BE TOU LAKE
❷ SOUTH FORK LITTLE COLORADO RIVER
❸ EAST FORK LITTLE COLORADO RIVER
❹ MOUNT BALDY WILDERNESS
❺ SHEEPS CROSSING

cinder knolls rise up on all sides. Lee Valley Reservoir, at 9,370 feet, is about as pretty a lake and setting as anyone could ask for. Mount Baldy forms the backdrop, while the lake sparkles blue against the deep greens of the large spruce and fir trees lining the shores.

Winn Campground is a few miles north of the byway and has 63 sites and a group area. You can walk up the West Fork Little Colorado River, beginning at Sheep's Crossing. The footpath enters the 7,000-acre Mount Baldy Wilderness and ascends the summit of Mount Baldy.

The byway passes White Mountain Reservoir and reaches Sunrise Park. The Sunrise Ski Area has restaurants, shops, equipment rentals, and ski instruction, and lifts go to ski runs on three adjacent mountains. Cross-country skiing, snowmobiling, and ice fishing are other very popular winter sports in the byway region.

At Sunrise Lake are a lodge, restaurant, boat rentals, and lounge. The lake is the most productive fishery in the White Mountains for rainbow and brook trout.

Route 273 ends at its junction with Route 260, just north of Sunrise Lake. Forest Road 87 is graveled and provides a shortcut between Greer and Highway 273. The final section of byway follows Forest Road 249 from Big Lake to Alpine. This gravel road breaks in and out of large meadows with dancing creeks, forests, and mountains nearby. There are many opportunities for primitive, dispersed camping. In winter, the road is usually plowed to Williams Valley, a popular snow play area about five miles west of Alpine. Chances are good for spotting elk along this route.

The Coronado Trail National Forest Scenic Byway also travels through Alpine, a small, mountain resort community with services for travelers. The ranger station has information on the national forest and both scenic byways. ☐

24 CORONADO TRAIL
Apache-Sitgreaves National Forest   Arizona

General description: A 123-mile paved highway through steep canyons and rolling mountains, with extensive views.

Special attractions: Spectacular views, mining, colorful autumn foliage, wildlife, fishing, camping, hiking, Bear Wallow and Escudilla wilderness areas, Blue Range Primitive Area.

Location: Eastern Arizona on the Apache-Sitgreaves National Forest, paralleling the Arizona-New Mexico border. The byway begins at highway milepost 165 at Morenci and proceeds north on U.S. Highway 666 to milepost 406 near Eagar.

Byway route number: U.S. Highway 666.

Travel season: Year-round, with occasional temporary winter closures for snow removal. There are impressive sharp curves and steep drop-offs along several sections of narrow road with no guardrails. This route is not for the fainthearted or those who get carsick. Not recommended for towed units or vehicles more than 20 feet long.

Camping: Eight national forest campgrounds with picnic tables, fire grates, and vault toilets. Some have drinking water. Not suitable for vehicles more than 20 feet in length. No hookups.

Services: All services in Clifton, Alpine, and nearby Springerville. Food and lodging at Hannagan Meadow.

Nearby attractions: White Mountains Scenic Highway, Inner Loop-Gila Cliff Dwellings Scenic Byway, Sunrise Ski Area, Lyman Lake State Park.

For more information: Apache-Sitgreaves National Forest, P.O. Box 640, Springerville, AZ 85938, (602) 333-4301. District Rangers: Alpine Ranger District, P.O. Box 469, Alpine, AZ 85920, (602) 339-4385; Clifton Ranger District, P.O. Box 698, Clifton, AZ 85533, (602) 865-4129.

Description: The Coronado Trail is an impressive route up a sheer-walled canyon and across high, rolling mountains. Sweeping panoramic views encompass hundreds of miles, and the terrain varies widely. The two-lane road is paved, traffic is usually light, and drivers are often white-knuckled and wide-eyed at the southern end through the canyon. Travel is generally slow, both for scenic viewing and for safety.

Elevations range from 4,710 feet to 9,400 feet. Summer visitors can expect daytime temperatures over 90 degrees, with cooler temperatures at the higher elevations. Winter snowfall is from two inches in the lower elevations to more than 70 inches around Alpine. Sudden and severe thunderstorms are to be expected, especially in July, August, and September.

The Coronado Trail takes its name from Francisco Vasquez de Coronado, a Spanish explorer. He and his armored conquistadores traveled this route in June and July 1540 in search of the mythical Seven Cities of Cibola, which were said to be filled with gold.

The steepest section of the byway is at the south end, and you may wish to climb north from there rather than ride the brakes from north to south. However, the views of the mountains and out over the high desert are a bit better when traveling from north to south.

At the south end, palm trees adorn neighborhoods in the small community of Clifton, set deep in a canyon. The historic downtown district is mostly boarded shut, but museum exhibits explain the late-nineteenth-century history of the mining camp. Nearby, rockhounds can find agates around Mulligan Peak, out Limestone Gulch.

The byway begins near Morenci and climbs 4,000 feet. Lining the route are eight miles of mines, processing plants, and smokestacks. The open-pit copper mine is huge on an awesome scale, and the colors exposed in the raw cuts are fascinating, ranging from blue to russet to purple to turquoise. The narrow road twists and winds and nearly meets itself in several places. A mine overlook has a taped interpretive message for visitors. The copper mine is the third largest in the world.

The byway continues its tortuous ascent up Chase Creek to the national forest boundary. Painted Bluff Trail leads west through the forest. Granville Campground has drinking water and nine sites in the cool forest. The Apache-Sitgreaves National Forest has the largest stand of ponderosa pines in the nation.

The byway climbs and climbs, and the views are magnificent—east into the Blue Range Primitive Area, west into the White Mountains, and south over

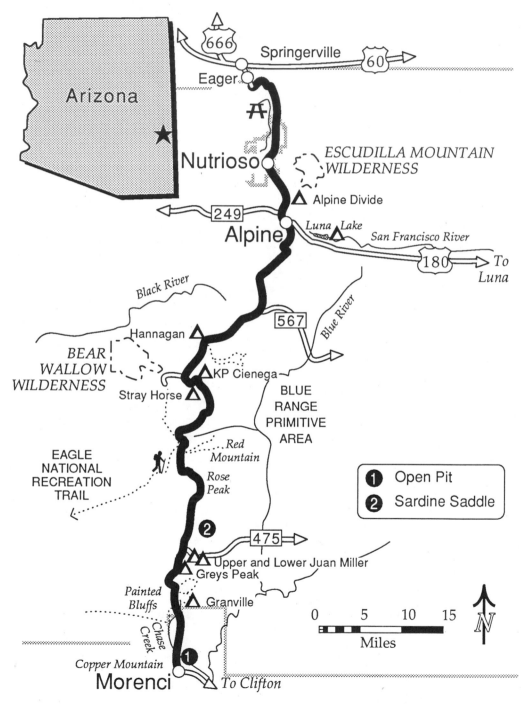

the high Sonoran deserts below. Sardine Saddle has a number of good foot-paths that lead to even better vantage points.

Greys Peak, Upper Juan Miller, and Lower Juan Miller campgrounds are all at about 6,000 feet elevation. They signal the end of the steep and winding stretch of the Coronado Trail. Greys Peak has seven sites and drinking water, and Upper and Lower each has four sites. A side trip east on graveled Forest Road 475 drops to the Blue River, where there is fishing for catfish and rainbow trout. Many of Arizona's important trout waters originate in this byway region. Of the 15 species of fish found on the national forest, two—the Apache trout and the Little Colorado spinedace—are endangered. Clearly this is crucial habitat for these fish and other wildlife.

More than 160 species of birds inhabit the byway area, including endangered peregrine falcons and bald eagles. Other interesting birds are spotted owls, pygmy nuthatches, hairy woodpeckers, olive warblers, and northern goshawks. The national forest also contains about 96 species of mammals. Common species include mule and whitetail deer, elk, Abert's squirrels, and coyotes.

Cattle graze in the large, grassy parks and meadows and among the pinyons and junipers. The topography here is gently rolling, and views are extensive. Whole thunderstorms can be seen off in the distance, while the byway area is sunny and clear. Or, conversely, the byway may be drenched in a major rainfall, while off in the distance the desert is lit by the sun. This is a wonderful stretch of road.

Rose Peak has a lookout at 8,154 feet. The lookout is manned between May and July, and the rough road leading to it is navigable by most passenger cars. A footpath leads to the top for expansive vistas. To the east, the Blue Mountains are primarily volcanic, and the major river valleys are filled with silt, sand, and gravel. The Blue River cuts a deep canyon through the Blue Range Primitive Area, which is located in the transition zone between the Colorado Plateau and the Basin and Range provinces. The strata are severely faulted. To the north, the White Mountains run east to west, covered with a thick ponderosa pine forest.

Hikers reach the Eagle National Recreation Trail from the byway just past Rose Peak. Gambel, gray, and white oaks dot the area.

Stray Horse Campground has drinking water and seven sites in the ponderosa pines near the highway. Blue Vista Point is at 9,100 feet elevation. From here, you can see Eagle Creek and the Black River to the west, the Graham Mountains to the southwest, and the Clifton area far to the south.

K P Cienaga Campground has five sites, drinking water, and a three-mile trail along a lush canyon bottom to a small waterfall. Watch for occasional patches of poison ivy. Hannagan Campground has eight sites.

Tucked into the spruce and fir forest at Hannagan Meadow is a lodge that also provides meals. Autumn is particularly nice here, when the aspens turn bright gold and shimmer in the sunlight. There are many footpaths in this area, and winter recreation includes cross-country skiing and snowmobiling.

Wildflowers are particularly abundant in August or after a summer rain. Look for black-eyed Susans, four o'clocks, sunflowers, evening primroses, penstemons, lupines, and asters.

The byway descends to Alpine through a forest of Douglas-firs and white firs, Englemann and blue spruce, and white and ponderosa pines. Alpine is a small, popular recreation-based community. There are numerous loop trips

The Coronado Trail Scenic Byway provides sweeping views of varied landscape along its 123-mile route through steep canyons and rolling mountains.

to drive from here, and hunting, horseback riding, hiking and skiing are common activities. The White Mountains Scenic Byway intersects the Coronado Trail in Alpine.

The byway travels north through forested ancient cinder cones. Four miles north of Alpine, Alpine Divide Campground has 12 sites in the ponderosa pines. The route travels through rabbitbrush, forested hills, and the timber-mill community of Nutrioso. Steep bluffs line the creek and road as it ascends, and the byway emerges from a small canyon to overlook Springerville, Becker Lake, and the adjacent rolling hills and fields. The byway ends at the national forest boundary near Eagar and Springerville. □

25 INNER LOOP—GILA CLIFF DWELLINGS SCENIC BYWAY
Gila National Forest   New Mexico

General description: A 110-mile paved loop through the Pinos Altos Mountains, including a spur trip to Gila Cliff Dwellings National Monument.

Special attractions: Prehistoric Indian cliff dwellings, far-reaching views into the Gila and Aldo Leopold wilderness areas, historic mining relics, hiking.

Location: Southwest New Mexico on the Gila National Forest, near Silver City. The byway is a loop, and it follows New Mexico Route 15 from Silver City north to Gila Cliff Dwellings National Monument, New Mexico Route 35 from the junction of Routes 15 and 35 east to San Lorenzo, New Mexico Route 152 from San Lorenzo west to the junction of Route 152 and U.S. Highway 180, and Highway 180 west to Silver City.

Byway route numbers: New Mexico Routes 15, 35, and 152, and U.S. Highway 180.

Travel season: Year-round.

Camping: Seven public campgrounds with toilets, picnic tables, and fire grates. Suitable for tents, truck campers, and trailers less than 17 feet in length. No hookups. Some campgrounds closed in winter.

Services: All services in Silver City. All services but limited availability in Gila Hot Springs, Lake Roberts, Mimbres, and San Lorenzo.

Nearby attractions: Gila and Aldo Leopold wilderness areas, City of Rocks State Park, The Catwalk of Whitewater Canyon, Coronado Trail Scenic Byway, and White Mountains Scenic Highway.

For more information: Gila National Forest, 2610 N. Silver St., Silver City, NM 88061, (505) 388-8201. District Rangers: Wilderness Ranger District, P.O. Box 79, Mimbres, NM 88049, (505) 536-2250; Silver City Ranger District, 2915 Highway 180 E., Silver City, NM 88061, (505) 538-2771.

Description: The two-lane, paved byway winds through the cooler altitudes of the Pinos Altos Mountains and crosses the Continental Divide twice. The byway from Pinos Altos to the junction of New Mexico Routes 15 and 35 is unsuitable for vehicles longer than 17 feet because it is narrow and makes sharp turns. There are scenic turnouts, traffic is light, and the highway is well-maintained. Views into the wilderness are extensive.

Expect variable mountain weather conditions. Temperatures may change as much as 40 degrees in a day. Generally, June through November mornings are clear and sunny, with daytime temperatures in the 70s and evening temperatures above freezing. Afternoon thunderstorms come with clockwork-like regularity. From December through February, temperatures range between 20 and 40 degrees, and from March through May between 30 and 60 degrees.

The active mining town of Silver City sits at about 6,000 feet. Early Indians found turquoise here, the Spanish mined copper, and in 1870 prospectors struck rich silver deposits. The community has two museums and a colorful history. Billy the Kid spent his childhood here.

Drive north out of Silver City on New Mexico Route 15 through fields of pinyons and junipers and private agricultural land. The "W" on the hillside above town stands for Western New Mexico University.

Six miles north of Silver City, the tiny community of Pinos Altos has a historic district worth seeing. Bear left at the marked junction and drive into town. You will find the first Protestant church in the Territory of New Mexico, a three-quarter-size replica of the old Santa Rita del Cobre Fort and Trading Post, an opera house, cabin, store, and museum. The road then loops back out to New Mexico Route 15.

Travel this very narrow, winding road through ponderosa pine forest. A short distance from Pinos Altos, an abandoned mining arrastra is interpreted. Here, mules dragged a boom around and around to crush the gold-bearing ore.

Farther north, a short walk to a rock outcrop leads to a good view into the forested mountains. You will also find a plaque that commemorates Ben Lilly, an early-day mountain man and hunter.

The byway gains elevation, and rock columns to the west rise over Cherry Creek and McMillen campgrounds, open April to November. Bring your own water as none is provided at these campgrounds.

Just before milepost 14, Forest Road 154 bears east to Signal Peak, elevation 9,001 feet. This dirt road winds up to the fire lookout, once the site of a heliograph station during the Apache Wars. The views extend into the Gila Wilderness and south to Mexico. The road can be traveled by most passenger cars.

Back on New Mexico Route 15, Lookout Point is situated at 7,000 feet amid pinyon pines, junipers, and cacti. Views, especially to the west, are extensive. This is good habitat for black bears, mule deer, elk, and wild turkeys. The byway then descends to the junction of Routes 15 and 35. Stay north on Route 15 toward Gila Cliff Dwellings National Monument, 23 miles away. This stretch of highway is named in honor of Senator Clinton P. Anderson, a nationally recognized conservationist. The road winds through the middle of the Gila Wilderness, climbing through a ponderosa pine forest. The Gila Wilderness encompasses 500,000 acres and has the honor of being the first federally designated wilderness in the world. The threatened Gila trout is making a slow comeback in the wilderness.

Copperas Vista is located on the edge of an ancient, collapsed caldera. The headwaters of the Gila River sparkle to the west, and views extend 50 miles or more, encompassing the Pinos Altos Range, the Black Range and the Mogollon Mountains. The road winds down a spur ridge to river level and numerous campgrounds, most open year-round. Upper and Lower Scorpion campgrounds have running water during warm months. Forks and Grapevine

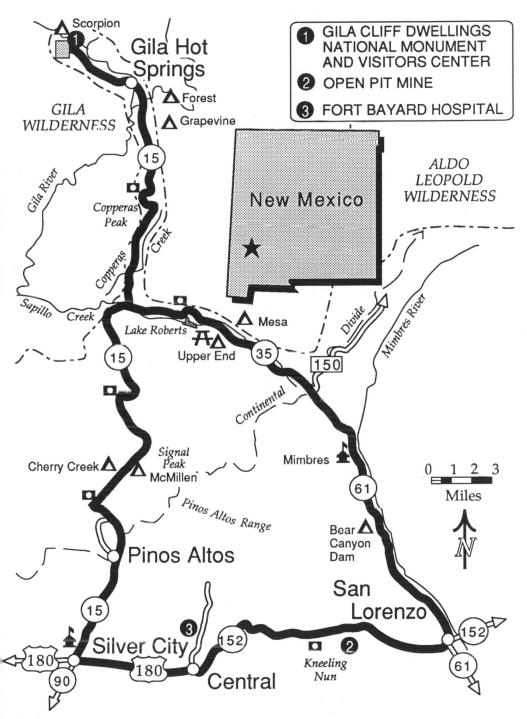

25

INNER LOOP—GILA CLIFF DWELLINGS SCENIC BYWAY

- **1** GILA CLIFF DWELLINGS NATIONAL MONUMENT AND VISITORS CENTER
- **2** OPEN PIT MINE
- **3** FORT BAYARD HOSPITAL

Scorpion

Gila Hot Springs

GILA WILDERNESS

Forest

Grapevine

New Mexico

ALDO LEOPOLD WILDERNESS

15

Gila River

Copperas Peak

Copperas Creek

Sapillo Creek

Lake Roberts

Upper End

Mesa

15

35

150

Divide

Mimbres River

Continental

Cherry Creek

Signal Peak
McMillen

Mimbres

61

Pinos Altos Range

Pinos Altos

Bear Canyon Dam

San Lorenzo

0 1 2 3
Miles

N

15

152

3

Silver City

180

180

Central

Kneeling Nun

2

152

61

90

A ranger explains the prehistoric Mogollon Indian culture at Gila Cliff Dwellings National Monument.

camping areas are less developed. Watch for poison ivy in the moist drainages.

Gila Hot Springs has privately owned services, open on a limited basis. A great blue heron rookery can be viewed in springtime, opposite the entrance to Heart Bar Wildlife Area.

Gila Cliff Dwellings National Monument lies at the edge of an ancient volcano, in the riparian Gila River bottom. The visitor center is open 8 a.m. to 5 p.m. throughout the year. A one-mile, moderately easy loop trail leads through the cliff dwellings inhabited by the Mogollon Indians seven centuries ago. A guidebook and rangers help interpret the area. Numerous hiking trails begin here, with opportunities for hour-long to week-long treks. Fishing for rainbow trout in the three forks of the Gila River can be rewarding. Peregrine falcons, golden and bald eagles, and red-tailed and Cooper's hawks may be spotted soaring above.

Return via the same highway, but turn east onto New Mexico Route 35. Lake Roberts has fishing, boating, camping, and hiking trails. The prehistoric Mimbres Indians inhabited the area from A.D. 200 to 1150, and a self-guided trail leaves from a fenced parking area just east of the Austin Roberts Vista Point and leads to Indian ruins. The museum at Western New Mexico University in Silver City has a large collection of Mimbres Indian pottery, valued for its distinctively intricate designs.

A pictograph trail and a swamp nature trail begin at Upper End campground. Purgatory Chasm Trail is another self-guided nature trail; it begins across from Lake Roberts picnic area and descends the chasm to a grotto and pond. Mesa Campground has improved facilities and is open May to September.

Farther along Rouute 35, Wall Lake Road (Forest Road 150) makes a nice side trip. This dirt road travels atop the Continental Divide and has good hiking trails and primitive campsites.

Near the Mimbres River, the byway descends through open terrain. Russet-colored canyon walls show horizontal bedding and the effects of erosion. Undeveloped campsites are scattered under the ponderosa pines beside the road.

The Mimbres Ranger Station is open during normal business hours. The byway travels through rolling topography and private agricultural land. Bear Canyon campground has four sites, and picnic tables. At San Lorenzo, turn west onto New Mexico Route 152 toward Silver City.

The Santa Rita Copper Pit can be viewed from a small turnout. An overlook a few miles farther west points out the Kneeling Nun rock formation. Continuing along the highway, bear right on U.S. Highway 180. Within a mile of the junction is the road to Fort Bayard, an interesting side trip. Now a hospital, the complex was once a cavalry post, complete with parade grounds, headquarters, and officers' and enlisted men's quarters. You will probably spot elk if you continue on the dirt road past the fort.

U.S. Highway 180 leads back into Silver City, completing the 110-mile loop. □

26 SANDIA CREST ROAD
Cibola National Forest   New Mexico

General description: A 13.4-mile highway that winds from high desert up to the 10,687-foot summit of forested Sandia Mountain.

Special attractions: Cool temperatures, thick forest, colorful autumn foliage, far-ranging views, hiking, and skiing.

Location: Central New Mexico on the Cibola National Forest, northeast of Albuquerque. The byway begins at the junction of New Mexico Route 14 and Forest Road 536, at Sandia Park, and ends at the upper parking lot at the top of Sandia Mountain.

Byway route number: Forest Road 536.

Travel season: Year-round. The byway winds around some very steep curves, and winter driving conditions may be hazardous at higher elevations. Chains or snow tires sometimes are required.

Camping: There are no developed campgrounds on the byway, but some opportunities exist for primitive and backcountry camping. There are many privately owned campgrounds in the vicinity, but the nearest public campgrounds are more than 50 miles away.

Services: Restaurant, phones, and restrooms at Sandia Peak Ski Area and at the summit. All services in nearby Tijeras and Albuquerque.

Nearby attractions: Salinas National Monument, Bandelier National Monument, Pecos National Monument, Bosque del Apache Wildlife Refuge, El Malpais National Monument, Indian pueblos and missions.

For more information: Cibola National Forest, 10308 Candelaria NE, Albuquerque, NM 87112, (505) 275-5207. District Ranger: Sandia Ranger District, 11776 Highway 14 S., Tijeras, NM 87059, (505) 281-3304.

Description: The Sandia Crest Road climbs 3,760 feet on the east side of the Sandia Mountains, offering cool mountain temperatures, wide views to the west, and plenty of opportunities to picnic and hike. The two-lane highway is paved and has frequent turnouts for scenic and recreational access. Traffic on weekends and holidays can be quite constant, but it is relatively light during the weekdays.

Summer visitors can expect temperatures ranging from the 40s to the 80s. Intense afternoon storms come regularly in July and August. The weather is always cooler and may be quite windy at the higher elevations. Spring and fall temperatures range from the 30s to the 60s. Winter can go below zero to above 50, and snows accumulate from late December through February.

The byway begins at the junction of New Mexico Route 14 and Forest Road 536, at 6,880 feet elevation. Follow Road 536 northwest through a woodland of pinyons, junipers, and oaks. Short side roads lead to Doc Long, Sulphur Canyon, and Cienaga Canyon picnic areas. Cienaga is well off the road, with many secluded sites in the rich riparian vegetation. Cienaga Nature Trail has facilities for the physically and visually handicapped, and nature lovers will find the scaly bark of the alligator juniper trees interpreted in Braille as well as print. A number of other easy but longer loop walks include Faulty and Cienaga trails. The latter provides access to the South Crest Trail, which is the main ridgetop path ascending Sandia Mountain.

The Doc Long Picnic Area was built by the Civilian Conservation Corps in the 1930s. It still has the original wood ramada, an interesting architectural structure. Bill Spring Trail is at the west end of Doc Long, offering very easy walking along the original crest highway that follows the bottom of Tejano Canyon. Thick streamside vegetation includes box elders, wild roses, maples, aspens, chokecherries, and poison ivy. This rich bird habitat hosts rufus-sided towhees, Audubon's warblers, Steller's jays, robins, red-breasted nuthatches, and chickadees. Other birds to be seen along the byway include turkey vultures, golden eagles, red-tailed hawks, and great horned owls. The tiny flammulated owl with the big hoot also resides here.

Dramatic color changes in the exposed roadcuts along the byway tell an interesting geological story. The granitic core of the Precambrian mountain system contacts a much younger Pennsylvanian limestone, but whole geologic eras are missing between them. This is known as the Great Unconformity, and it can be seen directly across from Doc Long Picnic Area. Look for gray rocks sticking out of the russet-colored, eroding limestone, with interesting stripes in the limestone where other rock was injected into fault lines. The Sandia Mountains were formed along a thrust fault, and displaced limestone and rock outcrops are visible throughout the byway area.

As the byway climbs, you can contrast the ponderosa-pine-covered north-facing side of the road with the hotter, drier south-facing side of the road, which supports a variety of shrub species. Vegetation changes as the route gains altitude, adding mixed conifers and then finally Engelmann spruces and corkbark firs at about 10,000 feet.

The Cibola National Forest is host to mule deer, black bears, striped skunks, raccoons, and the Abert's squirrel, which lives exclusively in ponderosa pine trees. In all, the forest has more than 180 species of birds, 11 species of bats, 58 species of mammals, 12 species of reptiles and amphibians, and more than 800 species of plants, including more than 20 species of trees.

Cienaga Nature Trail offers a lovely walk through alligator junipers not far off Sandia Crest Road.

Tree Spring Trail makes for an easy family hike. It winds along the side of the mountain and joins the 10K Trail and the South Crest Trail for a longer route. Wildflowers along the trails include Rocky Mountain wild irises, coneflowers, shooting stars, and a variety of penstemons.

At Dry Camp Picnic Area, walk up the saddle for a big view to the northeast, over Madera Canyon. The byway then comes to Sandia Peak Ski Area, a popular winter resort. In summer, there are phones, restrooms, and a restaurant open at the base. The lift is also usually open in summer and fall, but call ahead to be sure.

The view from the top of the lift is magnificent; it extends as far as 100 miles. Albuquerque spreads out to the west, while mountains rise to the south and east. The Forest Service operates the Four Seasons Visitor Center year-round at the upper tram terminal. A fine restaurant offers meals, and the Sandia Peak Aerial Tram rises from Albuquerque to this spot. There are also hiking opportunities at the top.

Balsam Glade Picnic Area sits near a side road (New Mexico Route 165) that leads down pretty Capulin Canyon and Las Huertas Creek to Placitas. Remains of a woolly mammoth and prehistoric projectile points were found in Sandia Man Cave along this creek. The remains may be more than 12,500 years old and are probably from the Clovis people. A spiral staircase leads to the mouth of the cave at the edge of the cliff, and there are beautiful views into the canyon, especially in autumn.

Capulin Springs Picnic Area is near Capulin Snow Play Area, which has colorful wildflowers in summer and tubing and cross-country skiing in winter. The byway then begins a series of switchbacks and passes Ninemile Picnic Area to reach the top of Sandia Mountain.

Wonderful vistas spread out below, making it easier to overlook the "forest

26

SANDIA CREST ROAD

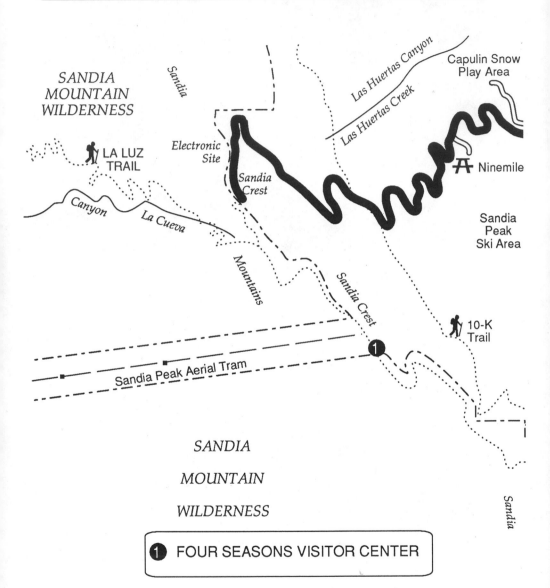

SANDIA
MOUNTAIN
WILDERNESS

LA LUZ
TRAIL

Sandia

Electronic
Site

Sandia
Crest

Canyon

La Cueva

Mountains

Sandia Crest

Las Huertas Canyon

Las Huertas Creek

Capulin Snow
Play Area

Ninemile

Sandia
Peak
Ski Area

10-K
Trail

Sandia Peak Aerial Tram

SANDIA

MOUNTAIN

WILDERNESS

Sandia

1 FOUR SEASONS VISITOR CENTER

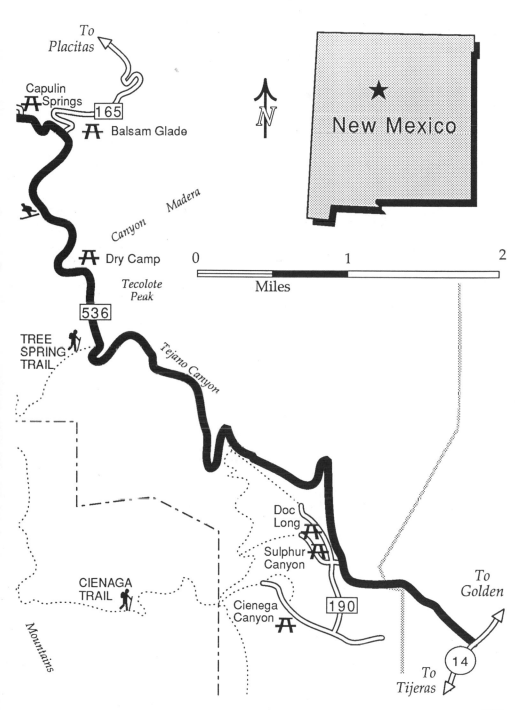

To
Placitas

Capulin
Springs

165

Balsam Glade

Canyon Madera

Canyon

Dry Camp

Tecolote
Peak

536

TREE
SPRING
TRAIL

Tejano Canyon

CIENAGA
TRAIL

Doc
Long

Sulphur
Canyon

Cienega
Canyon

190

Mountains

New Mexico

N

0   1   2

Miles

To
Golden

14

To
Tijeras

135

of steel" electronic site nearby. A restaurant and gift shop, restrooms, and telephones are located at the summit, and the dense spruce and fir forest gives some shelter from the wind. Rare dwarf coralbells grow only on this summit. Other species at the top are fairyslippers, penstemons, monkshoods, nodding onions, monument plants, and western wallflowers.

There's something about a mountaintop that exhilarates, and this summit is no exception. □

27 SANTA FE SCENIC BYWAY
Santa Fe National Forest   New Mexico

General description: A 15-mile paved route from the heart of historic Santa Fe up into the Sangre de Cristo Mountains.

Special attractions: Palace of the Governors and Santa Fe Plaza, Tesuque Canyon, Pecos Wilderness, Hyde State Park, far-ranging views, high elevations, colorful autumn foliage, Santa Fe Ski Area.

Location: North-central New Mexico on the Santa Fe National Forest. The byway begins at the Palace of the Governors on the plaza in downtown Santa Fe, heads north on New Mexico Route 590, turns northeast onto New Mexico Route 475/Forest Road 101, and ends at Santa Fe Ski Area.

Byway route numbers: New Mexico Route 475/Forest Road 101.

Travel season: Year-round. Winter driving conditions may be hazardous.

Camping: Three national forest campgrounds with picnic tables, fire grates, and vault toilets. One campground has drinking water. No hookups. Campgrounds open May through October. One state park campground with 72 sites (seven sites have electrical hookups), picnic tables, vault toilets, trailer dumping station, playground, nature trails, and drinking water. State park campground open year-round.

Services: All services in Santa Fe.

Nearby attractions: Bradbury Science Museum in Los Alamos, Bandelier National Monument, Pecos National Monument, Rio Chama Wild and Scenic River, Ghost Ranch Living Museum, Sunspot Highway, Indian pueblos, Indian Art and Culture Museum, International Folk Art Museum.

For more information: Santa Fe National Forest, 1220 St. Francis Drive, P.O. Box 1689, Santa Fe, NM 87504, (505) 988-6940. District Ranger: Espanola Ranger District, P.O. Drawer R, Espanola, NM 87532, (505) 753-7331.

Description: The Santa Fe Scenic Byway climbs from 7,000 feet in elevation at the city center, up Tesuque Canyon, and into the Sangre de Cristo Mountains. The two-lane paved road has narrow shoulders but frequent turnouts. Traffic can be heavy and may include vehicles, bicyclists, and joggers.

Summer visitors should expect warm temperatures from the 50s to high 80s, with lightning and thunderstorms most afternoons from late June until the end of August. It can rain up to an inch in an hour. Autumn is cooler and generally dry, with temperatures ranging from the 30s to the 60s. Snow and cold conditions stay throughout the winter above about 7,000 feet, while

Santa Fe Scenic Byway ascends from the arid high plateau desert of Santa Fe through the cooler, aspen- and conifer-covered Sangre de Cristo Mountains.

lower elevations have only occasional snow and temperatures in the 20s to 40s. Spring begins about April, and temperatures can warm rapidly.

Begin the drive right at the plaza in Santa Fe, but first walk around the historic area and note the Palace of the Governors, built in 1610. It is the oldest continuously occupied public building in the United States. In the past 300 years, Santa Fe has been ruled by the Pueblo Indians, Spain, Mexico, the Confederacy, and the United States.

Also of interest are the many adobe churches and chapels, the unusual state capitol building, six museums, a variety of pleasant shops, the performing arts (including the Santa Fe Opera), and the wonderful architecture of Santa Fe. The city is a visual delight; its buildings are mostly built in the Pueblo Revival or Territorial styles.

Driving north on New Mexico 475/Forest Road 101, you leave the city and encounter pinyon pines, junipers, and Gambel oaks on the rolling foothills. Brilliant yellow chamisa and sunflowers brighten the way in September. Residences are scattered among the tan- and rust-colored sandstone hills up to the national forest boundary. There, about five miles from town, the road enters the mountains and Tesuque Canyon.

This steep-walled, picturesque canyon leads to Little Tesuque Picnic Area and Black Canyon Campground. Little Tesuque has 11 picnic tables in the ponderosa pines, and it has barrier-free access. Black Canyon, elevation 8,400 feet, has drinking water and 44 campsites in a thick stand of pines and firs. The Black Canyon Trail is a two-mile loop that starts at Campsite 4.

The Sangre de Cristo Mountains are composed of brick-red sandstone and siltstone mixed with a lot of volcanic ash. The Precambrian core was pushed up on both sides, and the glaciation and erosion of later years cut deep, steep-walled canyons into the range.

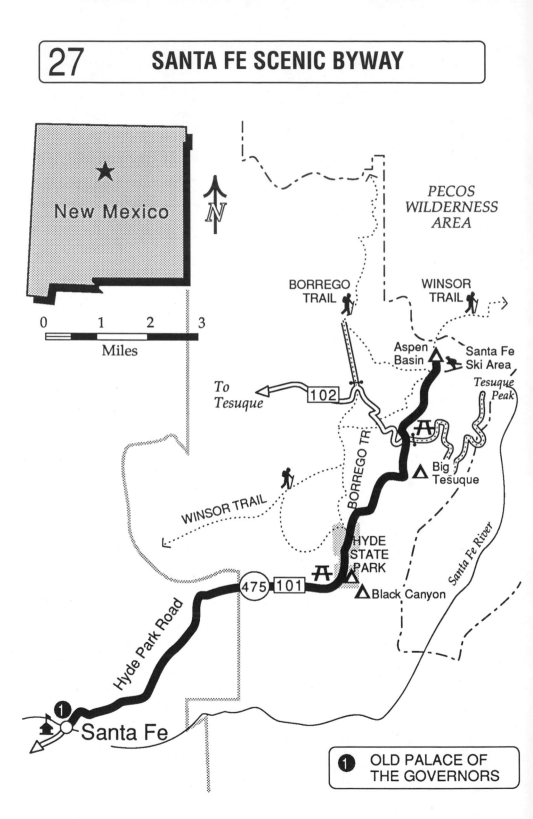

New Mexico

N

0   1   2   3
Miles

PECOS
WILDERNESS
AREA

BORREGO
TRAIL

WINSOR
TRAIL

Aspen
Basin

Santa Fe
Ski Area

Tesuque
Peak

To
Tesuque

102

BORREGO TR

Big
Tesuque

WINSOR TRAIL

HYDE
STATE
PARK

Santa Fe River

475   101

Black Canyon

Hyde Park Road

1

Santa Fe

1   OLD PALACE OF
THE GOVERNORS

A short distance beyond Little Tesuque, 350-acre Hyde Memorial State Park lies at an elevation of 8,500 feet. It has a good playground, a pond, camping, and picnicking. The Borrego-Bear Wallow Loop Trail is an easy three-mile hike. The trail leaves the byway at the northern edge of Hyde State Park and drops into a valley of forest and wildflowers. It climbs a ridge and then continues down to Big Tesuque Creek. After following the creek on Trail #254, it meets Bear Wallow and returns to the starting point. This moderately strenuous hike is popular and used year-round.

The byway continues north, paralleling the Pecos Wilderness boundary. The Pecos Wilderness is a heavily forested, rugged mountain area with peaks jutting higher than 13,000 feet. Steep slopes and cliffs furnish a backdrop to the small lakes and streams, and wildlife includes ptarmigans, turkeys, blue grouse, black bears, mule deer, bighorn sheep, elk, and pine squirrels. Brown trout lure anglers, and there are more than 100 miles of hiking trails in this 223,667-acre wilderness, all accessible from the scenic byway.

The byway twists and turns up to Big Tesuque Campground and Aspen Vista Picnic Area. Big Tesuque, at elevation 9,700 feet, has 10 sites in a lovely aspen grove. You can walk back into the aspens at Aspen Vista to get a view of Santa Fe far below, or you can hike Forest Road 150, a service road, up to 12,040-foot Tesuque Peak.

Raptors and ravens soar over the valley floor, while around the byway bird-watchers spot gray and Steller's jays, western tanagers, and a variety of warblers and sparrows.

A side trip on Forest Road 102 loops down a gravel road to Pacheco Canyon and the community of Tesuque. The narrow road winds down a mountain and then follows Pacheco Canyon and Rio Chupadero through stands of aspens and pines to New Mexico Route 590. Forest Road 102 is not passable in winter.

Near the top of the byway, frequent openings in the aspen forest offer good views of Santa Fe, the Rio Grande Valley, and the Pojoaque Valley. The autumn foliage is brilliant, usually beginning in late September. The byway ends at the Santa Fe Ski Area, where a new lift ascends to 11,320 feet and views extend over 8,000 square miles of the Southwest. The lift and related tourist services are open summer and winter.

Aspen Basin Campground is located in the parking loop of the ski area. It has 10 sites at an elevation of 10,300 feet. The popular Winsor Trail leads directly into the Pecos Wilderness and continues on to a multitude of wilderness hiking trails and their spectacular views. □

28 SUNSPOT SCENIC BYWAY
Lincoln National Forest   New Mexico

General description: A 14.8-mile route high atop the forested Sacramento Mountains.

Special attractions: Cool mountain elevations, guided and self-guided tours of a solar observatory, hiking, winter recreation.

Location: South-central New Mexico, on the Lincoln National Forest, east of Alamogordo. Turn south onto New Mexico Route 130 at Cloudcroft and then south again on New Mexico Route 6563, known locally as the Sunspot Highway. The byway travels the entire length of Route 6563.

Byway route number: New Mexico Route 6563.

Travel season: Year-round.

Camping: One group area by reservation only. However, seven national forest campgrounds with 246 sites are within a few miles of the byway.

Services: All services in Alamogordo. All services, with limited availability, in Cloudcroft.

Nearby attractions: Cloudcroft Ski Area, Ski Apache, Space Hall of Fame, White Sands National Monument, White Mountain Wilderness, Capitan Wilderness, The Lodge, cross-country skiing.

For more information: Lincoln National Forest, Federal Building, 11th Street and New York Avenue, Alamogordo, NM 88310, (505) 437-6030. Ranger District: Cloudcroft Ranger District, P.O. Box 288, Cloudcroft, NM 88317, (505) 682-2551.

Description: The paved, two-lane highway with scenic turnouts winds through a cool evergreen forest along the front rim of the Sacramento Mountains. Elevations range from 8,300 feet to 9,500 feet.

Expect variable mountain weather. Summer temperatures are likely to reach the 70s, and thunderstorms occur almost every afternoon. Fall and spring are usually dry with much lower temperatures, and winter brings snow to the upper elevations.

The byway begins a few miles south of Cloudcroft, at the start of New Mexico Route 6563. Travel by Slide group-camping area and find the first of many access points to the Rim Trail, a scenic and popular 13.5-mile hiking trail that parallels the edge of the Sacramento Mountains before dropping into Haynes Canyon.

The forest includes ponderosa pines, aspens, white firs, southwest white pines, New Mexico locusts, Engelmann spruces, and Rocky Mountain maples. Berry-lovers will find strawberries, raspberries, chokecherries, and blueberry elders. Occasional openings in the forest corridor afford glimpses west to the San Andres Mountains, White Sands National Monument, the Tularosa Basin, and the White Sands Missile Range.

The byway travels by a resort area for winter tubing and snowmobiling and continues to Nelson Canyon Vista Trail, a quarter-mile interpretive nature trail. Karr Canyon Road has numerous dispersed primitive campsites in the upper canyon, as well as a developed campground.

The Lincoln National Forest gets heavy use by snowmobilers, four-wheelers, motorcyclists, hunters, and firewood gatherers. You should also expect to see cattle grazing throughout the forest.

About halfway along the byway, Alamo Peak makes a good side trip. A paved road leads to the top, from which the view is splendid. The Tularosa Basin and San Andres Mountains spread out to the west, while forested slopes cover the mountains to the north, east, and south. The Sacramento Mountains are primarily composed of limestone. Rather than being thrust upward like the Rockies, the Sacramento and San Andres mountains stayed relatively still while the Tularosa Basin sank 5,000 feet between them along the Rio Grande Rift.

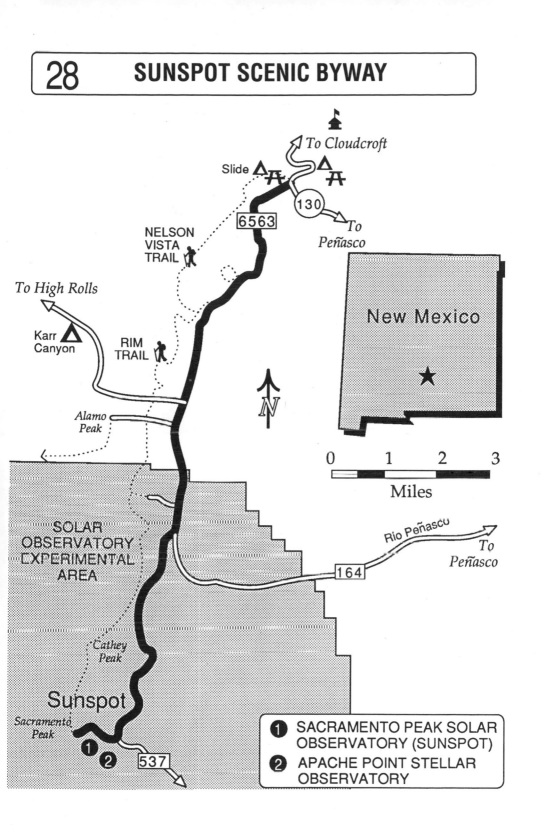

To Cloudcroft

Slide

130

6563

NELSON
VISTA
TRAIL

To
Peñasco

New Mexico

To High Rolls

Karr
Canyon

RIM
TRAIL

N

Alamo
Peak

0   1   2   3
Miles

SOLAR
OBSERVATORY
EXPERIMENTAL
AREA

Rio Peñasco

To
Peñasco

164

Cathey
Peak

Sunspot

Sacramento
Peak

537

❶ SACRAMENTO PEAK SOLAR
   OBSERVATORY (SUNSPOT)
❷ APACHE POINT STELLAR
   OBSERVATORY

Gambel oaks and shady conifers line the Nelson Canyon Vista Trail, just off the Sunspot Scenic Byway.

The Lincoln National Forest is home to rare Mexican spotted owls, found few other places in the world. Other unique species found in this forest are Sacramento Mountain salamanders and mescalero thistles. More commonly found are elk, mule deer, and black bears. Birdwatchers will likely spot red-tailed hawks, ravens, woodpeckers, warblers, and robins. Wildflowers include Indian paintbrushes, coneflowers, firecracker flowers, lupines, geraniums, daisies, and western yarrows.

Atkinson Point marks the last place to access the National Recreation Trail portion of the Rim Trail. Beyond the point, Cathey Vista, at more than 9,000 feet, is one of the highest places on the byway. There, a short interpretive trail winds through the spruce forest. A new stellar observatory is situated at Apache Point.

The byway ends at Sunspot, home of the National Solar Observatory. Here you will see lots of old-man's beard on the Douglas-fir and white fir trees. This wispy, moss-like plant is epiphytic, or air-breathing, and does no damage to the trees.

The solar observatory is open year-round for self-guided tours. A free guided tour is given at 2 p.m. each Saturday from May through October. The observatory houses the nation's largest coronagraph, a powerful tool used to study the sun's corona.

You can return to Cloudcroft via the byway or opt for a more circuitous route back. Forest Road 537, the Sacramento River Road, is a beautiful drive on a gravel road. Elk and deer may be spotted in spring and fall, and the route connects with the state highway system at Pinon. Alternatively, the Rio Penasco Road, Forest Road 164, goes past a little springs and waterfall before joining the Cox Canyon Road. This forms another nice scenic loop back to Cloudcroft. □

General description: A 29-mile paved highway through forests and rolling hills, past lakes, streams, and marshes.

Special attractions: Outstanding fishing in several lakes and streams, hunting, colorful foliage colors, historic logging-camp sites, and abundant wildlife.

Location: Northwest Wisconsin on the Chequamegon National Forest, southeast of Superior. The byway travels Wisconsin Route 77 on national forest land between Hayward and Glidden.

Byway route number: Wisconsin Route 77.

Travel season: Year-round.

Camping: There are no campgrounds located on the byway. However, there are three national forest campgrounds within a short drive, with 93 sites, water, picnic tables, fire rings, and vault toilets. No hookups.

Services: All services available in Hayward. Gas, phone, and food in Clam Lake and Glidden. Lodging at various byway resorts.

Nearby attractions: National Fresh Water Fishing Hall of Fame, Historyland, American Birkebeiner cross-country ski race, Lumberjack World Championships, Chequamegon Fat Tire Festival, Grandview Firehouse 50 Race.

For more information: Chequamegon National Forest, 1170 Fourth Ave. S., Park Falls, WI 54552, (715) 762-2461. District Rangers: Glidden Ranger District, P.O. Box 126, Glidden, WI 54527, (715) 264-2511; Hayward Ranger District, Route 10, Box 50, Hayward, WI 54843, (715) 634-4821.

Description: Located in the middle of the Chequamegon National Forest, the Great Divide Highway travels an obscure line that separates water flowing north to Lake Superior from water flowing south to the Gulf of Mexico. The two-lane paved road underwent extensive reconstruction in 1989. Traffic is light, allowing travelers a chance to enjoy the scenery of Wisconsin's northern lakes and timber country.

Weather conditions are variable in northern Wisconsin. Summer high temperatures are commonly around 80 with lows in the 60s, but cold fronts can drop daytime highs to the 50s. June and July are the only months in which an occasional nighttime frost is not normally expected. Winter temperatures range from daytime highs of 40 degrees to overnight lows of minus 40, though average temperatures are highs in the 20s with lows in the single digits.

The community of Hayward is known as the home of world-record muskies because of a series of fish caught in the area during the 1940s. Set among a number of both natural and man-made flowages, it is easy to see why tourism is the number-one industry, though logging is not far behind.

The scenic byway begins at the national forest boundary near Tiger Cat Flowage. Driving east from Hayward, you will find a number of resorts and tourism-related businesses lining the road, but the natural beauty of the area becomes more prevalent the farther you get from Hayward.

The landscape along the scenic byway varies. The topography features both

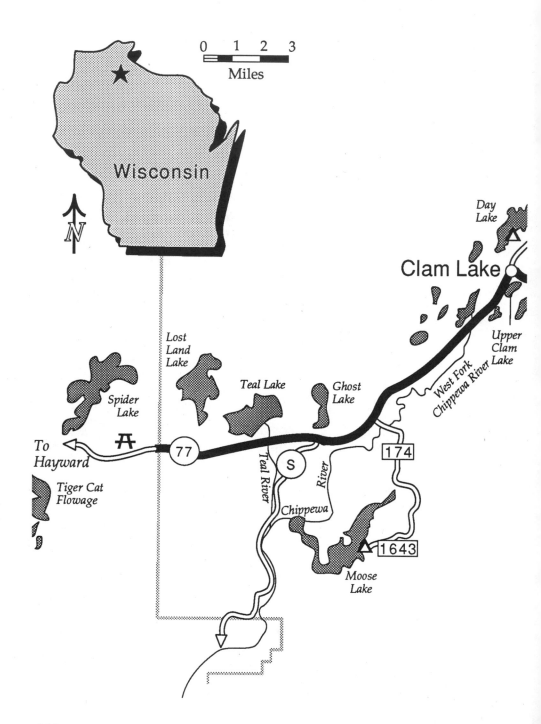

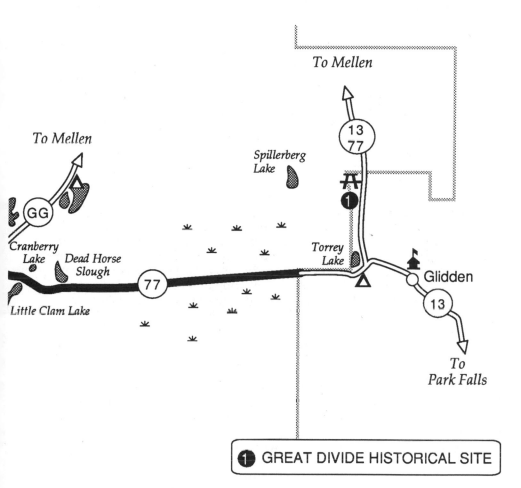

To Mellen

To Mellen

13
77

Spillerberg
Lake

GG

Cranberry
Lake

Dead Horse
Slough

Torrey
Lake

Glidden

77

13

Little Clam Lake

To
Park Falls

❶ GREAT DIVIDE HISTORICAL SITE

rolling hills and lowland areas, with American larches, spruces, pines, aspens, and maples predominating. Several noteworthy mixed forest stands are also found along the way, including white and yellow birches, hemlocks, basswoods, white ashes, and balsam firs. In autumn, the hardwoods and larches provide a spectacular display; colors usually peak during the last week of September.

The lakes and forests of the area provide good habitat for a number of abundant wildlife species, as well as endangered species. Whitetail deer, black bears, and ruffed grouse are commonly hunted on the Chequamegon National Forest. Hunting has long been a popular fall tradition in the area, dating back to the early settlers whose winter survival depended upon the autumn hunt. In the late 1800s and early 1900s, visiting hunters traveled by railroad for days to reach this popular spot. Today the region is hunted lightly compared with other areas of the state, but it is known for producing large-bodied, trophy-racked deer. And every year, northwestern Wisconsin produces more black bears for hunters than any other region of the state. Deer are especially abundant along the roadsides just after the snow melts in spring and again during the breeding season in fall. Drive with extra caution at these times.

Good fishing lakes along the route include Round, Spider, Lost Land, Teal, Ghost, Moose, Day, Upper Clam, and Lower Clam, as well as the Tiger Cat flowage. All have public access with adequate boat-launching facilities. Muskellunge, huge fish that must be at least 32 inches long before they can legally be kept, are commonly found in these lakes. Fine-tasting walleyes inhabit all but Day Lake. Crappies also provide an exceptional fishery.

The mournful cry of the common loon is often heard on the lakes along the Great Divide Highway, and bald eagles and ospreys can be seen soaring overhead. Their appearance can be the perfect cap to a good day of fishing.

Resorts are located on most of the lakes mentioned, but true wilderness fishing can be experienced on Moose and Day lakes. Both are actually flowages that provide a home to a wide variety of creatures, such as great blue herons, muskrats, beavers, and many species of ducks. It is quite common on these lakes to be fishing within only 50 yards of deer that come to the water's edge to feed on aquatic plants. Most of the land around these lakes is national forest retained in a wild state.

At the southern end of Ghost Lake, where Ghost Creek crosses the scenic byway, is a dam left over from the logging era.

You can reach a national forest campground on Moose Lake by driving 7.5 miles south on Forest Road 174, about 10 miles west of Clam Lake. It has 15 sites, a boat launch, and a swimming area.

The last seven miles of the byway heading toward Clam Lake generally follow the West Fork of the Chippewa River.

The Day Lake Campground is located seven-tenths of a mile north of the byway, on Ashland County Road GG. This campground has 66 sites, a boat launch, picnic area, two swimming areas, and barrier-free access. Also on Ashland County Road GG, 3.5 miles north of the byway, is the East Twin Lake Campground, with 12 sites, a picnic area, and a boat launch.

Besides hunting, fishing, camping, swimming, boating, picnicking, and exploring, other recreational activities along this route include snowmobiling, hiking, biking, and cross-country skiing.

Clam Lake, a tiny community in southern Ashland County, once served

A young child examines wildflowers near the beach at Day Lake along the Great Divide Highway. Steven C. Heiting photo.

as a hub for logging and fishing camps in the late 1800s and early 1900s. Wisconsin Route 77 evolved as a winding tote road in the 1890s, on which horse teams pulled large loads of lumbermen's supplies to the lumber camps of the Clam Lake area. Wagon and buggies traversed these tote roads during snow-free periods, while horse-drawn sleds were the only means of transportation in winter.

Glidden writer Joe A. Moran referred to the 18-mile tote road between Glidden and Clam Lake as a "seven-hour ordeal of lurching jolts through quagmire and the devil knows what, over hogbacks for a score of miles." The tote road between Clam Lake and Hayward "wiggled through untouched wilderness, where the hemlock parks were as velvet to one's tread," Moran wrote in the 1800s. Frederick Weyerhaeuser, a famous lumber baron, owned and inspected large tracts of white pine in the Clam Lake area.

A number of logging-camp sites as well as an old fire tower and Civilian Conservation Corps camp are located along this scenic byway. The national forest has pamphlets detailing the exact locations.

Today the exuberance of a child with a first fish, the splash of a swimmer, the huffing and puffing of hikers and bicyclists, the swish of cross-country skiers, and the whine of snowmobile engines have replaced the ring of the logger's axe, but the land remains mostly wild. Scattered old-growth white pines stand as a reminder of the day when lumbering, not vacationing, was king of northern Wisconsin.—*Steven C. Heiting* □

30 WHITEFISH BAY SCENIC BYWAY
Hiawatha National Forest   *Michigan*

General description: A 27-mile road along Lake Superior's Whitefish Bay, past beaches and through northern hardwood forests.

Special attractions: Clean sand beaches, historic lighthouse and museum, campgrounds, boat launches, national fish hatchery.

Location: Eastern Upper Peninsula of Michigan on the Hiawatha National Forest, west of Sault Ste. Marie. The byway travels Curly Lewis Highway (Forest Road 3150) and Forest Road 42 west from Brimley to the junction of 42 and Michigan Route 123.

Byway route numbers: Forest Roads 3150 and 42.

Travel season: Year-round.

Camping: Two national forest campgrounds with fire rings, picnic tables, drinking water, and toilets. Campgrounds open mid-May through mid-October.

Services: Gas, groceries, and restaurant in Bay Mills. All services in nearby Brimley, Sault Ste. Marie, Paradise, and Newberry.

Nearby attractions: Soo Locks, Tahquamenon Falls State Park, Brimley State Park, Great Lakes Shipwreck Museum, North Country hiking trail.

For more information: Hiawatha National Forest, 2727 N. Lincoln Road, Escanaba, MI 49829, (906) 786-4062; District Ranger: Sault Ste. Marie Ranger District, 4000 Interstate 75 Business Spur, Sault Ste. Marie, MI 49783, (906) 635-5311.

Description: Whitefish Bay Scenic Byway travels the shoreline of Whitefish Bay through white birches, pines, and spruce. The two-lane paved highway has frequent scenic turnouts, as well as one-lane dirt side roads that leads through the forest.

Summer temperatures range from the 50s to an idyllic 80 degrees. Although Lake Superior summer temperatures seldom rise above 68 degrees, the shallow bays are swimmable, if invigorating. Winter brings snowfalls averaging 100 inches a year, and temperatures can dip below zero. Cloudiness and precipitation are fairly constant, and heavy fogs reach a peak between August and October.

St. Marys River at Sault Ste. Marie brought early explorers, missionaries, and fur traders through the area, followed by timbermen who felled the virgin white pine forests and opened the area for further development. Except for scattered summer cottages, the area shows little disturbance. Forests are second-growth, and the lakes are unspoiled by development. Tourism and small industry form the basis of the area's economy, with Lake Superior the main attraction. Superior can be temperamental; its glassy surface can suddenly be rent by crashing waves brought in by gale-force winds.

Driving west from Sault Ste. Marie and Brimley, the scenic byway begins at the national forest boundary in a hardwood forest with scattered white pines and jackpines. The predominant hardwood species are birch, maple, and oak, which blaze red, orange, and gold during late September and early October.

Monocle Lake is near the byway's eastern entrance. There is serenity and silence in this forest campground, interrupted only by the sound of birds. Take the short drive to the Mission Hill Overlook for a panoramic view of the area, and enjoy the swimming beach. The campground has 39 sites.

A few miles west on the byway is the Point Iroquois Light Station. The light was activated in 1858, and the existing two-story brick keeper's residence and the light tower were built in 1870. The light was replaced by an automated beacon in 1962. The lighthouse museum and gift shop are open daily from May 15 through October 15 from 9 a.m. to 5 p.m. The tower is open until sunset. A footpath leads down the low bluff to the Lake Superior shoreline.

Across the wide expanse of water is the Canadian shore. Nineteen miles of accessible sand beach on the gently curving bay follow a shoreline of ancient sand dunes and glacial moraines. The bay is located on the north rim of the Michigan Basin, which was covered by glacial outwash. Scattered outcroppings of limestone and sandstone protrude from the surface, and past levels of the Great Lakes during the latest period of glaciation left generous lake-basin sand deposits.

The byway runs primarily within a quarter-mile of the shoreline and is never more than a few miles away. Whitefish Bay itself holds a double legacy: It was memorialized in Henry Wadsworth Longfellow's "Song of Hiawatha," and it is the historical site of many shipwrecks between the mid-1800s and the early 1900s. The Edmund Fitzgerald met her fate off Whitefish Point 20 miles to the north, an event that was the subject of a ballad by Canadian singer Gordon Lightfoot.

Forest and wildflowers line the byway, and colors change with the seasons. White trilliums introduce spring, a wild profusion of colors announces

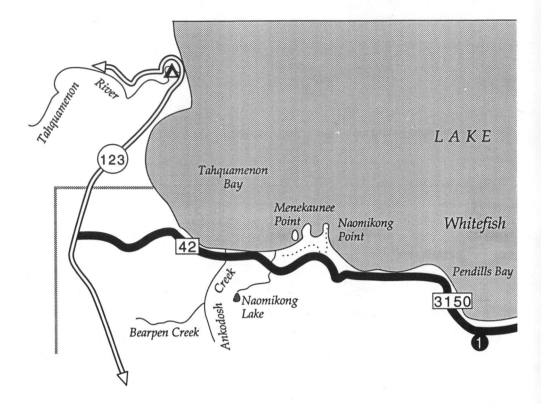

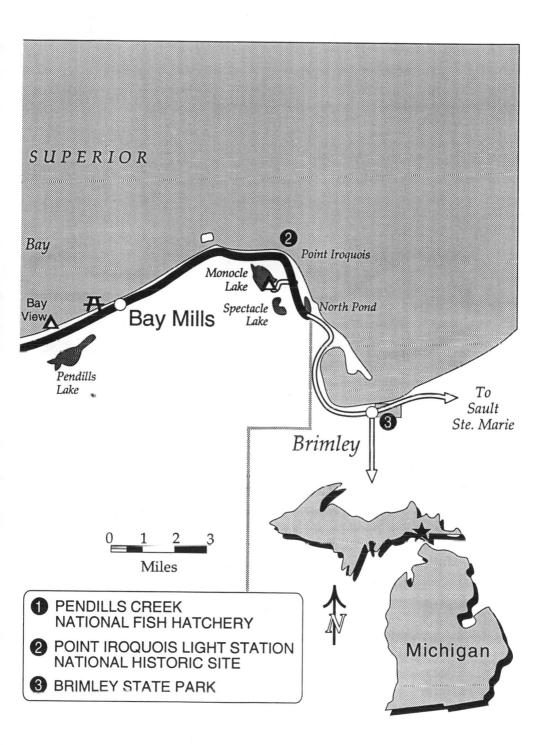

SUPERIOR

Bay

Bay View

Bay Mills

Monocle Lake

Spectacle Lake

Point Iroquois

North Pond

Pendills Lake

Brimley

To Sault Ste. Marie

0 1 2 3
Miles

N

Michigan

① PENDILLS CREEK
NATIONAL FISH HATCHERY

② POINT IROQUOIS LIGHT STATION
NATIONAL HISTORIC SITE

③ BRIMLEY STATE PARK

Families enjoy the wide beaches and vast views of Lake Superior along Whitefish Bay. Dixie Franklin photo.

summer, and deep blue asters and chickories rival the autumn leaves. In winter, the deep-green conifers stand out against the white snow.

At Bay Mills, a small general store has groceries, ice, and gasoline.

Big Pine Picnic Area stands in a red pine forest with scatterings of birches and maples. Bay View Campground is a mile farther west. The campground has 24 sites, and the long sand beach is lovely. Even if the lake is too cold for swimming, the shallows stretch some distance from shore and are good for wading.

Pendill's National Fish Hatchery is an interesting stop, and tours of lake-trout hatching ponds are available. There is good trout fishing in Pendill's Creek.

The trees are taller as you head west from Pendill's, and they stand farther back from the roadway. Wildflowers line the route. Scenic turnouts provide views of the bay, which stretches out wide and blue on a clear day. The byway climbs up and away from the lake and then returns to the shore and its open vistas.

The North Country National Scenic Trail intersects the byway about one mile east of Naomikong Creek and parallels the shore through old-growth hardwoods for about four miles. Several turnoffs and parking areas provide access to the trail along Tahquamenon Bay.

Scenic turnouts and beachside parking areas are at the end of the byway near Michigan Route 123, giving you plenty of opportunities to enjoy the blue waters, wide skies, and sand beaches.—*Dixie Franklin* □

General description: A 22-mile road alongside the scenic Au Sable River.
Special attractions: Lumberman's Monument, Iargo Springs Interpretive Site, paddle-wheel riverboat rides, historic and scenic sites, canoeing, trout and salmon fishing, colorful autumn foliage, beaches, camping.
Location: Northeast Michigan on the Huron National Forest, south of Alpena. The byway begins at the national forest boundary just west of Oscoda, travels the River Road west to its junction with Michigan Route 65, and continues west on Route 65 to the national forest boundary near Rollway Road.
Byway route numbers: River Road and Michigan Route 65.
Travel season: Year-round.
Camping: Two national forest campgrounds with picnic tables, fire grates, drinking water, and toilets. Campgrounds open from May 25 to October 15. One county campground with 500 sites, drinking water, and showers. Two hundred sites have hookups. Open April 1 to December 1.
Services: All services in Oscoda and in nearby Hale.
Nearby attractions: Michigan Shore-to-Shore Hiking and Riding Trail; Huron Snowmobile and ATV Trail; Eagle Run, Highbanks, and Corsair cross-country ski and hiking trails; Kiwanis Monument.
For more information: Huron-Manistee National Forests, 421 S. Mitchell St., Cadillac, MI 49601, (616) 775-2421; District Ranger: Tawas Ranger District, 326 Newman St., Federal Building, East Tawas, MI 48730, (517) 362-4477.

Description: River Road follows the south bank of the Au Sable River near Lake Huron. The scenic byway begins a short distance from the river's mouth at Oscoda and follows the river across low, sandy plains. The two lane paved highway has frequent turnouts for scenic and recreational access.

Summer visitors enjoy contrasts in weather, varying from early spring and late autumn temperatures in the 50s to occasional sultry summer days of 90 degrees. Winters normally average around the 20s, with a few days below zero.

River Road follows the old Saginaw to Mackinaw Indian Trail of the Chippewas and other Michigan tribes that inhabited the area. The byway travels through a serene landscape along the lazy river, which snakes between white sandy bluffs and long corridors of green forest spires. This is a glaciated landscape of the Michigan sedimentary basin. Outwash and deltas were carved by the latest ice age.

Oscoda, on the Lake Huron shoreline, is a former lumber-mill town that now depends largely upon tourism for its livelihood. Evidence of the old logging days is visible at the concrete Au Sable bridge, where decaying piers and log-boom sorting ponds are still visible.

Oscoda was leveled by fire in 1911, and scars of more recent blazes can be seen along River Road. Green sprouts of new vegetation in the burned areas are the result of work done by nature and the Forest Service.

West on the byway, the burned area gives way to lowland timber such

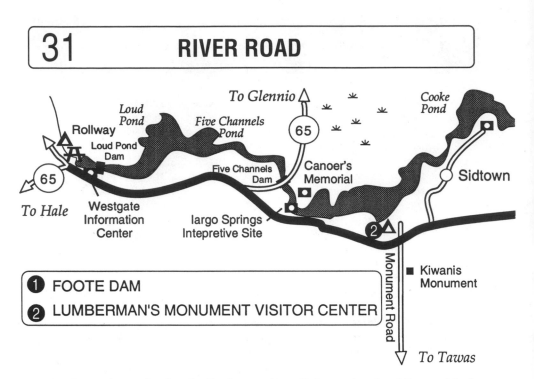

To Glennio

Loud Pond

Rollway

Loud Pond Dam

Five Channels Pond

65

Cooke Pond

Five Channels Dam

Canoer's Memorial

Sidtown

65

To Hale

Westgate Information Center

Iargo Springs Intepretive Site

Monument Road

Kiwanis Monument

❶ FOOTE DAM

❷ LUMBERMAN'S MONUMENT VISITOR CENTER

To Tawas

as maples, oaks, and ashes in the lower sites. Oaks, and red, white, and jack pines are the primary species on the upper sandy plains. The burned area, about 2,500 acres adjacent to the byway, is classified as essential habitat for the Kirtland's warbler. It will be ready for occupancy by the warbler in the late 1990s.

A short distance west of the national forest boundary, Eastgate Information Center provides easy access to the Eagle Run cross-country ski and nature trails. Trails lead through the forest to the scenic Whirlpool canoe and boat launch. The popular Whirlpool launch is also accessible by a half-mile unpaved road. This section of stream is fed by the spill from Foote Dam hydroelectric site upstream, and the water is very cold.

You can fish Whirlpool from its sandy banks or from its accessible fishing pier. The Au Sable River offers anglers the chance to catch trophy-size steelhead, in addition to coho, chinook, and Atlantic salmon. Other wildlife along the byway includes whitetail deer, wild turkeys, foxes, coyotes, and small mammals such as squirrels.

The Au Sable is slowed by a number of hydroelectric dams, forming wide, blue pools that are known for producing walleyes, muskellunge, bass, northern pikes, bluegills, and sunfish. The waterway is used by anglers, canoeists, two river paddle wheelers, and careful boaters conscious of deadheads (jammed logs) left over from logging days.

Groceries and supplies are available at Foote Site Village, at the intersection of the byway and Rea Road. A short side trip on Rea Road leads to Foote Dam powersite, where there are public launch ramps and a 500-foot fishing pier.

About eight miles farther west on the byway, you can see a wide stretch of beach along Foote Pond. The colorful red, white, and blue Au Sable River

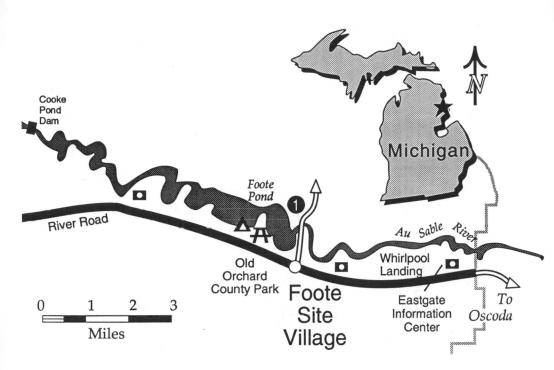

Queen paddle wheeler takes passengers for cruises up and down the 1,800-acre pond, among the scattered islands and around the forested shoreline.

Nearby, Old Orchard County Park offers a campground, picnic area, playground equipment, toilets, a boat-launch area, and swimming beaches. Paved roads wind through the forested park along the banks of Foote Pond.

The next few miles of scenic byway cut through 50- to 60-year-old mixed red pine and jackpine forest. A short side trip on Cooke Dam Road drops down to the river through Sidtown, a small village and country store with camping and vacation supplies. The road passes beneath trees that turn spectacular colors in autumn. Several scenic turnouts provide views of Cooke Pond, and fishing is good. There are boat launches above and below the dam.

A main attraction on the byway is Lumberman's Monument. The statue portrays three loggers standing over a fallen log; one has a cross-cut saw balanced over his shoulder, another wields a peavey, and the third contemplates his compass. The rustic visitors center has barrier-free access to outdoor exhibits and a 263-step wooden stairway down to Cooke Pond. Across the road, Kiwanis Monument is another historic site.

River Road continues through red and Norway pines to the Canoer's Memorial. Canoer's Memorial, erected in the early 1950s, pays tribute to the many thousands of marathon canoeists who have participated annually in a grueling 240-mile race down the Au Sable, from its headwaters near Grayling to Oscoda.

Eye-catching wildflowers along the byway include smooth asters, goldenrod, bracken ferns, blazing stars, fireweeds, and blue vervains.

Iargo Springs is farther west. According to legend, early Indians used the

The scenic Au Sable River, which runs alongside River Road, provides opportunities for canoeing, riding paddle wheelers, fishing, swimming, camping, and hiking. Dixie Franklin photo.

springs as a gathering place and partook of its "mystical" waters. In the 1930s, the site was developed as a scenic area with a low waterfall. Iargo Springs also serves as the trailhead for the popular Highbanks Trail, which winds along the high bluffs of Cooke Pond and offers many panoramic views.

River Road intersects Michigan Route 65, and the scenic byway continues west (left). A short side trip north on 65 takes you across the iron Five Channel Bridge.

Rollway Resort and Campground mark the western end of the scenic byway, and provide access to Loud Pond. A country store has basic vacation supplies, gasoline, and canoe rental. A national forest and campground located nearby provide scenic views of majestic white pines rising above the mixed hardwood forest.—*Dixie Franklin* □

---

32 KANCAMAGUS HIGHWAY
White Mountain National Forest   New Hampshire

General description: A 28-mile paved road through the heart of the White Mountains.

Special attractions: Brilliant autumn foliage, trout fishing, swimming, skiing.

Location: Central New Hampshire on the White Mountain National Forest, north of Laconia. The byway travels New Hampshire Route 112 between Lincoln and the junction of 112 and New Hampshire Route 16.

Byway route number: New Hampshire Route 112.

Travel season: Year-round. Expect winter driving conditions from November through May

Camping: Six national forest campgrounds with drinking water, picnic tables, fireplaces, and toilets. No hookups. Campgrounds open late April through early to mid-October. There are numerous additional national forest campgrounds within a short drive of the byway.

Services: All services in Lincoln, Conway, and North Conway.

Nearby attractions: Old Man of the Mountain; Clark's Trading Post; Mount Washington; Fantasy Farm; ski areas; Conway Scenic Railroad steam-train ride; and Presidential Range-Dry River, Sandwich Range and Pemigewasset wilderness areas.

For more information: White Mountain National Forest, P.O. Box 638, 719 Main St., Laconia, NH 03247, (603) 528-8721. District Rangers: Pemigawasset Ranger District, RFD 3 Box 15, Plymouth, NH 03264, (603) 536-1310; Saco Ranger District, RFD 1 Box 94, Kancamagus Highway, Conway, NH 03818, (603) 447-5448.

Description: The Kancamagus Highway climbs from Lincoln, elevation 811 feet, to an altitude of 2,855 feet in its first 10 miles. Then it slowly descends the remaining 18 miles through a variety of outstanding scenery. The two-lane highway is paved and has numerous turnouts, and traffic can be heavy

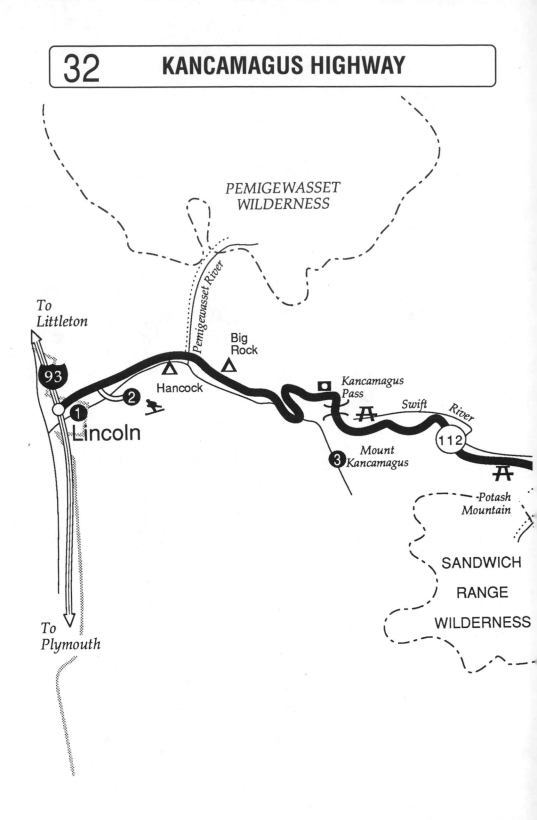

32 **KANCAMAGUS HIGHWAY**

PEMIGEWASSET
WILDERNESS

Pemigewasset River

To
Littleton

93

Big
Rock

Hancock

2

1

Lincoln

Kancamagus
Pass

Swift River

112

3 Mount
Kancamagus

-Potash
Mountain

SANDWICH

RANGE

WILDERNESS

To
Plymouth

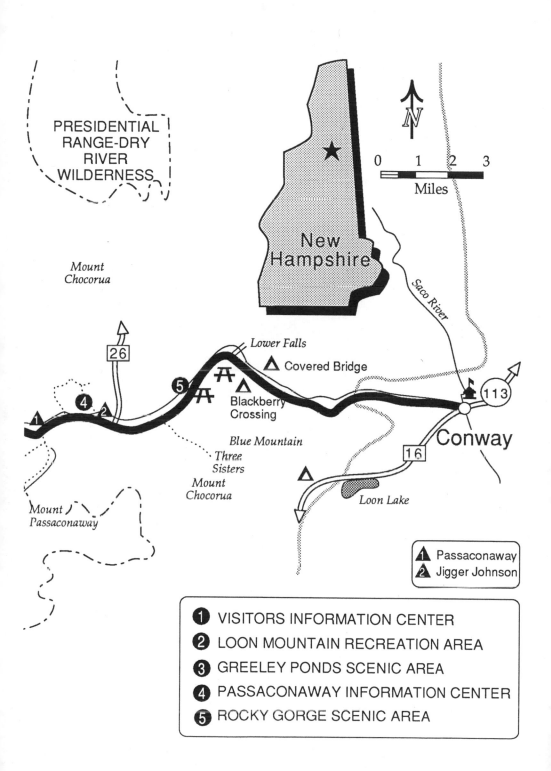

PRESIDENTIAL RANGE-DRY RIVER WILDERNESS

N

0   1   2   3
Miles

New Hampshire

Saco River

Mount Chocorua

Lower Falls

△ Covered Bridge

⑤

Blackberry Crossing

④ ▲ ②

① ▲

Blue Mountain

Three Sisters

Mount Chocorua

Mount Passaconaway

Loon Lake

Conway

113

16

🅰 Passaconaway
🅱 Jigger Johnson

❶ VISITORS INFORMATION CENTER
❷ LOON MOUNTAIN RECREATION AREA
❸ GREELEY PONDS SCENIC AREA
❹ PASSACONAWAY INFORMATION CENTER
❺ ROCKY GORGE SCENIC AREA

depending upon the season. Kancamagus Highway is considered one of the best highways in the United States from which to view fall foliage.

The weather here is extremely variable, which is typical for New England. Spring can be rainy, or the byway may still be wrapped in snow and cold into June. Generally, summer visitors will experience temperatures as high as the low 90s, but plenty of shaded areas and cool mountain breezes keep the drive comfortable.

The town of Lincoln, at the western end of the byway, caters to the traveler. Loon Mountain and Cannon Mountain ski areas have attracted many top-quality gift shops that are open year-round.

The byway follows the Swift River and the East and Hancock branches of the Pemigawasset River. The Swift River is stocked with brook and rainbow trout, and fishing is both popular and rewarding. Most stretches can be fished without waders either by moving from rock to rock or by taking advantage of the river's delightful summer temperatures and simply wading in shorts.

The name "Kancamagus" comes from a famous New Hampshire Indian who began his rule as chief of the Penacook Confederacy in 1684. History relates that Kancamagus tried to encourage peace between the Indians and the whites until harassment from the English aggravated him too much and he retaliated. When in 1691 the confederate tribes scattered, Kancamagus and his followers moved either to northern New Hampshire or into Canada.

East of Lincoln, Loon Mountain Recreation Area offers skiing and a year-round gondola ride. There is a nature trail at the top of the mountain, and the view is excellent.

Hancock Campground, situated in a beautiful birch stand, has 56 sites, fishing, and hiking.

Almost five miles east of Lincoln on the byway is the popular Lincoln Woods Trail, which leads into the Pemigewasset Wilderness. The trail parallels the East Branch of the Pemigewasset River. It is a very popular and easy hike which follows an old logging railroad bed. Hikers are offered views of the river and will see old logging ties.

The byway travels alongside the Hancock Branch of the Pemigawasset River and climbs to Big Rock Campground, which has 28 sites adjacent to the river. The campground was named for the large rock just inside its entrance. Swimmers enjoy dipping in Upper Lady's Bath, a five-minute walk from the campground.

Scenic overlooks permit frequent stops to admire the scenery. The area is ablaze with bright foliage in autumn. Each bend in the road reveals a new montage of yellows, reds, and oranges vividly splashed against the ever-constant green of stately spruces and hemlocks. To the north are the Pemigawasset and the Presidential Range-Dry River wilderness areas. The Presidential Range-Dry River Wilderness features distinctive geologic formations and mountain peaks varying in elevation from 3,000 to 4,000 feet. The Appalachian Trail, a National Scenic Trail, runs along the northern and western boundaries. Hardwoods occupy the lower slopes; mixed birches, maples, spruces, and firs the middle slopes; and spruces and firs the upper slopes. A portion of the major ridges are above timberline and are dotted with typical "krummholtz" vegetation. Wildlife is not a prominent feature of the wilderness, although deer, black bears, grouse, hares, and a variety of birds associated with high mountain slopes are found here.

The Kancamagus Highway winds 28 miles through the heart of the White Mountains.
Warren B. McGranahan photo.

There are three mountains over 4,000 feet within or on the edge of the Pemigewasset Wilderness: Mount Hancock, Mount Bond, and Owl's Head. Major attractions of the area are trails along the long, gentle valley bottoms, constant views of adjacent streams, and isolation. The view from Bond Cliff is unsurpassed in the White Mountains.

Most exposed mountains are granitic, based on Paleozoic Plutonic bedrock formations. The Passaconaway Gravel Pits hold smoky quartz crystals, and other area mountains yield magnetite, tin, and adularia feldspar.

Greeley Ponds Scenic Area can be reached via a 1.5-mile hike over forest trails.

C.L. Graham Wangan Ground has picnicking and a nice view. The headwaters of the Swift River emerge from Lily Pond, and the byway follows the deep cleft the river has carved into the rock over the years. Wangan ground is an Indian term for meeting place.

Whitetail deer, moose, black bears, grouse, and a variety of songbirds inhabit the byway region.

Passaconaway Campground has 33 sites, fishing, and hiking. The UNH Trail is a moderately strenuous four-mile hike that leads to the open ledges on the summit of Hedgehog Mountain for views of the Sandwich Range.

A short distance farther along the byway is the Passaconaway or Albany Intervale, a parcel of rich, flat land first settled about 1790. The Russell-Colbath House, listed in the National Register of Historic Places, is located here, and interesting tours are available in the summer months.

The Rail 'n' River Hike follows an easy half-mile trail that begins at the Passaconaway Information Center. Self-guiding interpretive points along the trail are being developed.

161

Jigger Johnson Campground has 75 sites located on the intervale. A side trip on Bear Notch Road allows you to explore the surrounding area.

Champney Falls Trail wends an easy 1.5 miles to the falls, which are spectacular in the spring and after heavy rains but somewhat meager in dry seasons. Champney was a pioneer White Mountain artist. Another path goes about 200 yards beyond Champney Falls to the base of Pitcher Falls, which usually have plenty of water.

Farther east along the byway, the Swift River has worn a cleft in the rock. The area is now known as Rocky Gorge Scenic Area. Within this area is Falls Pond, a five-minute walk on a graded path that crosses the gorge via a rustic footbridge. A trail circles the pond. Lower Falls, a short distance below Rocky Gorge, is a popular swimming area.

Covered Bridge Campground has 49 sites along the river. A three-mile interpretive trail tells the story of the formation of soils in the area and the origin and growth of the forest. There are several good views of Mount Chocorua and the Swift River from the ledges along the trail. The Boulder Loop Trail is also located near the campground. It is just under three miles long, and its gradual climb is interrupted occasionally by steep pitches. The view of Mount Chocorua and the Swift River is lovely.

Across from Covered Bridge, Blackberry Crossing Campground has 20 sites. Remains of an old Civilian Conservation Corps camp are still visible.

The byway continues east along the Swift River and ends near Conway, at the junction of New Hampshire Routes 112 and 16. A side trip on Forest Road 16 leads to Loon Lake, another campground, and hiking trails. You will be able to see Mount Chocorua, named after a brave Indian thought to be a chief of the Ossipee tribe.—*Warren B. McGranahan* □

33 GLADE TOP TRAIL
Mark Twain National Forest   *Missouri*

General description: A 23-mile, well-maintained gravel road through the glades and forests of the Ozark Plateau.

Special attractions: Wildlife, birdwatching, hunting, hiking, spring blossoms, colorful autumn foliage, horseback riding.

Location: Southwest Missouri on the Mark Twain National Forest, southeast of Springfield. The byway is shaped like an upside-down Y. It begins at the national forest boundary on Forest Road 147 and travels south to Longrun, and it also travels on Forest Road 149 from the junction of 149 and 147 to the junction with Missouri Route 125.

Byway route numbers: Forest Roads 147 and 149.

Travel season: Year-round. Winter driving conditions may be hazardous.

Camping: No national forest campgrounds on the byway. Primitive camping permitted along the byway, except at picnic areas. Other public campgrounds are located nearby.

Services: All services in Ava. Gas and store in Thornfield. Store, phone, and gas in Bradleyville.

Nearby attractions: Hercules Glade Wilderness, Laura Ingalls Wilder home in Mansfield, old grist mills, fox-trotting horse shows in Ava, Our Lady of Assumption Abbey.

For more information: Mark Twain National Forest, 401 Fairgrounds Road, Rolla, MO 65401, (314) 364-4621. District Ranger: Ava Ranger District, 1103 S. Jefferson, Ava, MO 65608, (417) 683-4428.

Description: Situated in the rolling hills of the Ozark Plateau, Glade Top Trail has changed very little since the Civilian Conservation Corps built the two-lane gravel road in the late 1930s. The entire road is well-marked and has frequent pullouts.

Summer visitors can expect very humid weather and an average temperature of 89 degrees. Fall and spring are more moderate, and average temperatures are in the 40s through 60s. Winter ranges from 10 to 50 degrees, with precipitation falling in the form of snow or sleet. Roads may be icy in the winter.

The glades are home to numerous species of wildflowers, such as purple coneflowers, columbines, Indian paintbrushes, chickories, jonquils, and daffodils. Dogwoods, redbuds, and serviceberries add to the profusion of spring color, and local communities celebrate the season with festivals and tours.

Driving the byway from north to south, the first point of interest about a mile from the beginning of the byway is Haden Bald, across from Smoke Tree Scene. This area is called "bald" because of the extensive, open limestone glades. Haden Bald is a State Natural Area of 40 acres. Management includes a controlled burn every four to six years, and no grazing. Other areas of the national forest permit open grazing, so watch for cattle along the road.

Bare knobs such as this were common meeting places for the Baldknobbers, bands of vigilantes who emerged primarily in Taney, Christian, and Douglas counties during a period of relative lawlessness following the Civil War. The men eventually ran amok, donning horned, white masks and conducting raids on townsfolk for several decades following the war.

Smoke Tree Scene is an interpretive site. Smoke Trees are known locally as yellowwood because of the tree's color when the bark is removed. The trees dot the entire hollow and turn magnificent deep hues of red and orange in autumn.

The flora and fauna along this trail truly accentuate the beauty of the Ozark Plateau. Limestone glades and gentle rolling hills are home to central hardwood forests of oaks, hickories, walnuts, and ashes. Redcedars, smoke trees, rare ashe junipers, and flowering trees provide more variety. Native prairie grasses line the roadway and dot the open hillsides; these grasses include big and little bluestems, and Indian grasses. Wildlife such as whitetail deer, wild turkeys, bobwhites, squirrels, cottontail rabbits, and chipmunks inhabit the area, as do the less common roadrunners, collared lizards, pygmy rattlesnakes, scorpions, and endangered Bachman sparrows.

Arkansas View, a mile and a half past Smoke Tree Scene, overlooks a panorama that includes the Boston Mountains, about 40 miles south. There is a picnic table and plenty of shade for an enjoyable family outing.

A mile south, Watershed Divide separates the Beaver Creek watershed to the west and the Little North Fork White River watershed to the east. This is a good place to see native hardwoods such as oaks—black, white, post, chinquapin, and northern red. Winged elm trees are also fairly common. From

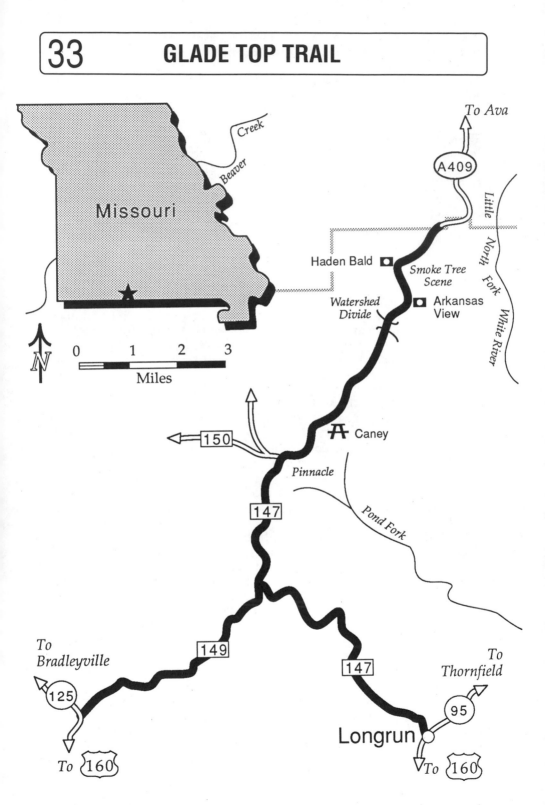

Missouri

Creek

Beaver

To Ava

A409

Little

North

Fork

White River

Haden Bald

Smoke Tree
Scene

Watershed
Divide

Arkansas
View

0   1   2   3

N

Miles

150

Caney

Pinnacle

147

Pond Fork

To
Bradleyville

149

147

To
Thornfield

125

95

Longrun

To 160

To 160

The Glade Top Trail offers pretty views over the rolling Ozark Plateau, which is especially colorful in autumn. John Lowell Lumb photo.

the divide, you can see Caney Lookout Tower to the south. This historic tower was built by the Civilian Conservation Corps in 1937.

Caney Picnic Area is a very popular spot. There are picnic tables, a stationary grill, an open-air stage, restrooms, and split-rail benches. The annual Glade Top Trail Festival (or Flaming Fall Revue) is held here in mid-October. This three-day event celebrates the brilliant red and orange foliage of the smoke trees and the overall beauty of the Ozarks. There are activities in Ava, such as arts and crafts shows, and a Sunday afternoon barbeque and music festival at the Caney Picnic Area.

North of the Caney parking lot, a vague trail wanders off to an interesting cave. A mile south of the picnic area is the Pinnacle, and on top of the Pinnacle is Mrs. Murray's Gold Mine. According to legend, Mrs. Murray had a vision in which she was instructed to dig on the Pinnacle to find gold. Although she never found it, evidence of her digging remains.

Local hillfolk used to gather on the Pinnacle for church services the first Sunday in May. It was not uncommon for a crowd of 500 to be present for the all-day event.

The first whites in this area were hunters, trappers, and farmers. During the Depression years, settlers came from all areas, lured by the cheap land. The Ozarks became a melting pot for immigrants. The Lee Houseplace was a schoolhouse attended by about 40 children in the 1930s.

Eastern redcedar trees, actually members of the juniper family, are able to grow in the shallow soils atop the limestone ridges. Their distinctive, twisted shapes are easily recognized. The waxy blue berries on the female tree are a favorite food of birds in the area, and they are also used in distilling gin.

The byway forks a few miles south of the Pinnacle. You may follow either Forest Road 147 or 149. Route 147 goes southeast and ends at Longrun, while

Route 149 goes southwest and ends at the junction of 149 and Missouri Route 125. From both, you will have lovely panoramic views of farms, hills, and forest.—*John Lowell Lumb* □

34 HIGHLAND SCENIC BYWAY
Monongahela National Forest   *West Virginia*

General description: A 44-mile route through the green, rolling Allegheny Mountains, past flowing rivers.

Special attractions: Fishing, hiking, Cranberry Mountain Visitor Center, camping, colorful autumn foliage, Cranberry Glades Botanical Area.

Location: Southeast West Virginia on the Monongahela National Forest. The byway begins east of Richwood and follows West Virginia Route 39/55 to the Cranberry Mountain Visitor Center. From there it follows West Virginia Route 150 northeast to U.S. Highway 219.

Byway route numbers: West Virginia Routes 39/55 and 150.

Travel season: West Virginia Route 39/55 is open year-round. West Virginia Route 150 is open from about mid-March through mid-December and then closed by winter snows.

Camping: Three national forest campgrounds within five miles of the byway, with drinking water, toilets, picnic tables, fire grates, and fishing available. Numerous additional national forest campgrounds in the area.

Services: All services in Richwood and in nearby Marlinton.

Nearby attractions: Cass Scenic Railroad and historic lumber town, Pearl S. Buck Birthplace, Green Bank National Radio Astronomy Observatory, Civil War battlefields, rafting, cross-country and alpine skiing, spelunking, music and crafts festivals, Droop Mountain Battlefield, Watoga and Beartoown state parks.

For more information: Monongahela National Forest, 200 Sycamore St., Elkins, WV 26241, (304) 636-1800. District Rangers: Gauley Ranger District, P.O. Box 110, Richwood, WV 26261, (304) 846-2695; Marlinton Ranger District, P.O. Box 210, Marlinton, WV 24954, (304) 799-4334.

Description: The Highland Scenic Highway travels from Richwood east through wildflowers and forests and then turns north and parallels the Cranberry Wilderness border. The two-lane road is paved. Traffic on the byway is generally light, and the route has frequent viewpoints and recreational opportunities.

Summertime high temperatures average 65 to 75 degrees. Winter temperatures may drop below zero, but daytime temperatures are generally between 10 and 25 degrees. The average annual precipitation of 50 to 65 inches is relatively evenly distributed throughout the year, with snowfall averaging 120 to 140 inches a year.

Beginning at Richwood, drive east on West Virginia Route 39/55. A side road just outside of town, West Virginia and Forest Road 76, leads five miles to Woodbine Picnic Area. Nearby, Big Rock Campground has five sites. Another six miles on Forest Road 76 brings you to Cranberry Campground,

Big Spruce Viewpoint overlooks lush wildflowers and extensive forest along the Highland Scenic Highway. Ken Haltenhoff photo.

with 30 sites. These three recreation areas are located along the Cranberry River, one of West Virginia's best trout streams.

Trout fishing along the scenic byway is some of the best in the state. Awaiting your line are brook, brown, rainbow, and golden trout. Summit Lake, the North Fork Cherry River, Williams River, and nearby Cranberry River are stocked with trout, while several smaller streams support native brook trout populations.

Throughout its length, the byway passes through predominantly hardwood forests consisting of yellow poplars, red and white oaks, sugar and red maples, beeches, yellow and black birches, black cherries, white ashes, basswoods, and others. Eastern hemlock is a common conifer, and red spruce occurs at higher elevations, sometimes in pure stands. Wildlife in the area includes black bears, bobcats, whitetail deer, raccoons, opposums, showshoe hares, red and gray foxes, squirrels, wild turkeys, ruffed grouse, and several species of hawks and owls as well as many songbirds.

The byway begins at the national forest boundary near the Gauley Ranger Station, which has visitor information available. North Bend Picnic Area is a pleasant stop. Just beyond it, a side trip on West Virginia 39/5 leads north two miles to Summit Lake Campground, which has 33 sites. The 42-acre lake provides opportunities for boating and fishing, including a barrier-free fishing pier and a boat ramp. An easy 1.5-mile footpath offers attractive views of the lake, and numerous other trails are nearby for more strenuous hiking through the national forest.

Back on the byway, Falls of Hills Creek Scenic Area is 16 miles east of Richwood. It features three waterfalls—25-, 45-, and 63-feet high—in the midst of rich northern hardwood forests. Footpaths and stairways lead to observation points for each of the falls.

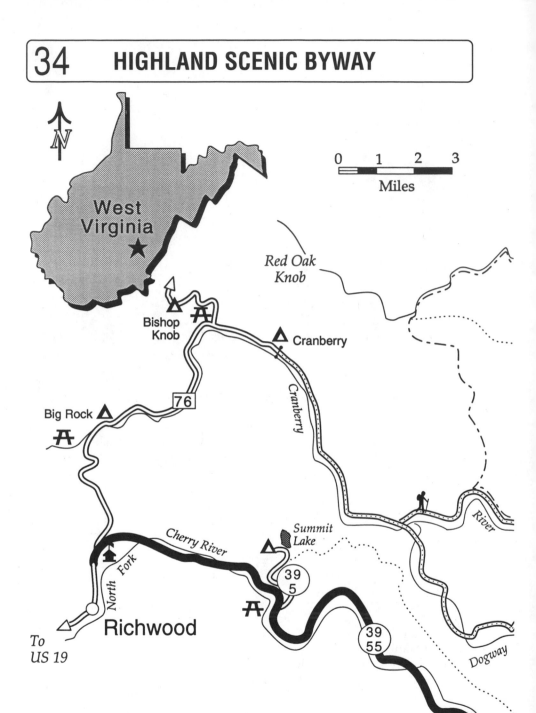

West Virginia

Red Oak Knob

Bishop Knob

Cranberry

Cranberry

76

Big Rock

Summit Lake

Cherry River

North Fork

Richwood

39 5

39 55

Dogway

River

To US 19

0   1   2   3
Miles

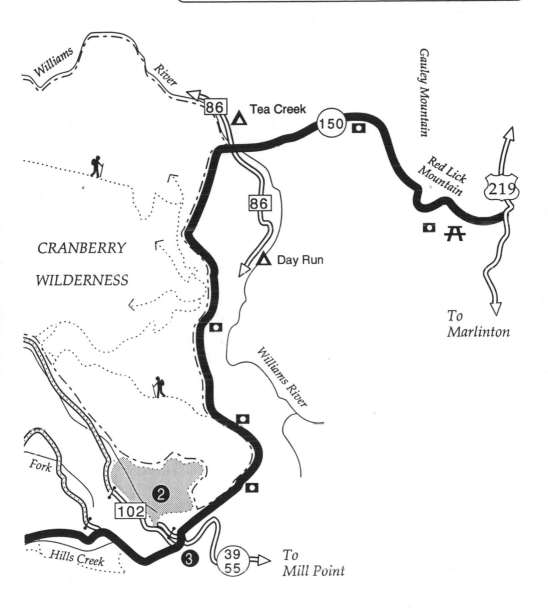

1 FALLS OF HILLS CREEK SCENIC AREA
2 CRANBERRY GLADES BOTANICAL AREA
3 CRANBERRY MOUNTAIN VISITORS CENTER

Williams River

86

Tea Creek

150

Gauley Mountain

Red Lick Mountain

219

86

Day Run

CRANBERRY

WILDERNESS

Williams River

To
Marlinton

Fork

102

2

3

39
55

To
Mill Point

Hills Creek

A wide variety of wildlife calls the Monongahela National Forest home, including the black bear. Christopher Cauble photo.

Three miles east of the Falls of Hills Creek, the byway crosses Kennison Mountain at an elevation of 3,964 feet. Then it descends into the headwaters drainage of the Cranberry River. Forest Road 102 is a side trip leading 1.5 miles north to the unique 750-acre Cranberry Glades Botanical Area. A half-mile boardwalk with interpretive signs provides safe access to one of five open bogs and their associated shrub/forest communities. Numerous plants and animals that normally live far to the north can be found here.

You can drive Forest Road 102 another mile north to the gate at the boundary of the Cranberry Backcountry. Beyond the gate, the road provides nonmotorized access to the 26,000-acre area. Fishing is excellent in the Cranberry River. Road 102 also provides access to the Cranberry Wilderness and its extensive system of hiking trails, and to the seven-mile Cowpasture Trail, which circles the botanical area.

The scenic byway continues east from Road 102 to Cranberry Mountain Visitor Center, located at the junction of Routes 39/55 and 150. The center offers traveler information, has exhibits, interpretive programs about local ecology and history, and naturalist-led tours of the Cranberry Glades. The visitor center is open daily throughout the summer and on weekends in May and early October.

The byway turns north at the visitor center and travels West Virginia Route 150. This section of the byway is managed primarily for scenic and recreational use. Roadside camping is prohibited, and a 45-mile-an-hour speed limit encourages leisurely recreational travel.

This portion of the Highland Scenic Highway is the highest major road in West Virginia. Sixty percent of the parkway is above 4,000 feet, and more than 88 percent is above 3,500 feet. The highway forms the eastern boundary of the 35,864-acre Cranberry Wilderness. More than 70 miles of hiking trails provide access for hiking and backcountry camping within and near the wilderness area. Several trailheads are signed along the parkway.

In this area, the byway passes through red spruce, hardwood, and shrub forests along the crest of Black Mountain, reaching a maximum elevation of 3,544 feet before descending to cross the Williams River at 3,038 feet. Three developed overlooks provide views of Cranberry Glades and the Williams River Valley. Another overlook, accessible by the mile-long High Rocks Trail, affords a spectacular view across the Greenbrier River Valley to the southeast.

Forest Road 86, a side road on the Williams River 13.5 miles north of the visitor center, leads one mile north to Tea Creek Campground, with 29 sites. Day Run Campground, with 14 sites, is four miles south on Forest Road 86. The Williams River is a popular fishing stream for stocked rainbow, brook, and brown trout.

The byway turns east and climbs Tea Creek Mountain and then crosses Gauley Mountain, where a trailhead provides access to more than 20 miles of hiking trails. The nearby Little Laurel Overlook provides a panoramic view of Black Mountain, Spruce Mountain, and the Williams River Valley.

On the east side of Gauley Mountain, the highway overlooks the upper Elk River drainage, with Cheat Mountain, Buzzard Ridge, and Cloverlick Mountain in the background. The parkway passes east of Red Spruce Knob and then south of Red Lick Mountain to Red Lick Overlook and Picnic Area, from which you can get expansive views of the Greenbrier River Valley. The route descends gradually to U.S. Highway 219 at an elevation of 3,525 feet on Elk Mountain, seven miles north of Marlinton.—*Ken Haltenhoff* □

35 PIG TRAIL SCENIC BYWAY
Ozark National Forest   Arkansas

General description: A 19-mile route that meanders through the scenic Boston Mountains.

Special attractions: Colorful autumn foliage, canoeing, fishing, hunting, Ozark Highlands Trail, camping, spring wildflowers, spectacular panoramic views.

Location: Western Arkansas on the Ozark National Forest, northeast of Fort Smith. The byway follows Arkansas Route 23 on national forest land between Brashears and Ozark.

Byway route number: Arkansas Route 23.

Travel season: Year-round.

Camping: One national forest campground near the byway, with picnic tables, toilets, fire grates, and drinking water. No hookups.

Services: Small store, gas, and canoe rental at Turners Bend. All services in nearby Ozark and Fayetteville.

Nearby attractions: Fort Smith Historical Site; White Rock Mountain Recreation Area; Arkansas River and Ozark Lake; War Eagle Craft Fair; Shores Lake; and Ozark Highlands, Arkansas Highway 7, and Mount Magazine national forest scenic byways.

For more information: Ozark-St. Francis National Forests, P.O. Box 1008,

605 W. Main, Russellville, AR 72801, (501) 968-2354. District Ranger: Boston Mountain Ranger District, Highway 23 N., P.O. Box 76, Ozark, AR 72949, (501) 667-2191.

Description: The Pig Trail Scenic Byway crosses the Boston Mountains in the Ozark Highlands, offering far-ranging views of the heavily forested, rolling landscape. The two-lane road is paved and has turnouts for scenic and recreational access. It is a major thoroughfare, and traffic is moderately heavy in spring, summer, and fall. It is lighter in winter.

Summer temperatures range from the 60s at night to the 80s and 90s during the day. Spring and autumn range from the 50s to the 80s, and winter days reach the 40s, with temperatures dropping below freezing at night.

This byway was given its unusual name for several reasons. It winds and meanders through the mountains much as a game or wild-pig trail does, and it is the route traveled by many of the fans who attend the University of Arkansas' Razorbacks football games. If you drive this byway on an autumn weekend, you may encounter carloads of people wearing bright-red hog hats and yelling ''Wooo-pig-sooee'' out the windows as they drive by.

If you plan to travel the byway from north to south, you begin at the national forest boundary at Brashears. Canoeing, kayaking, and fishing are popular on the nearby White River. The byway winds alongside a sparkling stream, part of the headwaters of the White River, and climbs Allard Mountain. The region is forested with a mixture of oaks and hickories, as well as smaller stands of pines, cedars, and hardwoods. Autumn colors are spectacular, and spring blossoms are equally splendid.

Drive south through Fly Gap, the highest spot on the Pig Trail at an elevation of 1,953 feet. South of Fly Gap, the 165-mile-long Ozark Highlands Trail crosses the byway at Cherry Bend, near milepost 37 on the highway. This National Scenic Trail is an east-west trending footpath across the entire Boston Range. It begins at Lake Fort Smith State Park on the western end of the national forest and goes out the northeastern edge of the forest to the Buffalo National River. You may wish to walk a portion of it. The trail is steep east of the byway, and it leads to Cherry Bend Hollow and broad vistas. West of the byway, the trail is fairly easy and goes around the mountain. About a quarter-mile west of the byway, the ruins of an old rock house lie under the bluff near the trail.

The byway continues south across the rolling ridges and hills of the highlands, and the views are different at each bend in the road. The Mulberry River drainage, mountains, and the hardwood overstory are visible from byway viewpoints.

A side trip three miles east on Forest Road 1003 leads to Redding Campground's 27 sites along the Mulberry River. An 8.5-mile loop trail begins at Redding and climbs to Spy Rock for a wonderful view of the Mulberry River Valley. The foot trail also intersects the Ozark Highlands Trail. Anglers fish the Mulberry for smallmouth bass, warmwater perches, and catfish.

The community of Cass sits in the deep valley along the Mulberry River, just south of the 1003 turnoff. In the 1920s and '30s, the Cass-Combs Railroad used some unusual techniques for getting lumber up to the ridge tops: a windlass lowered empty railcars to the riverside lumbermill, and then oxen

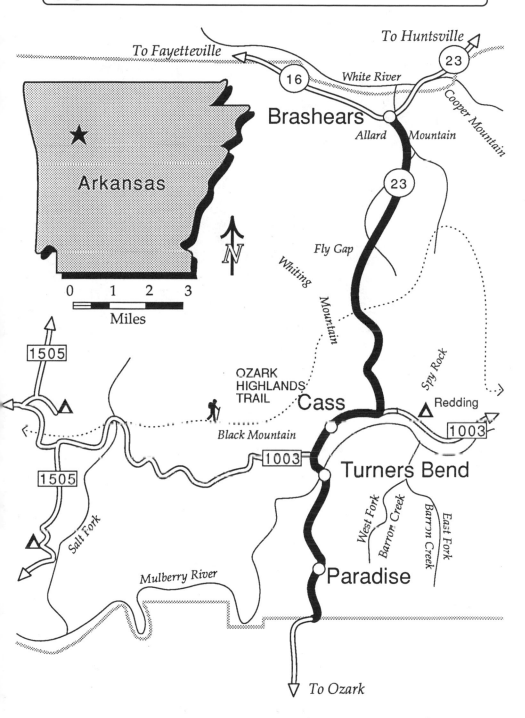

The Pig Trail Scenic Byway winds alongside a stream and travels through hardwood forests and pasturelands in the Boston Mountains. Ozark National Forest photo.

pulled the loaded cars up the steep roads to the ridge top. From there, the lumber was hauled by rail to St. Paul or Fayetteville. Also in Cass, the Job Corp Civilian Conservation Center trains more than 200 young people a year in various occupational skills, such as carpentry, plumbing, masonry, painting, and heavy-equipment operation. Visitors may tour the facilities, or stop for information on the Ozark Naitonal Forest.

The byway crosses the Mulberry River, which is navigable between mid-March and early June and again in late fall. The river drops about a foot per mile in elevation and is classified as class III white water. You may see canoeists and kayakers negotiating the white water where the byway crosses the river. Just beyond the river crossing, a side trip west on Forest Road 1003 will lead to several campgrounds.

Turners Bend has a small store and rents canoes. Farther south, the byway ascends Bend Hill through pines and cedars and past picturesque old homesteads with barns and stone fences. It continues through Paradise and ends at the national forest boundary north of Ozark.

The Boston Ranger Station in Ozark has visitor information about the national forest. Nearby, the Arkansas River provides numerous recreational opportunities, such as fishing, waterskiing, and boating. □

General description: A 24.9-mile drive through hardwood forests to the top of Mount Magazine.

Special attractions: Colorful autumn foliage, high sandstone bluffs, spring blossoms, camping, extensive views of mountain and pastures.

Location: Northwest Arkansas on the Ozark National Forest, southeast of Fort Smith. The byway follows Arkansas Route 309 between Paris and Havana and includes spur roads into the Mount Magazine Recreation Area.

Byway route numbers: Arkansas Route 309, Forest Roads 1606, 1636, and 1606A.

Travel season: Year-round.

Camping: Two national forest campgrounds with picnic tables, drinking water, fire grates, and toilets. No hookups.

Services: No services on the byway. All services in nearby Paris and Havana.

Nearby attractions: Blue Mountain Lake; Dardanelle Reservoir; numerous local festivals; Logan County Museum in Paris; historic city of Fort Smith; winery tours; Spring Lake Recreation Area; and Pig Trail, Ozark Highlands, and Arkansas Highway 7 national forest scenic byways.

For more information: Ozark-St. Francis National Forests, P.O. Box 1008, 605 W. Main, Russellville, AR 72801, (501) 968-2354. District Ranger: Magazine Ranger District, P.O. Box 511, Highway 22 East and Kalamazoo Road, Paris, AR 72855, (501) 963-3076.

Description: The Mount Magazine Scenic Byway climbs from the Arkansas River Valley up to flat-topped Mount Magazine and then winds down to the Petit Jean River Valley. The two-lane road is paved and has turnouts for scenic and recreational opportunities. Traffic is steady on weekends and light on weekdays.

Summers are hot and humid, with temperatures averaging in the 90s and sometimes exceeding 100 degrees. The top of the mountain averages 10 to 15 degrees cooler than the surrounding valleys. The region gets about 45 inches of rain a year. July through September are generally dry, and the rains begin in October. Autumn and spring are pleasant, with daytime temperatures in the 60s. Winter days reach the 40s, with freezing weather common at night in January and February.

To drive the byway from north to south, begin in Paris, where the Magazine Ranger Station has national forest information. The byway starts at the national forest boundary just south of Paris and immediately starts to climb.

The forest is composed primarily of shortleaf pines, with mixed stands of red and white oaks, hickories, gums, and maples. The lush understory includes wild plums, wild roses, mulberries, and spice bushes, as well as osage oranges, sassafras, and edible berries such as huckleberries, blackberries, dewberries, and gooseberries. The forest is spectacular when the leaves have turned color, from late October through early November. In the spring, blossoming shrubs and trees are also lovely.

The first campground is located at 160-acre Cove Lake Recreation Area. There are 28 campsites, restrooms, and showers in the summer. Additionally,

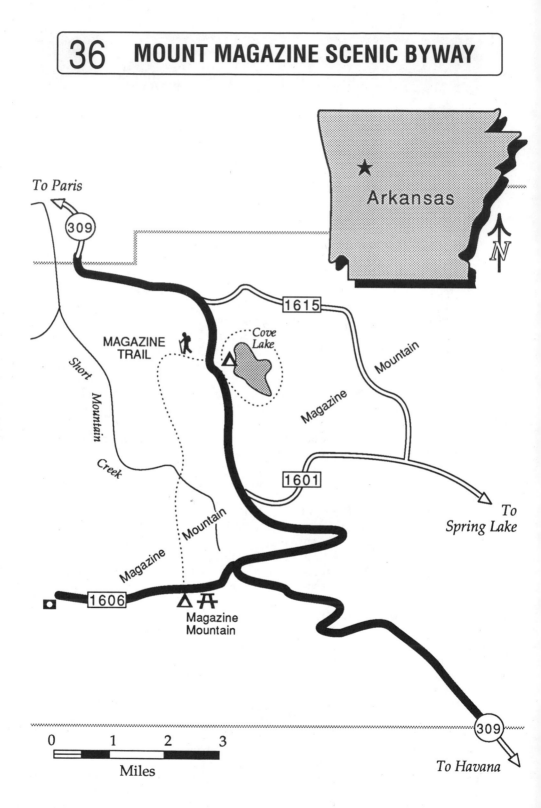

Rock formations and bluffs await visitors to the Mount Magazine Scenic Byway. Ozark National Forest photo.

Cove Lake has picnicking, swimming, fishing, a hiking trail, and a boat-launch ramp. Naturalists lead occasional interpretive programs at the outdoor amphitheater. Anglers fish for largemouth bass, catfish, and bream. The hiking trail encircles Cove Lake in a three-mile loop, with a spur to a vista point. Another trail leads to an old CCC campsite.

The byway climbs through scattered private land and farms. Logging, grazing, wildlife management, and watershed protection are activities that are promoted on the national forest. The Forest Service maintains picnic areas and scenic overlooks on the byway, which allow views north over the forest to the Arkansas River Valley.

Wildflowers are abundant and varied, both along the roadside and in the forest. Spring beauties, johnny jumpups, jack-in-the-pulpits, and violets bloom each spring, and summer blossoms include May apples, columbines, and many varieties of orchids and lilies. Autumn flowers are predominantly asters and sunflowers.

The byway climbs and turns onto the national forest spur roads that lead into the Mount Magazine Recreation Area. Here you will find three picnic areas, numerous vista points, hiking trails, and a campground. The campground has 13 sites in the forest on the mountaintop. Signal Hill Trail is a short route to the very top of Mount Magazine. East End Trail goes from the campground through the woods to East End Picnic Area. The Magazine Trail leaves Mount Magazine Recreation Area and parallels the west side of the byway 10.8 miles down to Cove Lake. This foot path through young and old stands of hardwoods and pines is moderately difficult, but it offers beautiful views along the way.

Mount Magazine, at 2,753 feet in elevation, is the highest mountain in Arkansas. It is about seven miles long and three miles wide, and it dominates the landscape. Views from the flat top on a clear day can extend 50 miles and can include Blue Mountain Lake in the Petit Jean River Valley, Dardanelle Reservoir in the Arkansas River Valley, high sandstone bluffs and cliffs, and dense forests and pastures on the rolling hills that surround the mountain. The mountain is primarily sandstone and shale, uplifted along with the Arkansas River millions of years ago.

Back on Arkansas Route 309, the byway descends the south side of Mount Magazine, again offering extensive views. The road winds and twists down the mountain and through the pine and hardwood forest. Forest inhabitants include raccoons, deer, foxes, black bears, bobcats, oppossums, skunks, and squirrels. Songbirds are plentiful and include indigo buntings, purple martins, whip-poor-wills, mockingbirds, and cardinals. Seeing painted buntings, scarlet and summer tanagers, and rufous-crowned sparrows would be a rare treat. Naturalists are interested in the threatened Mount Magazine middle-toothed land snail and the maple-leaved oak tree. Both are found only on Mount Magazine.

The byway ends at the national forest boundary north of Havana. ☐

37 OZARK HIGHLANDS SCENIC BYWAY
Ozark National Forest   Arkansas

General description: A 35-mile route traversing the upper ridges and highlands of the Boston Range in the Ozark Mountains.

Special attractions: Colorful autumn foliage, spring blossoms, extensive views, abundant wildlife, Upper Buffalo Wilderness, hunting, Ozark Highland Trail.

Location: West-central Arkansas on the 1.1-million-acre Ozark National Forest, east of Fort Smith and north of Interstate 40. The byway follows Arkansas Route 21 on national forest land between Boxley and Clarksville.

Byway route number: Arkansas Route 21.

Travel season: Year-round.

Camping: One national forest campground with picnic tables, drinking water, fire grates, and toilets. No hookups.

Services: Ozone, Fallsville, and Edwards Junction have gas and groceries. All services in nearby Clarksville, Boxley, and Jasper.

Nearby attractions: Buffalo National River; Dardanelle Reservoir; Eureka Springs; Silver Dollar City in Branson, Missouri; War Eagle Craft Fair; Peach Festival in Clarksville; Dogpatch USA; and Mount Magazine, Arkansas Highway 7, Pig Trail, and Sylamore national forest scenic byways.

For more information: Ozark-St. Francis National Forests, P.O. Box 1008, 605 W. Main, Russellville, AR 72801, (501) 968-2354. District Ranger: Pleasant Hill Ranger District, P.O. Box 190, Highway 21 North, Clarksville, AR 72830, (501) 754-2864 or 754-8864.

Description: The Ozark Highlands Scenic Byway travels some of the highest elevations of the Ozarks, and panoramic views are extensive. The two-lane

Backpackers enjoy a winter trek along the 140-mile-long Ozark Highland National Recreational Trail, accessible from the Ozark Highlands Scenic Byway. Tim Ernst photo.

highway is paved and has pullouts for scenic and recreational access. This is a major highway, and traffic is light to moderately heavy.

Summer temperatures range from the 60s through the 90s, and humidity is moderate. Spring and autumn are cooler, with temperatures in the 40s to 80s, while winter temperatures drop below freezing at night and climb to the 40s or 50s by day.

Driving from north to south, begin near the Buffalo National River, a popular recreation area with floating, swimming, fishing, hiking, and camping opportunities.

The byway runs just east of the Upper Buffalo Wilderness, which protects the headwaters of the Buffalo River. The wilderness encompasses 12,035 acres of hardwood forest with scenic sandstone and limestone outcrops and mountainous terrain.

The byway goes south through Edwards Junction, where Arkansas Route 16 joins Route 21 for 8.5 miles. The byway runs atop high ridges, paralleling Moonhull Mountain and the headwaters of the Mulberry River, which has premier canoeing farther down, beginning in Oark. This upper section is very scenic and offers seasonal fishing.

The forest vegetation is thick, with several species of oaks and hickories and scattered stands of native shortleaf pines represented. The understory is rich with springtime blossoms of redbuds, dogwoods, serviceberries, wild plums, and vacciniums, or berry bushes. In autumn the sumacs, sassafras, and Virginia creepers add bright colors to the forest foliage.

Forest inhabitants include whitetail deer, black bears, and wild turkeys, as well as abundant songbirds such as indigo buntings, cardinals, bluejays, and finches. There are red-tailed hawks, crows, and barred owls, and in winter bald and golden eagles are occasionally sighted along the river or soaring over the ridges.

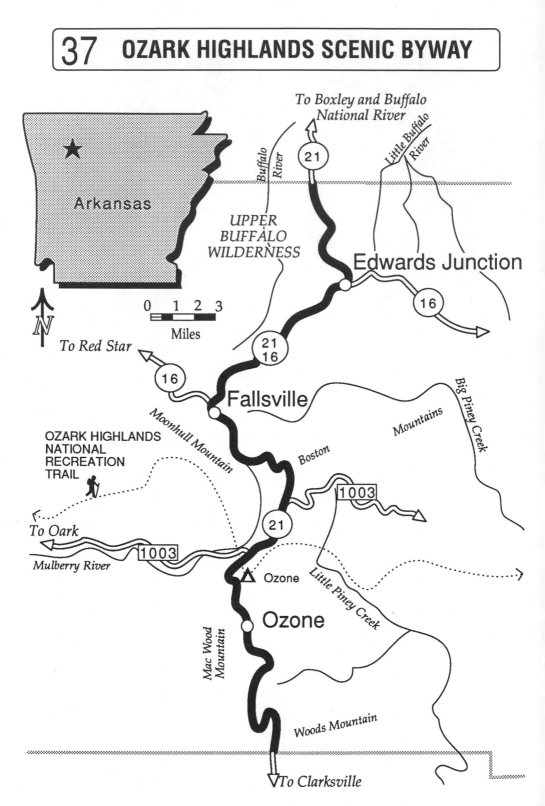

Ozone Campground is situated in the tall pines and has eight sites. The 165-mile-long Ozark Highlands National Recreation Trail runs through the campground, and it is a pleasure to hike. You can stroll along the trail just a short distance from the campground and see a good example of the varied Ozark Highlands topography and vegetation. Backpackers hike east to the Hurricane Creek Wilderness or west along the hollows and ridges of the highlands.

The Ozark Mountains are actually an eroded plateau that was uplifted millions of years ago. The southern section is predominantly sandstone, while the northern section, around the Buffalo River, is mostly limestone.

The byway winds south through Ozone and Lynwood and ends at the national forest boundary north of Clarksville. Pleasant Hill Ranger Station is just north of Clarksville and has information on the national forest. The Walton Fine Arts Center has exhibits and shows at the University of the Ozarks, also in Clarksville. Nearby, Dardanelle Reservoir impounds the Arkansas River and offers fishing, boating, camping, and swimming. □

38 ARKANSAS HIGHWAY 7 SCENIC BYWAY
Ozark and Ouachita National Forests   Arkansas

General description: Two sections of highway totaling 60.6 miles, through the Ouachita Mountains and the Boston Mountains in the Ozark Highlands.
Special attractions: Brilliant autumn foliage, spring wildflowers, Ozark Highlands National Recreation Trail, Rotary Ann Overlook.
Location: West-central Arkansas on the Ozark and Ouachita national forests, east of Fort Smith. One section of the byway follows Arkansas Route 7 north of Hot Springs National Park, on national forest lands between Jessieville and Fourche Junction. The other section travels Arkansas Route 7 north of Russellville, on national forest lands between Dover and Jasper.
Byway route number: Arkansas Route 7.
Travel season: Year-round.
Camping: Four national forest campgrounds with picnic tables, drinking water, fire grates, and toilets. No hookups.
Services: Scattered limited services along the byway. All services in nearby Hot Springs National Park, Russellville, and Harrison.
Nearby attractions: Alum Cove Natural Bridge and Interpretive Trail; Pedestal Rocks; Sam's Throne; Buffalo National River; Dardanelle Reservoir; Big Piney, Richland, and Hurricane creeks; Hot Springs National Park; Lake Ouachita State Park; Ozark Highlands, Pig Trail, Mount Magazine, and Talimena national forest scenic byways; and Hurricane Creek, Richland Creek, Upper Buffalo, and East Fork wilderness areas.
For more information: Ouachita National Forest, P.O. Box 1270, Hot Springs National Park, AR 71902, (501) 321-5202; Ozark-St. Francis National Forests, P.O. Box 1008, 605 W. Main, Russellville, AR 72801, (501) 968-2354. District Rangers: Buffalo Ranger District, P.O. Box 427, Jasper, AR 72641, (501) 446-5122; Bayou Ranger District, Route 1 Box 36, Hector, AR 72843, (501)

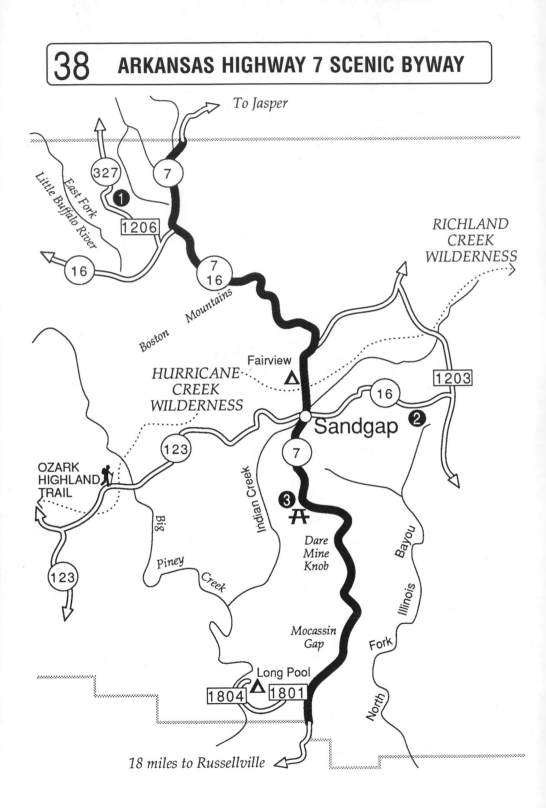

To Jasper

327

7

1

1206

East Fork

Little Buffalo River

16

7
16

Boston Mountains

RICHLAND
CREEK
WILDERNESS

Fairview

HURRICANE
CREEK
WILDERNESS

1203

16

2

Sandgap

7

123

OZARK
HIGHLAND
TRAIL

Indian Creek

3

Dare
Mine
Knob

Big

Piney

Creek

Bayou

Illinois

123

Mocassin
Gap

Fork

Long Pool

1804   1801

North

18 miles to Russellville

182

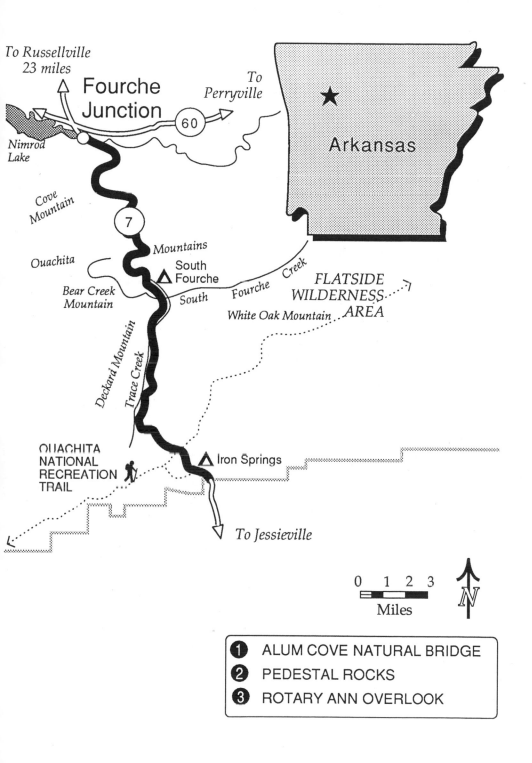

To Russellville
23 miles

Fourche
Junction

To
Perryville

60

Nimrod
Lake

Cove
Mountain

7

Arkansas

Ouachita

Mountains

South
Fourche

FLATSIDE
WILDERNESS
AREA

Bear Creek
Mountain

South

Fourche

Creek

White Oak Mountain

Deckard Mountain

Trace Creek

OUACHITA
NATIONAL
RECREATION
TRAIL

Iron Springs

To Jessieville

0 1 2 3
Miles

N

❶ ALUM COVE NATURAL BRIDGE
❷ PEDESTAL ROCKS
❸ ROTARY ANN OVERLOOK

284-3150; Jessieville Ranger District, Highway 7 N., Jessieville, AR 71949, (501) 984-5313.

Description: The Arkansas Highway 7 Scenic Byway is actually two separate sections of the same north-south highway. The section through the Ouachita National Forest is 24.3 miles long, and the section on the Ozark National Forest totals 36.3 miles. The byway segments are separated by about 40 miles of the populated Arkansas River Valley. The winding two-lane highway is paved and has turnouts for scenic and recreational access.

Summers are generally hot, with daytime temperatures in the 80s and 90s and evenings somewhat cooler. Spring and autumn range from the mid-50s to 80s, and winter days often reach the 50s and 60s, with freezing nights and ice or sleet in January and February, especially on the northern portion of the byway.

Beginning at the north and traveling south, enter the byway at the national forest boundary south of Jasper. The Buffalo Ranger Station in Jasper has information about the national forest, the byway, and the nearby Buffalo National River, which winds through high limestone bluffs and is popular for fishing and for white-water kayaking and canoeing in springtime.

The byway heads south alongside Henderson Mountain. A side trip west on Arkansas Route 16 and Forest Road 1206 leads five miles to Alum Cove Natural Bridge Recreation Area. There are picnic tables, restrooms, drinking water, and a one-mile interpretive nature trail. Walkers see the caves and rock formations along the bluffs and stroll through stands of American beeches, umbrella magnolias, and dogwoods. The natural bridge is 130 feet long and 20 feet wide, and it was carved by the erosive action of wind and water.

Back on the byway, you travel south, gaining elevation and rolling through the hardwood forest. Fairview Campground has 11 sites on a small hill above the highway. The dogwoods and redbuds are beautiful in spring.

The Ozark Highlands Trail crosses the byway at Fairview Campground. This 165-mile national recreation trail follows clear streams and ascends mountains on its scenic east-west route. You can hike a portion of it from the campground; the trail goes about five miles west to the Hurricane Creek Wilderness Area or about 17 miles east through Richland Creek Wilderness to Richland Creek Campground. Hurricane Creek Wilderness encompasses 15,427 acres of upland southern hardwoods, as well as flat-topped mountains and limestone bluffs. Richland Creek Wilderness has 11,801 acres of slightly steeper terrain and higher elevations.

Continue south on Route 7. Tiny Sandgap lies about midway through this section of the byway. Here, a side trip east on Arkansas Route 16 leads five miles to unique pedestal rock formations carved into the bluff.

Back on the byway, the route goes south through Piney Creeks Wildlife Management Area. This area is inhabited by big and small game species, notably whitetail deer, turkeys, and black bears. Ruffed grouse were recently reintroduced to the area.

The highway climbs to the popular Rotary Ann Overlook and Picnic Area. This popular overlook allows a splendid view of forests and mountains.

The route crosses rolling terrain past Freeman Springs and Dare Mine Knob and through Moccasin Gap before dropping down to its end at the national forest boundary. A side trip just before the boundary, west on Forest Roads

Arkansas Highway 7 Scenic Byway meanders through the lovely hardwood forests in the Ouachita and Boston mountain ranges. Ozark National Forest photo.

1801 and 1804, leads to Long Pool Recreation Area on Big Piney Creek. Long Pool has 19 campsites, picnicking, a swimming beach, and canoe access. Large, natural pools make great swimming holes under the high bluffs. Anglers fish for smallmouth, largemouth, and spotted bass, along with several species of sunfish. Floaters enjoy seasonal canoeing and kayaking in the creek.

The northern end of the second part of the byway is at the community of Fourche Junction on Nimrod Lake. Nimrod has boating and fishing opportunities.

From the junction, drive south on the winding road through the Ouachita National Forest. Ouachita is the French phonetic spelling for an Indian word that means good hunting grounds. The well-known Ouachita whetstones and quartz crystals come from this area. The Ouachita Forest hosts whitetail deer, wild turkeys, beavers, squirrels, rabbits, raccoons, quail, turtles, and various waterfowl such as great blue herons, egrets, and wood ducks. Canada geese and mallards pass through during migration.

This southern section of the byway crosses through a dense forest of shortleaf pines and occasional stands of hardwoods. The Ouachita Mountains are unique in being an east-west trending range. Most ranges in North America trend north and south.

About midway through this section of the byway is South Fourche Campground, with seven roadside campsites near South Fourche Creek. Anglers try for brown perch, bass, and catfish in the creek. Nights spent camping in Arkansas are filled with the sounds of frogs, toads, locusts, owls, and whip-poor-wills. Mornings are brightened by the songs of birds.

Continuing south, the byway ascends beside Trace Creek, a pretty stream that sparkles and murmurs under the forest canopy. There are abundant and beautiful wildflowers along the byway and in the adjacent forest. They include lilies, columbines, orchids, crested irises, and asters. The 8,200-acre Deckard Mountain Walk-In Turkey Hunting Area is west of the byway.

Ouachita National Recreation Trail crosses the byway a mile north of Iron Springs Campground. This footpath is 192 miles long and runs east to west from Pinnacle Mountain State Park, through the Ouachita National Forest, to Talemina State Park in Oklahoma. West of the byway, the four- to five-mile-long loop known as Hump's Trail connects with the Ouachita Trail and Iron Springs Recreation Area. Hikers can reach the Ouachita Trail and Hump's Trail from the byway or from Iron Springs Recreation Area. The loop is moderately difficult and best hiked in a counterclockwise direction. There is a spectacular view south from the rocky bluff atop Short Mountain.

Iron Springs Campground has 13 sites in the woods near a spring and stream. A pleasant wading area and a picnic shelter are available.

The byway ends at the national forest boundary near Jessieville. The ranger station in Jessieville has a visitor information center. Travelers continuing south reach Lake Ouachita and Hot Springs National Park. □

39 SYLAMORE SCENIC BYWAY
Ozark National Forest Arkansas

General description: A 26.5-mile drive through the hardwoods forests of the rolling Ozark Mountains to Blanchard Springs Caverns.

Special attractions: Blanchard Springs Caverns and Information Center, colorful autumn foliage, White River.

Location: North-central Arkansas on the Ozark National Forest, northwest of Batesville. The route follows Arkansas Route 5 from Calico Rock south to Allison and Arkansas Route 14 from Allison west to Blanchard Springs Caverns.

Byway route numbers: Arkansas Routes 5 and 14.

Travel season: Year-round.

Camping: One national forest campground with picnic tables, showers, drinking water, fire grates, and trailer dumping station. Two additional national forest campgrounds nearby.

Services: All services in Calico Rock, and nearby Mountain View.

Nearby attractions: Ozark Folk Center, regional festivals and celebrations, Leatherwood and Lower Buffalo wilderness areas, Buffalo National River.

For more information: Ozark-St. Francis National Forests, P.O. Box 1008, 605 W. Main, Russellville, AR 72801, (501) 968-2354. District Ranger: Sylamore Ranger District, P.O. Box 1279, Highway 14 N., Mountain View, AR 72560, (501) 269-3228.

Description: The Sylamore Scenic Byway is a J-shaped route that parallels the White River atop its plunging white limestone cliffs, climbs a high ridge, and winds along the top to Blanchard Springs Caverns. The two-lane highway is paved and has turnouts for scenic and recreational opportunities. Traffic is moderate from June through October and very light the rest of the year.

The Arkansas Folk Festival at Mountain View kicks off the tourist season the third weekend in April.

Spring and autumn temperatures are generally very pleasant, with daytime temperatures in the 50s and 60s. Summers are humid, and there are frequent afternoon thunderstorms. Daytime temperatures are usually in the 80s and 90s. Winter days are usually above freezing and may get up to the 60s. Nights drop below freezing, and ice or sleet is common in January and February.

The byway can be entered at either end or at Allison via Arkansas Route 9. Driving from north to south, begin in Calico Rock, a rural community on the White River. This broad, meandering river is floatable year-round. Anglers will enjoy fishing for brown and rainbow trout.

The byway passes fenced pastures and agricultural lands near the White River and then climbs rapidly up Government Hill. Views down to the river are very pretty from City Rock Bluff, an overlook perched atop high limestone cliffs. The area is part of the northern Arkansas limestone belt, deposited by ancient seas 460 million years ago. The oval-shaped Ozark Dome was uplifted, and breaks and fractures developed to relieve the internal pressures. Limestone, sandstone, shale, and chert were exposed by the fractures and by subsequent stream erosion.

The byway crosses Sugarloaf Creek and continues south through Optimus to follow Livingston Creek. The hills are primarily blanketed in white oaks, hickories, and stands of shortleaf pines. The byway area is managed as a scenic corridor by the Forest Service, and clearcutting is prohibited within sight of the route. Numerous fields host sassafras, blackberry bushes, and flowering plums.

Ozark National Forest inhabitants include whitetail deer, wild turkeys, squirrels, rabbits, oppossums, skunks, and raccoons. Birdwatchers can look for more than 150 species of birds, including cardinals, robins, bluejays, warblers, and finches. Bald eagles are occasionally seen in winter. Caves on the national forest are inhabited by endangered Indiana and gray bats. About 250,000 gray bats winter in one cave on the district; they represent about a sixth of the known population of that species. Ticks and chiggers can be annoying in spring and summer, and walkers should watch for poison ivy and oak and stinging nettle, as well as occasional poisonous snakes.

The byway continues south across rolling hills, offering pretty views of the forest and fields. The White River flows below, contained within high limestone cliffs. The route turns west at Allison, onto Arkansas Route 14.

A six-mile side trip through Allison to Mountain View brings you to this charming Ozark community that emphasizes folk arts. The Ozark Folk Center State Park has more than 24 activities and interpretations that recreate the turn-of-the-century mountain lifestyle. Live music and jigs, clogging, and waltzes brighten the dance floor, and the arts and traditional crafts flourish. There is lodging and a restaurant at the state park, and Mountain View offers all services to travelers.

Back at Allison, turn west onto Route 14. The road climbs to the ridge top, which provides far-reaching views of the Ozark Mountains. The winding route runs atop the ridge to Blanchard Springs Caverns Recreation Area, the end of the byway.

Blanchard Springs offers a variety of activities, including hiking, camping,

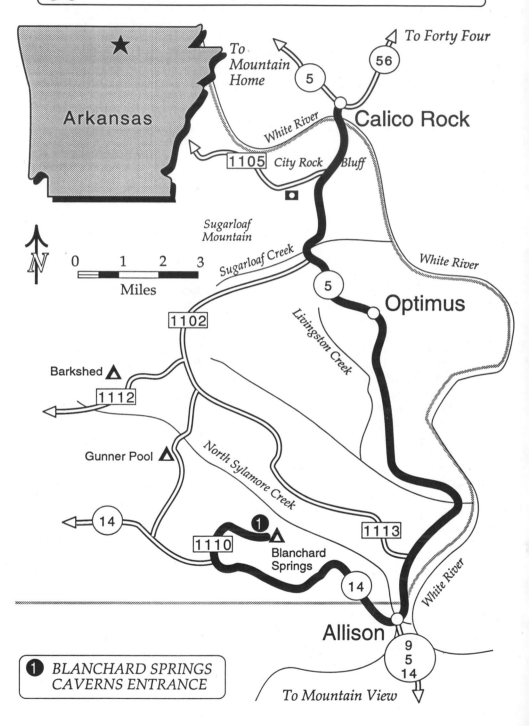

39 SYLAMORE SCENIC BYWAY

Arkansas

To Mountain Home

To Forty Four

56

5

Calico Rock

White River

1105 City Rock Bluff

Sugarloaf Mountain

Sugarloaf Creek

White River

0 1 2 3
Miles

N

5 Optimus

1102

Livingston Creek

Barkshed

1112

Gunner Pool

North Sylamore Creek

White River

14

1 ▲

1110 Blanchard Springs

1113

14

Allison

9
5
14

1 BLANCHARD SPRINGS CAVERNS ENTRANCE

To Mountain View

188

Springtime blossoms along the Sylamore Scenic Byway include flowering plums, dogwoods, and redbuds. Ozark National Forest photo.

swimming, fishing, boating, nature programs, cavern tours, and picnicking. You could easily spend a few days here.

The campground has 32 sites along North Sylamore Creek. The creek has some great swimming holes, and it is fun to tube. Anglers fish for smallmouth bass in the creek and rainbow trout in Mirror Lake. During the summer Forest Service naturalists lead evening programs about the many interesting features of the Ozark National Forest, their topics ranging from natural history to local folk culture. The programs are held in the Shelter Cave Amphitheater, at the base of a big sandstone bluff.

Blanchard Springs Caverns has a visitor center and guided tours. Information and exhibits explain the caverns, and a movie provides a good introduction to the area.

The limestone caverns are still growing and changing. You can choose to walk the .7-mile Dripstone Trail through the upper levels of the caverns, which is easy walking, or you can follow the 1.2-mile Discovery Trail through a stream-carved corridor. Speleothems, or cave formations, include giant columns, travertine dams, fragile soda-straw stalactites, and gleaming crystalline flowstones. Minerals color the formations in shades of orange, brown, yellow, blue, black, and gray. Unusual insects and animals have adapted to the unique environment. They include the endangered gray bat and the colorless Ozark blind salamander.

This area offers plenty of hiking opportunities. Sylamore Creek Hiking Trail follows the creek 15 miles, beginning near Allison and passing through Blanchard Campground to reach Barkshed Picnic Area to the northwest. There are several access points, and you can hike anywhere from 1.5 to the full 15 miles. The footpath sometimes meanders close to the creek and other times climbs the adjacent limestone bluffs. Hikers may see a shy deer or startle a lizard sunning on the rocks. □

40 TALIMENA SCENIC BYWAY
Ouachita National Forest   Oklahoma and Arkansas

General description: A 54-mile winding highway atop the crest of the Ouachita Mountains.

Special attractions: Robert S. Kerr Memorial Arboretum and Nature Center, Queen Wilhelmina State Park and Lodge, historical sites, far-ranging views, camping.

Location: The border between east-central Oklahoma and west-central Arkansas, on the Ouachita National Forest. The byway follows Oklahoma Route 1 and Arkansas Route 88 from the national forest boundary just north of Talihina, Oklahoma, to the community of Mena, Arkansas.

Byway route numbers: Oklahoma Route 1 and Arkansas Route 88.

Travel season: Year-round. The highway is occasionally closed because of snow, and winter driving conditions may be hazardous.

Camping: One national forest campground with picnic tables, flush toilets, fire rings, and drinking water. One state park campground with picnic tables, fire grates, electric and water hookups, bathhouse, laundry, and trailer dumping station. Open April through mid-November.

Services: No services on the byway, but all services available in Talihina and Mena.

Nearby attractions: Black Fork Mountain and Upper Kiamichi wilderness areas, Broken Bow Reservoir.

For more information: Ouachita National Forest, P.O. Box 1270, Hot Springs National Park, AR 71902, (501) 321-5202. District Rangers: Kiamichi Ranger District, P.O. Box 577, Talihina, OK 74571, (918) 567-2326; Mena Ranger District, Route 3 Box 220, Highway 71N, Mena, AR 71953, (501) 394-2382; Choctaw Ranger District, Box B, Heavener, OK 74937, (918) 653-2991.

Description: The Talimena Scenic Byway crosses the Ouachita Mountains, the highest range between the Appalachians and the Rockies. The byway route varies in elevation from 1,150 to 2,681 feet as it travels the crest of Rich Mountain and Winding Stair Mountain. The two-lane highway is paved and has frequent turnouts for scenic and recreational access. There are some steep grades and sharp curves.

The average summer temperature in this area is about 80 degrees. Spring and fall have moderate temperatures, and the haze of summer humidity is generally blown away by thunderstorms. Winters average 43 degrees, with occasional light snowfalls. Temperatures dip below freezing at night, and the wind blows constantly. Tornadoes occur periodically.

The byway can be driven from either direction or entered at about its midpoint via U.S. Highway 259. It is named for the two communities at either end: Talihina and Mena.

Driving from west to east, the Talimena Scenic Byway begins about six miles northeast of Talihina, Oklahoma. Talihina was a missionary settlement established in 1888 and named for the Choctaw Indian word for iron road, meaning the railroad. Talimena State Park, near the byway entrance, has 40 campsites, picnic tables, toilets, and some hookups. Talihina Visitor Center, at the beginning of the byway, has displays, exhibits, and information about the area. Nearby, picnicking is pleasant at Old Military Road Picnic Area.

The byway heads east on Oklahoma Route 1 on the Ouachita National Forest. Ouachita takes its name from the Choctaw Indian word Owachita, which means hunting trip.

The mountains here run east and west rather than north and south. They are primarily composed of sandstones and shales of the Mississippian and Pennsylvanian formations, thrust upward with tight folding and faulting. Many of the faults are visible from the byway.

The byway climbs Winding Stair Mountain. Ouachita National Recreation Trail parallels the highway, and there are a number of access points for hiking portions of the trail. The trail tends to be rough and quite steep in places.

About 16 miles from the beginning of the byway is Horsethief Spring, a historic site. In the 1830s, the Fort Towson Trail, a much-used military road, crossed this site. It was also the probable stopover for many a horse thief en route from stealing horses in Arkansas and driving them to Texas to sell. You can picnic here or hike four miles to Cedar Lake. A mile and a half past Horsethief Spring a side trip north leads to 84-acre Cedar Lake, which has camping, showers, boating, picnicking, and hiking and nature trails.

Emerald Vista Picnic Area offers views of the scenic byway, the Poteau River Valley, Cedar Lake, and Lake Wister. Winding Stair Campground has 27 campsites in the forest.

About midway through the scenic byway, the road crosses U.S. Highway 259 and continues east on Route 1. Robert S. Kerr Memorial Arboretum and Nature Center is a few miles past the intersection. Named for the late senator from Oklahoma, the center has three interpretive trails, each less than a mile in length. One focuses on soil formation, another identifies various plants and trees, and the third explains plant succession and communities. The arboretum and nature center is a delightful place to spend a few hours or a whole day. The experience offered there is both interesting and challenging.

The byway area is home to a great variety of birds, including warblers, grosbeaks, vireos, finches, and owls. Mammals include whitetail deer, oppossums, raccoons, foxes, bobcats, skunks, and squirrels.

The forest is composed of a variety of tree species. The north slopes and ridge tops are covered mostly with oaks, gums, hickories, elms, maples, cherry trees, and black walnuts. The south slopes have shortleaf pines and mixed hardwoods, as well as flowering shrubs such as dogwoods and redbuds. Spring is lovely along the byway, with the blossoming shrubs and wildflowers creating a colorful display. Autumn brings a photographer's and sightseer's dream; the palette of bright colors reaches from the underbrush to the tops of the trees.

The byway goes east to the Oklahoma-Arkansas state line and continues on as Arkansas Route 88. Queen Wilhemina State Park lies a few miles east of the state line atop Rich Mountain. Views of the surrounding mountains are extensive. There is a lodge, restaurant, activities, store, summer visitor center, amphitheater, hiking trails, and naturalist programs. The campground

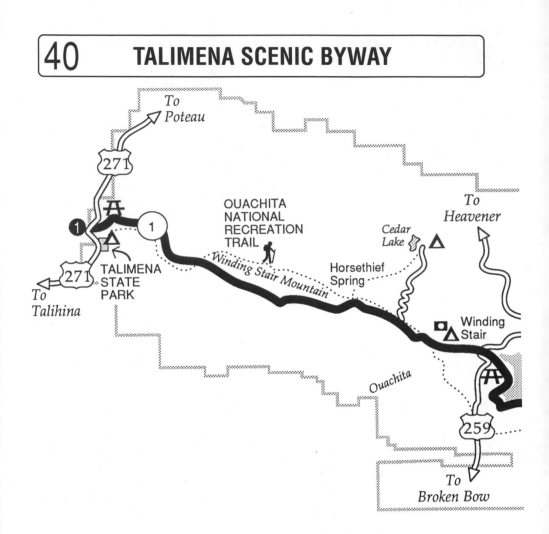

To
Poteau

271

OUACHITA
NATIONAL
RECREATION
TRAIL

Cedar
Lake

To
Heavener

1

1

Winding Stair Mountain

Horsethief
Spring

TALIMENA
STATE
PARK

271

To
Talihina

Winding
Stair

Ouachita

259

To
Broken Bow

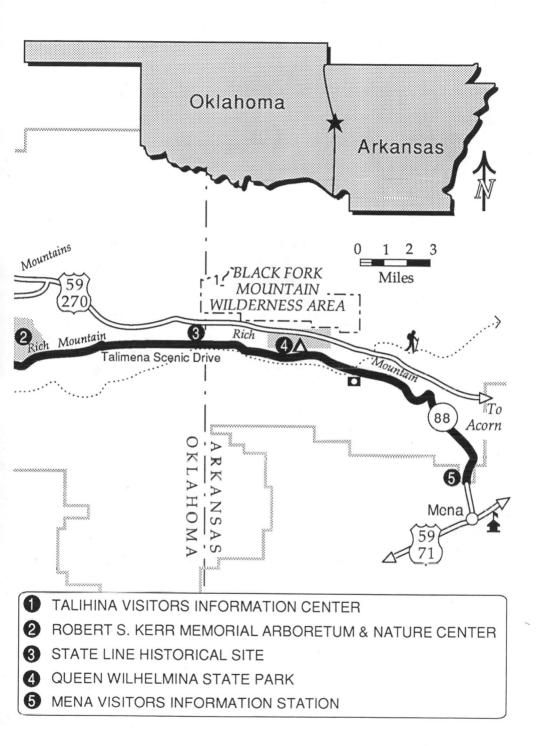

Oklahoma

Arkansas

N

Mountains

59
270

0 1 2 3
Miles

BLACK FORK MOUNTAIN WILDERNESS AREA

1

2 Rich Mountain

Talimena Scenic Drive

3 Rich

4

Mountain

88

To Acorn

OKLAHOMA ARKANSAS

5

Mena

59
71

1 TALIHINA VISITORS INFORMATION CENTER
2 ROBERT S. KERR MEMORIAL ARBORETUM & NATURE CENTER
3 STATE LINE HISTORICAL SITE
4 QUEEN WILHELMINA STATE PARK
5 MENA VISITORS INFORMATION STATION

The Talimena Scenic Drive offers far-ranging views as it winds along the crest of the Ouachita Mountains. Ouachita National Forest photo.

has 40 sites, a bathhouse, laundry, trailer dumping station, and hookups.

Rich Mountain Lookout is the highest point on the byway, at elevation 2,681 feet. You can picnic here, and the breathtaking view includes Queen Wilhemina State Park, Black Fork Mountain Wilderness Area, and the Mill Creek area.

The highway descends Rich Mountain, and there are frequent scenic overlooks. The byway ends at Mena Visitor Information Station, at the national forest boundary. □

41 ST. FRANCIS SCENIC BYWAY
St. Francis National Forest — Arkansas

General description: A 20-mile paved and gravel route along the top of Crowleys Ridge, offering extensive views of forests and Mississippi River delta.
Special attractions: Far-ranging views, Bear Creek Lake, Storm Creek Lake, boating, fishing, regional festivals.
Location: East-central Arkansas on the St. Francis National Forest, near the border with Mississippi. The route follows Arkansas Route 44 from the national forest boundary near Marianna, south to Forest Road 1900, and continues south on 1900 to its terminus at the national forest boundary near West Helena.
Byway route numbers: Arkansas Route 44 and Forest Road 1900.
Travel season: Year-round.

41   ST. FRANCIS SCENIC BYWAY

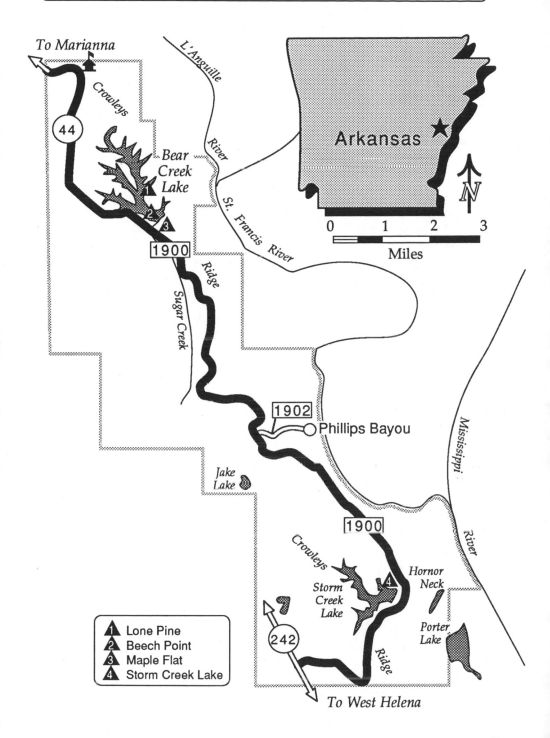

To Marianna

L'Anguille

Crowleys

44

Bear
Creek
Lake

River

St. Francis River

Arkansas

N

0   1   2   3

Miles

1900

Sugar Creek Ridge

1902

Phillips Bayou

Jake
Lake

Mississippi

1900

Crowleys

Storm
Creek
Lake

Hornor
Neck

Porter
Lake

River

242

Ridge

▲1 Lone Pine
▲2 Beech Point
▲3 Maple Flat
▲4 Storm Creek Lake

To West Helena

Camping: Four national forest campgrounds with picnic tables, drinking water, toilets, fire grates, and boat-launch facilities. No hookups.

Services: No services on the byway. All services in Marianna, Helena, and West Helena.

Nearby attractions: St. Francis, L'Anguille, and Mississippi rivers; White River National Wildlife Refuge; agricultural museum in Stuttgart; regional festivals and celebrations; Memphis music festivals; King Biscuit Blues Festival in Helena.

For more information: Ozark-St. Francis National Forests, P.O. Box 1008, 605 W. Main, Russellville, AR 72801, (501) 968-2354. District Ranger: St. Francis Ranger District, P.O. Box 356, Route 4 Box 14A, Marianna, AR 72360, (501) 295-5278.

Description: The St. Francis Scenic Byway winds atop a unique ridge in eastern Arkansas through a beautiful hardwood forest. The 20-mile route is paved for about nine miles and is well-maintained, graded gravel the remaining miles. Traffic is constant in the summer and light the rest of the year.

Summers here are humid and hot, with temperatures ranging from 70 to 100 degrees. Spring and autumn temperatures range from 50 to 80 degrees, and winters average in the 40s to 60s. Most precipitation falls between March and May.

Driving north to south, the route begins near Marianna, where a ranger station has national forest and byway information. The city also has a small museum, and the Chamber of Commerce is housed in a restored historic building.

The byway crosses five miles of rolling terrain south to Bear Creek Lake. The 625-acre lake is rated as one of the best fishing lakes in Arkansas. Fish species include bass, crappie, catfish, and bream.

Bear Creek Lake has two campgrounds and an overflow group campground, for a total of 46 sites. The peaceful campgrounds are situated in the trees and fields near the shore. Swimming, picnicking, fishing, and boating are popular recreational activities at Bear Lake. Bring mosquito repellant. A 0.5-mile loop trail in the lakeshore area was completed in 1992.

The byway continues south atop the ridge on Forest Road 1900. The surrounding forest is one of the largest hardwood stands in eastern Arkansas. The soils on the ridge are very fertile, and the trees grow large. Foliage colors in autumn are spectacular. The forest includes white and red oaks, hickories, sumacs, yellow poplars, American beeches, cypresses, swamp black gums (locally called tupelos), and American sycamores. The lush understory includes papaws, ironwoods, hydrangeas, spicebushes, dogwoods, redbuds, ferns, and Carolina magnolia vines. In spring the flowering shrubs are lovely, with blossoms hovering like a cloud of mist in the forest.

About midway through the scenic byway, Forest Road 1902 leads east to the small community of Phillips Bayou, on the St. Francis River. There are boat launches and fishing opportunities on the river here.

Forest inhabitants include whitetail deer, wild turkeys, rabbits, raccoons, armadillos, skunks, oppossums, and a variety of squirrels. Birdwatchers will see many species. Waterfowl such as colorful wood ducks and great blue herons are on the lakes, and songbirds include bluebirds, orioles, cardinals, jays, and wrens. Crowleys Ridge is on the Mississippi Flyway, and spring and fall bring the unmistakable sound of thousands of honking geese flying overhead.

St. Francis Scenic Byway brings motorists to 625-acre Bear Lake, considered one of the best fishing lakes in Arkansas. St. Francis National Forest photo.

The byway route runs atop Crowleys Ridge, a unique geological formation. The north-south ridge is about 200 miles long and four to nine miles wide. The ridge has a thick accumulation of windblown soil, or loess. Surrounding lands below the ridge are typical river-bottom deltas—flat, productive farmlands. For many decades, early farmers along the ridge burned off the thick vegetation, and the fine soils eroded into steep gullies and slopes. In 1932 the Soil Conservation Service acquired the ridge and let hardwood trees reclaim the badly damaged land. Today the ridge supports a thriving and productive hardwood forest. Most of the harvested timber goes to the furniture and flooring industries.

Continuing south on Road 1900, you will reach Storm Creek Lake, which covers 420 acres. The lake features popular swim and picnic areas, as well as a fishing pier. Anglers fish for striped bass, crappie, catfish, and bream. The campground has 12 sites near the lakeshore. At the northwest end of the lake, a Research Natural Area hosts a 400-acre forest of hundred-year-old trees. One yellow poplar has a trunk three feet in diameter. The area somehow escaped human interference during the early settlement years, and today national forest managers have a policy of no management so that researchers and students may study the largely untouched area.

The byway follows Forest Road 1900 south to its terminus at Arkansas Route 242, near West Helena. In nearby Helena, the Delta Cultural-Historical Center located in a historic train station, is open for public tours. □

42 LONGLEAF TRAIL SCENIC BYWAY
Kisatchie National Forest   Louisiana

General description: A 17-mile paved highway offering lovely views of the pine uplands of the Kisatchie Hills.

Special attractions: Rugged terrain and fast-flowing streams, warm-water fishing, Kisatchie Hills Wilderness, National Red Dirt Wildlife Management Preserve, hiking trails, logging and pioneer history.

Location: Central Louisiana on the Kisatchie National Forest, south of Natchitoches. The byway follows Forest Road 59 on national forest lands between Louisiana Routes 119 and 117.

Byway route number: Forest Road 59.

Travel season: Year-round.

Camping: Seven national forest campgrounds. Some have drinking water, tables, and vault toilets. Best suited to tents or truck campers, but some sites can accommodate larger motorhomes. No hookups.

Services: All services in Natchitoches. Gas, groceries, and phones at several nearby communities, including Derry, Kisatchie, Rosepine, Gorum, and Provencal.

Nearby attractions: Natchitoches, the oldest settlement in the Louisiana Purchase; historic Fort St. Jean Baptiste; several antebellum homes predating the Civil War and statehood.

For more information: Kisatchie National Forest, P.O. Box 5500, 2500 Shreveport Highway, Pineville, LA 71360, (318) 473-7160. District Ranger: Kisatchie Ranger District, P.O. Box 2128, Natchitoches, LA 71457, (318) 352-2568.

Description: The Longleaf Trail Scenic Byway winds along a ridge top through the unique Kisatchie Hills and features outstanding views of rocky outcrops, distant hills and buttes, and Kisatchie Bayou's sparkling water and white sand beaches. Elevations range from 80 feet in the creek bottoms to 400 feet in the hills. Visible from some distance, the hills are flanked by countryside that ranges from pastoral pecan orchards and cotton fields to heavily forested bayous and hill country. The Kisatchie Hills are a real jewel in the heart of Louisiana.

The two-lane road is paved and has numerous scenic turnouts at overlooks and interpretive areas. Gravel side roads lead to campgrounds and other areas of interest.

The central Louisiana climate is characterized by hot, humid summers with intense, local thunderstorms. July and August are the hottest months, with average temperatures of about 82 degrees. Winters are short and mild; the temperature averages about 47 degrees in December and January. Winter rains often last several days. The frost-free season usually extends from the end of March to the beginning of November.

The picturesque city of Natchitoches boasts waterfront architecture reminiscent of that in New Orleans. The old main street looks out on Cane River, a placid oxbow lake abandoned long ago by the meandering Red River. Northwestern State University, agriculture, and the wood-products industry are important factors in Natchitoches' commerce. Tourism has increased in recent years, primarily because of the area's rich history and unique scenery.

Driving Longleaf Trail from east to west, the byway sweeps gently up from flat, bottomland agricultural country into the pine uplands. The route then parallels the southern boundary of the Kisatchie Hills Wilderness for about seven miles. The Longleaf Trail was constructed as a single-lane road by the Civilian Conservation Corps in about 1935.

The Kisatchie Hills area is composed of two ancient sandstone beds that stand higher than the sandstone in the surrounding area. The area is known as the Kisatchie Wold, part of a unique line of upland hills that cross central Lousiana from Toledo Bend Reservoir on the Sabine River to Sicily Island, near the Mississippi River.

The wold is composed of silica-cemented sandstone, a result of the weathering of volcanic ash. It is highly resistant to erosion, and as surrounding countryside wore down and the Gulf of Mexico sank, the wold remained prominently high. Petrified wood and opals are found in this area.

Just west of Bayou Cypre Overlook, for about two miles, the byway follows the original Opelousas-to-Fort Jesup Military Road, an important route used during the Civil War.

Longleaf Vista has picnic tables, restrooms, and drinking water, as well as the 1.5-mile Longleaf Vista Nature Trail. The trail passes near the remains of a late-nineteenth- and early-twentieth-century turpentine still, and it also provides access to the old narrow-gauge railbed used for hauling timber and naval supplies. The vista point offers a sweeping panorama of Kisatchie Hills Wilderness and its unspoiled forest setting. This rugged 8,700-acre wilderness is known locally as the "Little Grand Canyon," and it has popular hiking trails. The Backbone Hiking and Equestrian Trail is a moderately difficult 12-mile path into the wilderness area. It follows ridge lines, allowing wonderful views of the sandstone bluffs and rock formations unique to the Kisatchie Hills area.

Kisatchie Ranger District lies within the traditional range of late prehistoric Caddo Indians. Several unmarked sites occupied during that time are within one mile of the byway.

About one mile west of Longleaf Vista, the 12.5-mile Caroline Dormon Hiking and Horse Trail extends to Kisatchie Bayou Campground. It is named in memory of the woman credited with pushing through legislation that resulted in the creation of Kisatchie National Forest, the only national forest in Louisiana.

Early loggers would occasionally leave a fine tree, possibly as a seed source. The Statesman Tree, just beyond the Caroline Dorman Trailhead, is about 175 years old—very old for a southern pine. It is typical of the trees that covered the Kisatchie Hills in the centuries before logging.

Forest Roads 360 and 321 lead to Kisatchie Bayou Campground. This scenic area is located on the bluffs overlooking white sand beaches, rocky rapids, and sandy bottomlands of mixed hardwoods and pine. You can camp, picnic, fish, canoe, and hike. There are vault toilets and drinking water available. Anglers fish for Kentucky striped bass, sunfish, and catfish.

Loblolly and longleaf pines dominate the forest, with mixed hardwoods such as hickories, dogwoods, and black, post, southern red, and white oaks in the drainages and along ridge tops. Spring is brightened by blossoming dogwoods and wild azaleas.

Farther west along the byway, Forest Roads 339, 341, and K1A make a nice side trip through the forest to Custis Campground, which is inside the

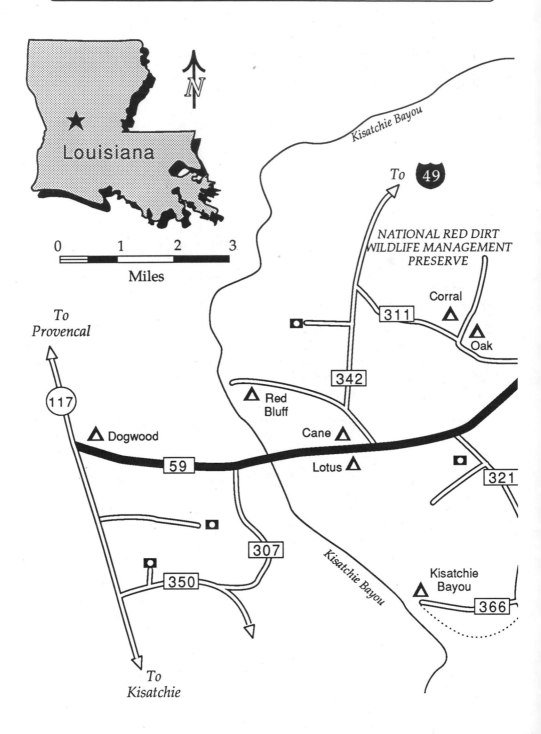

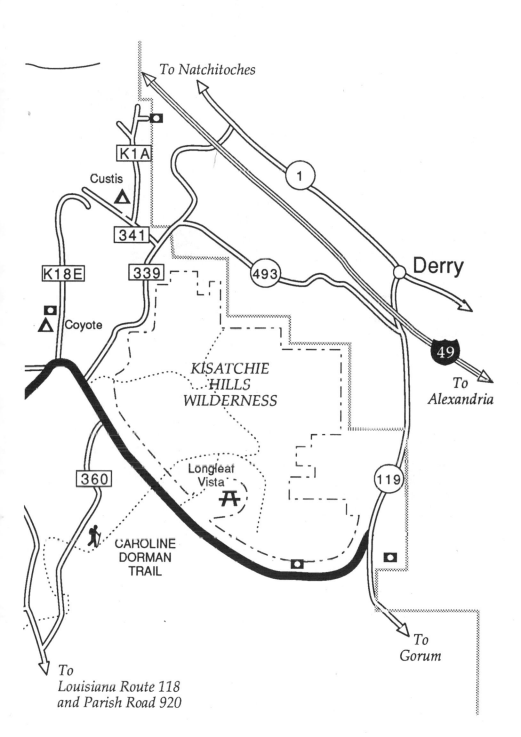

To Natchitoches

K1A

Custis

341

K18E

339

493

Derry

Coyote

49

To
Alexandria

KISATCHIE
HILLS
WILDERNESS

360

Longleaf
Vista

119

CAROLINE
DORMAN
TRAIL

To
Gorum

To
Louisiana Route 118
and Parish Road 920

Fine stonework and picturesque settings enhance the many scenic overlooks along the Longleaf Trail Scenic Byway. Jim Caldwell photo.

38,450-acre National Red Dirt Wildlife Management Preserve. This is a popular hunting camp, but it has no facilities. A bit north of the campground, on Forest Road K1A, is Melrose Overlook, from which you can see eastward over fields and farms. Roadside wildflowers include asters and coreopsis.

About midway along the byway, you will find Coyote Campground and Overlook, Oak Campground, and Corral Campground. These areas are popular with hunters from October 1 until April 30, and they have no developed facilities.

As turn-of-the-century loggers moved through the virgin forests of the Kisatchie Hills, they sometimes left small or deformed trees. Two of these trees, about 135 years old (just north of the byway between Forest Roads 311 and 321), are reminders of past consumptive logging operations. They are infected with red heart disease, a decay common to mature southern pines. Trees such as these are favorite nesting and roosting places for the endangered red-cockaded woodpecker, the only woodpecker known to build nests in cavities within living trees. Nest trees are banded with white paint for easy identification.

Other forest inhabitants include whitetail deer, foxes, squirrels, raccoons, oppossums, coyotes, quail, songbirds, and occasional roadrunners.

Forest Road 321 passes by forested Middle Branch Overlook and provides another access to Kisatchie Bayou Campground. Red Bluff Campground and Eagle Overlook are found off Forest Road 342. Red Bluff is located on the lower stretches of Kisatchie Bayou, where the bayou is deeper and less sandy than in other areas. Vault toilets are provided.

Across from Cane Campground, Lotus Campground, which has drinking water and vault toilets, is situated in a pretty upland hardwood forest. An old well is all that remains of the Lotus School site, the first school in the area. A historic stagecoach route from southern Louisiana intersects the byway near here.

Kisatchie Bayou crosses Longleaf Trail just east of Forest Road 307. The bayou is included in the Louisiana Natural and Scenic Stream system. Local Indians referred to it as Kisatchie, meaning "Cane Country," because of the switch cane patches that grow along the stream. Kisatchie Bayou is unique among the characteristically quiet bayous of Louisiana; it has a steep enough stream gradient that its rapids and falls greet you with exciting sights and sounds that you normally would expect to find only in the mountains of the eastern or western United States.

At its western end, Longleaf Trail Scenic Byway intersects with Louisiana Route 117. Near this junction, more than 100 years ago, Bellwood Academy was located on the present site of the Kisatchie Work Center. The academy offered advanced studies in several fields, but it closed in 1863. Also nearby is Dogwood Campground, set among the pines, hardwoods, and, of course, dogwood trees. This campground has drinking water, restrooms, and an interpretive display.—*Ron Couch* □

43 ZILPO ROAD
Daniel Boone National Forest — *Kentucky*

General description: A 9.1-mile road across forested ridges and hollows to Cave Run Lake.

Special attractions: Colorful autumn foliage, hiking and horseback trails, an old fire tower, blossoming shrubs, diverse wildlife, examples of timber-harvesting methods and wildlife-management practices, wildflowers.

Location: Eastern Kentucky on the Daniel Boone National Forest, east of Mount Sterling. The byway travels the entire length of Forest Road 918. To find it, follow Kentucky Route 211 south of U.S. Highway 60, turn east onto Forest Road 129, and follow the signs for Zilpo Campground.

Byway route number: Forest Road 918.

Travel season: Year-round.

Camping: Two national forest campgrounds with drinking water, toilets, picnic tables, and fire grates. Campgrounds open from mid-April to mid-October. Select units have hookups.

Services: All services in Morehead. Gas, telephone, and food in Salt Lick.

Nearby attractions: Clear Creek Recreation Area, Sheltowee Trace National Recreation Trail, Cave Run Lake, Red River Gorge Geological Area, Minor Clark Fish Hatchery, Natural Bridge State Park.

For more information: Daniel Boone National Forest, 100 Vaught Road, Winchester, KY 40391, (606) 745-3100. District Ranger: Morehead Ranger District, Box 910, Morehead, KY 40351, (606) 784-6429.

Description: Lying within the northern half of the Daniel Boone National Forest, the byway meanders a little more than nine miles across forested ridges and hollows and around hills before ending at the entrance gate to the Zilpo Recreation Area. There are a few sharp curves and steep grades along the route.

Spring weather is characterized by crisp mornings, sunny days, and cool

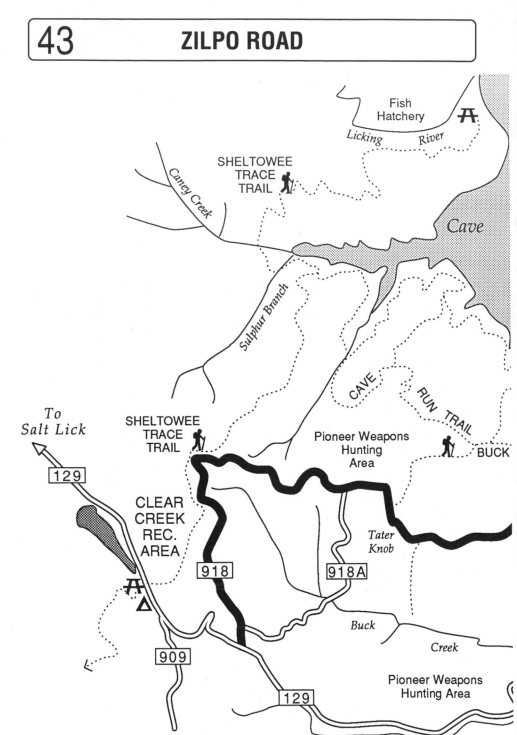

Fish Hatchery

Licking   *River*

SHELTOWEE TRACE TRAIL

Caney Creek

Cave

Sulphur Branch

CAVE

RUN TRAIL

SHELTOWEE TRACE TRAIL

Pioneer Weapons Hunting Area

BUCK

To *Salt Lick*

129

CLEAR CREEK REC. AREA

Tater Knob

918

918A

909

Buck

Creek

129

Pioneer Weapons Hunting Area

Leatherwood Creek

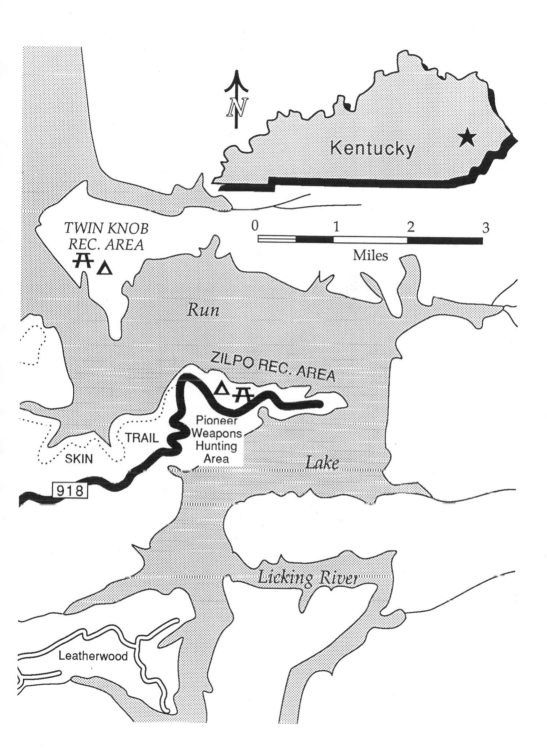

N

Kentucky

TWIN KNOB
REC. AREA

0   1   2   3
Miles

Run

ZILPO REC. AREA

Pioneer
Weapons
TRAIL   Hunting
Area

SKIN   Lake

918

Licking River

Leatherwood

evenings. There are occasional thunderstorms, but for the most part weather is pleasant. Daytime temperatures can reach the mid-60s, and nighttime lows in the 20s are not unusual. Summer temperatures are often in the upper 80s, and humidity levels can be high. Fall weather is similar to that of spring. Typical winter temperatures are in the 20s, and two to six inches of snow is the average.

The southern hardwood forest consists of oaks, yellow poplars, hickories, redbuds, dogwoods, maples, beeches, scattered clumps of pines, sycamores, and occasional black walnuts. In the autumn, the varied reds, oranges, and golds of changing leaves make for excellent color viewing. In spring, the redbud and dogwood blossoms are striking.

You may see whitetail deer feeding along ridge tops and in hollows. The best time for viewing wildlife is around sunrise or sunset. Deer are relatively abundant in this part of the national forest, and hunting is a popular activity.

In addition to deer, look for red foxes, groundhogs, rabbits, skunks, squirrels, wild turkey, geese, wood ducks, mallards, grouse, ospreys, hawks, owls, and a variety of songbirds.

The ridges are composed of Newman limestone over a thick bed of siltstone, all covered with a shallow layer of soil. The hollows are transported soils and siltstone carried from higher elevations by area streams.

The Zilpo area has a rich history of Indian settlement. Banks of flint are abundant, and there are signs that early Indians worked their tools here. Scrapers, arrowheads, and other Indian artifacts are often uncovered. As in all national forests, no artifacts may be removed.

Clear Creek Lake and Recreation Area is located on Forest Road 129 near the beginning of the byway. The 43-acre lake is stocked with largemouth bass, channel catfish, and sunfish. There is also a boat launch, and the lake is perfect for canoeing. Motors are not permitted.

Situated around the lake are nesting boxes for wood ducks and nesting platforms for Canada geese. The Forest Service is establishing a resident goose flock, and a large number of banded geese are present. Wood ducks nest between March and May, geese between March and July.

The Clear Creek Iron Furnace is also part of the recreation area. Though only the crumbling stone stack remains today, the furnace was once the site of frenzied activity. Each summer between 1839 and 1857, the furnace, built to smelt pig iron, gobbled up huge amounts of surrounding forest to keep itself running. The environmental impact of these logging practices was catastrophic, even in that day and age.

In contrast to the way the iron furnace was fed are today's methods of harvesting timber. The first interpretive stop on the byway details modern timber-harvesting techniques and how they are used as a tool for wildlife management, providing browse for deer, berries for ruffed grouse, and cover for wild turkeys.

Just beyond the first overlook, the byway enters the Pioneer Weapons Hunting Area. In season, hunters may hunt this area only with bow and arrow, crossbow, flintlock, or percussion cap rifle. Many hunters use the old forest roads in the vicinity for foot travel during the season. The roads are also open to backpackers, horseback riders, and cross-country skiers. Hikers using the area during hunting season should wear fluorescent orange for safety reasons.

Another interpretive site features a trailhead and wildlife exclosure. The

Interpretive sites add to the enjoyment of scenery along the Zilpo Road. Barbara Elliott photo.

trail, which is about 100 yards long, intersects the Sheltowee Trace, a 254-mile-long National Recreation Trail. Sheltowee means "Big Turtle" in the Shawnee language. The tribe gave this name to Daniel Boone when it adopted him, and the trail was named in honor of Boone, who explored the land over which it passes.

Just after the trails intersect, a fenced plot keeps wildlife out. Here trees and plants are protected so that wildlife biologists can compare vegetative utilization by deer and estimate browsing pressure.

The next interpretive site on the byway is called "A Rest in the Forest." A short trail meanders through the forest to a simple wooden bench. Sunlight filtering through the leaves, the buzz of bees, and the odor of decaying leaves all serve to highlight the regenerative powers of the forest on the mind and soul.

Sitting atop the next ridge is the Tater Knob Fire Lookout Tower, one of the highest points in the area at elevation 1,388 feet. The tower was manned from 1932 until the early 1970s. The lookout is scheduled for restoration.

Leaving Tater Knob, the road dips into a hollow and climbs to the summit of the next ridge and overlook. A panoramic view includes forested lands running down to the shores of Cave Run Lake, a large portion of the lake itself, and a section of the byway as it curves around a hill.

Cave Run Lake holds largemouth bass, bluegills, crappies, catfish, and an excellent muskellunge fishery. There are two marinas on the lake to serve boaters. Numerous coves are host to the many houseboats that ply the waters of the 8,270-acre impoundment. Swimmers enjoy two beaches, including the sand beach at the Zilpo Recreation Area. The lake is home to the Cave Run Sailing Association, sponsor of several regattas each season.

From the Cave Run overlook, the byway descends into a hollow that leads to Forest Road 918C. This is a camping area for horseback riders and their mounts. A horse trough is fed by a spring, but the campsite has no other water and no hookups.

The Zilpo Scenic Byway ends at the gates of Zilpo Campground and Recreation Area. The campground has 196 sites spread over 355 acres of trees and brush. Each site has a lantern holder. Water is available at centrally located sites, and there are 10 bathhouses with hot showers—five of them solar-heated. Select sites have electricity.—*Barbara Elliott* □

44 MOUNT ROGERS SCENIC BYWAY
Jefferson National Forest   *Virginia*

General description: A 55.5-mile paved highway through the scenic forests and countryside surrounding Mount Rogers, highest point in Virginia.

Special attractions: Mount Rogers National Recreation Area, the Appalachian Trail, Lewis Fork and Little Wilson Creek wilderness areas, historic logging towns.

Location: Southwest Virginia on the Jefferson National Forest, south of Marion. Mount Rogers Scenic Byway is divided into two parts: 23 miles of Virginia Route 603, from Troutdale southwest through the center of Mount Rogers National Recreation Area to the intersection with U.S. Highway 58; and 32 miles of U.S. Highway 58, from Damascus east to Volney, along the south edge of the Mount Rogers National Recreation Area.

Byway route numbers: U.S. Highway 58 and Virginia Route 603.

Travel season: Year-round.

Camping: Two national forest campgrounds with individual and group sites, picnic tables, fire grates, toilets, drinking water, and trailer dumping stations. No hookups.

Services: Lodging, store, food, and gas in Damascus. Gas and convenience store in Troutdale and Konnarock. All services in nearby Marion, Abingdon, and Bristol.

Nearby attractions: Grayson Highlands State Park, Barter Theatre in Abingdon, Salt Mine Museum, and numerous regional festivals.

For more information: Jefferson National Forest, 210 Franklin Road SW, Caller Service 2900, Roanoke, VA 24001, (703) 982-6270. Mount Rogers National Recreation Area, Route 1 Box 303, Marion, VA 24354, (703) 783-5196.

Description: The Mount Rogers Scenic Byway winds through forested areas and open countryside. Portions of U.S. Highway 58 are unsuitable for vehicles or trucks more than 35 feet long. The byway has moderately heavy traffic, with July and August the busiest months. The two-lane, paved route is lined by a diversity of established private farms and the more recently dedicated forest land set aside in 1966 for public recreational activities. The entire Jefferson National Forest encompasses more than 702,000 acres of valleys and rolling hills of the Blue Ridge Mountains.

Summer visitors can expect daytime temperatures of about 75 degrees, with nights in the 50s to 70s. Spring and autumn range from about 40 to 70 degrees, and winter temperatures may rise to 60 or plunge well below freezing.

Virginia Route 603 begins at Troutdale, where a population of 3,000 once thrived during the area's logging boom of the early 1900s. Troutdale was the home of author-publisher Sherwood Anderson, and the dwelling is now a historical monument open to visitors. Quietly reminiscent of its earlier heyday, Troutdale is a pleasant stopover as well as a good restocking point for campers in need of supplies.

The forest here is composed of typical eastern hardwoods, such as maples, oaks, walnuts, poplars, ashes, and locusts. Alpine meadows often sprout fraser firs and red spruces.

A multi-use area located in four-mile-long Fairwood Valley is at about 3,500 feet in elevation. Within this strikingly beautiful stretch of open pasture, wildflowers bloom year-round, horses and cattle graze, and fruit trees entice pickers to harvest their seasonal crops. Many miles of trails are devoted to the enjoyment of hikers and horseback riders.

Prior to 1900, Fairwood was the site of a large residential community of employees and officials of the Hassinger Lumber Company. Once a part of that community, the Fairwood Livery now offers seasonal horse rentals for rides into the high country of Pine Mountain (elevation 5,000 feet). One of the trails, the Virginia Highlands Horse Trail, provides 67 miles of riding paths and is accessible from the byway four miles west of Troutdale. Nearby is Fairwood Horse Camp, a camping area for those who bring their own horses.

The next two miles of byway will pass several trailheads. The Appalachian Trail crosses the byway at Fox Creek. The Lewis Fork Wilderness Trail lets hikers and cross-country skiers enjoy the seasonal variations of the forested landscape year-round. A third trailhead, six miles west of Troutdale, offers another path into the Lewis Fork Wilderness and connects with trails to Mount Rogers, at an elevation of 5,729 feet the highest peak in Virginia. The mountain is noted for its open meadows, abundant wildflowers, and extensive summit cover of spruces and firs.

In all, there are 450 miles of multi-use trails in the byway area, for hiking, bicycling, skiing, and horseback riding. The Appalachian Trail crosses the scenic byway three times and covers about 60 miles in the byway area.

Trout fishing in this byway area is some of the best in the southern Appalachians. There are native brook trout and stocked varieties of brook and rainbow trout. Thirty-five streams on the national forest are designated for native brook trout, and about 150 miles of streams have mixed trout species. Warm-water fishing for striped and largemouth bass is good in South Holsten Reservoir, just south of the byway. The New River on the east end of Mount Rogers National Recreation Area is considered excellent for smallmouth bass fishing.

Grindstone Campground has 108 sites and restrooms with showers. Also featured are a 400-seat amphitheater, the Whispering Waters Nature Trail, and several other paths that connect with the Appalachian and Mount Rogers trails. Other activities include swimming, trout fishing, and horseback riding.

Several miles west of Grindstone Campground, a side trip south on Virginia Route 600 and then west on Forest Road 89 leads to the summit of Whitetop Mountain. Whitetop derives its name from the snow or frost that sometimes covers its summit. From the summit, at 5,500 feet, you will have a spectacular

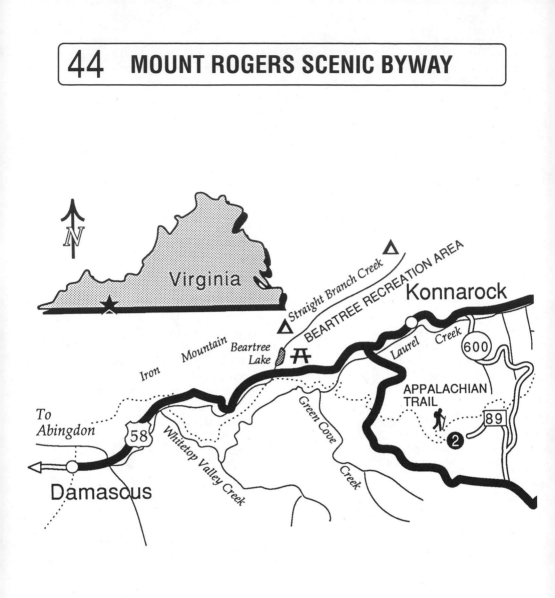

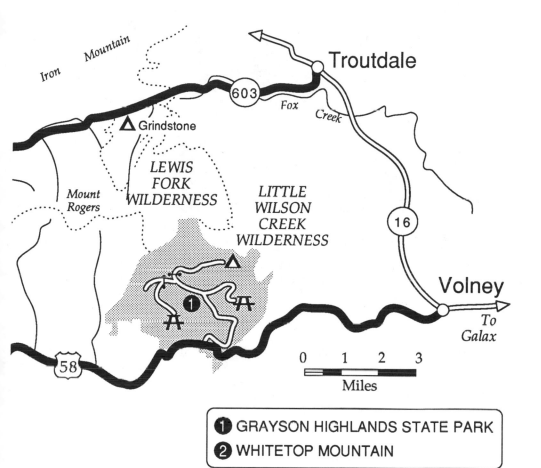

Iron Mountain

Troutdale

603

Fox Creek

△ Grindstone

16

LEWIS FORK WILDERNESS

LITTLE WILSON CREEK WILDERNESS

Mount Rogers

△

Volney

To Galax

58

0   1   2   3
Miles

❶ GRAYSON HIGHLANDS STATE PARK
❷ WHITETOP MOUNTAIN

Hikers on the Virginia Creeper National Recreation Trail cross this scenic railroad bridge in Mount Rogers National Recreation Area. Ken Haltenhoff photo.

view of Mount Rogers and vicinity. The landscape is unusual because it is the divide between geologic formations that show evidence of volcanic action, as well as oceanic and coastal sedimentation. Glaciation, continental uplift, and erosion are evident in the area.

Returning to the byway, you can replenish camping supplies in Konnarock. Historically reminiscent of the logging boom is the Lutheran Girls School, built during the late 1880s by the Hassinger Lumber Company. The school provided board and education for the daughters of loggers. Completely sided with chestnut bark, the school has weathered many years. It remained operational until the 1960s. The lumbermill remains, and period residences and a Lutheran church made entirely of stone are all historic attractions of this community.

This portion of the byway ends at the junction of Virginia Route 603 and U.S. Highway 58. The second segment of byway is on this adjacent stretch of U.S. Highway 58, between Damascus and Volney.

Beginning at Damascus, the byway winds through a mixed hardwood forest and pastures as it skirts the southern flanks of Whitetop Mountain, visible from various points along the route. The route parallels much of Straight Branch Creek, which provides good fishing. You can see portions of the old Virginia Creeper Railroad bed, now a National Recreation Trail that provides easy hiking and bicycling.

Beartree Campground features a lake with picnic facilities, swimming, boating, and fishing. The campground has 84 individual sites and 32 group sites. Wildlife viewing is a popular pastime. You may enjoy locating beaver ponds and watching the animals' busy routine. Other animals on the Jefferson National Forest include deer, foxes, turkeys, grouse, opossums, racoons, and skunks.

Grayson Highlands State Park is located near the terminus of the scenic byway, near Volney. This park provides good, year-round access to the high country of the Mount Rogers National Recreation Area, and it features seasonal cultural events that are regionally popular.—*Ken Haltenhoff* □

45 BIG WALKER MOUNTAIN SCENIC BYWAY
Jefferson National Forest   Virginia

General description: A paved, 16-mile open loop around and up Big Walker Mountain.

Special attractions: Trout fishing, southern Appalachian hardwood forest, wildflowers, diverse wildlife, scenic views, camping, hiking trails, historical Civil War site.

Location: Southwest Virginia on the Jefferson National Forest, northwest of Wytheville. From Wytheville, head northwest on Interstate 77, exiting at Exit 52 onto Virginia Route 717. The byway travels west on 717 to its junction with U.S. Highway 52 and then follows 52 back north and east to the interstate.

Byway route numbers: Virginia Route 717 and U.S. Highway 52.

Travel season: Year-round.

Camping: One national forest campground with bathhouses, picnic tables, fire grates, and drinking water.

Services: No services on the byway. All services in nearby Wytheville.

Nearby attractions: The Appalachian Trail, Mount Rogers Scenic Byway and National Recreation Area, Wytheville State Fish Hatchery, Rock House Museum in Wytheville.

For more information: Jefferson National Forest, 210 Franklin Road SW, Caller Service 2900, Roanoke, VA 24001, (703) 982-6270. District Ranger: Wytheville Ranger District, 1625 W. Lee Highway, Wytheville, VA 24382, (703) 228-5551.

Description: The Big Walker Mountain Scenic Byway, nestled in the southwestern arm of Virginia, is bordered by century-old stands of white pines, as well as southern Appalachian hardwoods such as oaks, hickories, hemlocks, chestnuts, redbuds, dogwoods, and a mix of Virginia, pitch and table mountain pines.

The byway ranges in elevation from 2,500 feet at each end to 4,000 feet at the Big Bend Picnic Area. Summers are hot, humid, and often rainy and overcast, with temperatures reaching 90 degrees. Fall temperatures are moderate, and there are extensive periods of rain and cloud cover. Winter is snowy, and the thermometer dips into the teens. Spring brings sunny days in the 50s and 60s.

From early spring through mid-July, you can see rhododendrons, mountain laurels, and wild azaleas in bloom. The forest explodes with other wildflowers, such as pink and yellow lady slippers, native orchids, and lobelias. Forest inhabitants include whitetail deer, wild turkeys, grouse, groundhogs, squirrels, cardinals, robins, bluejays, and a variety of songbirds.

Once ocean bottom, the area is primarily sedimentary rock, with large deposits of sandstone. The southern slopes of Big Walker and Little Walker mountains are gentle, while the northern slopes are quite steep and many strata are exposed. The soils, especially along Stony Fork Creek, are fertile but rocky. Early settlers devoted a great deal of time to rock removal before they could plant. At best, the soils supported kitchen gardens and limited grazing.

Settlement took place as early as the 1740s. This was the frontier, and settlers, building on traditional hunting lands, were subjected to frequent raids by Indians. Big Walker and Little Walker mountains were considered prime hunting lands, with plentiful deer and bear. Several tribes fought pitched battles for the right to hunt this section. The Shawnee likely were victorious; archaeological explorations have uncovered numerous Shawnee artifacts.

The byway is an open loop and can be traveled in either direction. If you start the byway tour from the junction of Interstate 77 and Virginia Route 717, you will travel in a clockwise direction. About one mile from the beginning of the byway is the trailhead for the Seven Sisters Hiking Trail (also open to mountain bikes). The trail is 4.3 miles long and terminates at Stony Fork Campground.

Just beyond the side road is the Astin homesite. Ollie and Buck Astin lived here and raised a family from the early 1900s through the 1970s. They cut pulp wood for sale, skidded logs with horses and mules, dug ginseng, and fed themselves and their children by cultivating a large garden and hunting wild game. All that remains of the homestead are the posts of an old pen, some fruit trees, and an overgrown blackberry patch. Deer can frequently be observed feasting on the berries.

Stony Fork Campground lies about four miles from the beginning of the byway. There are 53 sites and a trailer dump station nearby. A nature trail forms a 1-mile loop, and the trees and flowers along the way are identified. The East Fork of Stony Fork Creek runs through the campground, offering fishing, wading, and wildlife-watching opportunities. There are rainbow trout and panfish varieties such as sunfish and pumpkin seed fish in the creek.

Just beyond the campground, turn north onto U.S. Highway 52. A side trip on Virginia Route 686 leads west to Deer Trail Park Campground. The byway climbs Big Walker Mountain, ascending from 2,500 feet to 3,700 feet in less than three miles. Dry Gulch Junction is on the east, the skeleton of a defunct western-theme park. Deer are often seen moving through the tall grass past the boarded-up buildings.

Forest Road 206 makes a sharp intersection with the byway; the turn is difficult for large motor homes to navigate. The route leads four miles east to Big Bend Picnic Area, constructed in the 1930s by the Civilian Conservation Corps. From here, you have a view of the ridge and valley terrain to the south. There are picnic tables, grills, and fireplaces scattered in the orchard grass under a canopy of oaks. Vault toilets are provided.

Back on the byway, Big Walker Lookout is a privately owned 100-foot fire tower open to tourists for a fee. A platform to the right of the tower offers a magnificent view of the valley and surrounding ridges. A nearby plaque commemorates Toland's Raid and Molly Tynes. Colonel Toland commanded a force of Union troops bivouacked near Tazewell, Virginia, during the Civil War. It was common knowledge that he and his men planned to cross the

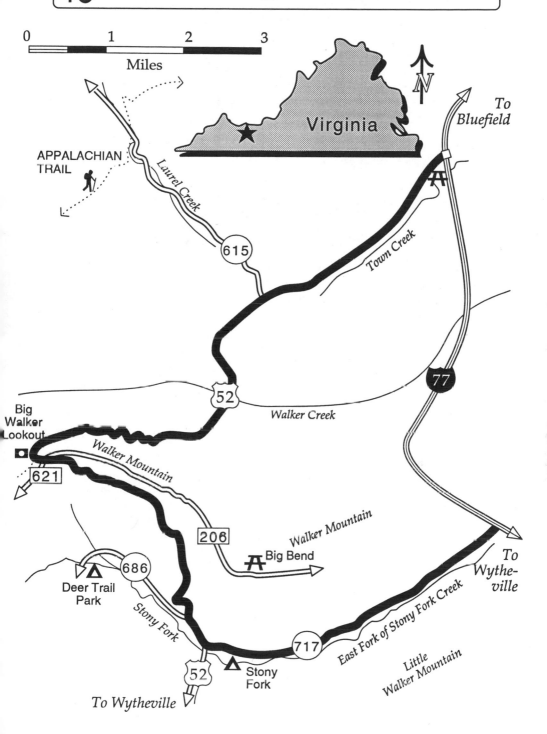

45 BIG WALKER MOUNTAIN SCENIC BYWAY

0   1   2   3

Miles

Virginia

To
Bluefield

APPALACHIAN
TRAIL

Laurel Creek

615

Town Creek

77

52

Walker Creek

Big
Walker
Lookout

Walker Mountain

621

206

Walker Mountain

Big Bend

686

Deer Trail
Park

Stony Fork

717

East Fork of Stony Fork Creek

Little
Walker Mountain

To
Wythe-
ville

52

Stony
Fork

To Wytheville

Travelers on Big Walker Mountain Scenic Byway enjoy far-ranging views over the rolling hills, fields, and forests of southwest Virginia. Jefferson National Forest photo.

mountains and capture the railroad depot at Wytheville. Young Molly Tynes took it upon herself to ride over the mountains and warn the citizenry of the impending raid. With no Confederate troops in the area, a group of Home Guards—older men, young boys, and a few women—turned out to defend the position. They repulsed the Union forces and killed Colonel Toland during the battle.

West of the lookout, the Walker Mountain Trail provides a 1-mile hike along the crest of Big Walker Mountain. This trail provides good views of the valley below.

About three miles down the mountain from the lookout, a historical marker notes the homesite of S.H. Newberry, a member of the "Big Four" in the Virginia Senate. It was this group that put an end to an influx of carpetbaggers and helped Virginia recover financially from the Civil War.

The byway traverses rolling fields planted in crops or used for grazing horses and cattle. Virginia Route 615 leads north to provide access to the Appalachian Trail. There are 79 miles of the Appalachian Trail within this ranger district. The byway ends at the intersection of U.S. Highway 52 and Interstate 77.—*Barbara Elliott* □

General description: A 79-mile loop through forest and countryside.

Special attractions: Cradle of Forestry in America, Pisgah State Fish Hatchery, Looking Glass Rock Scenic Area, Looking Glass Falls, Sliding Rock, Shining Rock and Middle Prong wilderness areas, hiking and nature trails, exceptional trout fishing, abundant wildlife, spring blossoms.

Location: Western North Carolina on the Pisgah National Forest and in Haywood and Transylvania counties, south of Asheville. The byway is a loop that travels from Brevard northwest on U.S. Highway 276, south on North Carolina Route 215, and northeast back to Brevard on U.S. Highway 64.

Byway route numbers: U.S. Highway 276, North Carolina Route 215, U.S. Highway 64.

Travel season: Year-round. Occasional snow and ice may require use of chains in winter.

Camping: Six national forest campgrounds, two for individual camping, four for groups. All have drinking water, picnic tables, fire grates, and toilets. Some with showers and trailer dumping station. Suitable for tents, truck campers, and trailers less than 16 feet in length. No hookups. Campgrounds generally open from April through November.

Services: All services in Brevard and in nearby communities of Balsam Grove, Canton, Rosman, and Waynesville.

Nearby attractions: Blue Ridge Parkway, Folk Art Center and Biltmore House in Asheville, Brevard Music Center, Carl Sandburg Home National Historic Site, Flat Rock State Theater near Hendersonville.

For more information: National Forests in North Carolina, P.O. Box 2750, Asheville, NC 28802, (704) 257-4200. District Ranger: Pisgah Ranger District, 1001 Pisgah Highway, Pisgah Forest, NC 28768, (704) 877-3265.

Description: North Carolina's first scenic byway provides a sampling of some of the state's best mountain scenery. The route passes through dense forests of conifers and hardwoods, along bold mountain trout streams, through picturesque farmlands, and across high mountain ridges. Part of the route follows old settlement roads and logging railroads that were developed in the late 1800s and early 1900s.

Much of the forest in this area was heavily logged in the early 1900s, but recovery has been so complete that today the forest looks nearly untouched. It is composed primarily of oaks, yellow poplars, and birches. Forest inhabitants include deer, black bears, gray squirrels, groundhogs, wild turkeys, gray foxes, and oppossums.

Elevations range from a low of 2,230 feet at Brevard to more than 5,340 feet where the byway crosses the Blue Ridge Parkway at Beech Gap.

Western North Carolina has four distinct seasons. Summers and winters are moderate. Even the hottest months seldom reach the 90s. But watch for sudden and severe thunderstorms during late summer. Foliage is at its most colorful around the second and third weeks of October, sometimes lasting until early November. The area has occasional snow and ice during the winter, but winter storms are usually short-lived.

The Pisgah District is one of the most popular areas in the state, and traffic can be heavy, particularly in summer and during the fall color season. The paved highways are steep and winding with frequent sharp curves. Pisgah is the biblical name of the mountain from which Moses saw the promised land, and the name was probably introduced here by a local pastor in the late 1700s.

Anglers can choose from several excellent trout streams. The upper section of the Davidson River was rated by *Trout* magazine as one of the 100 best streams in America. Limited to fly fishing, the stream is renowned for its hefty populations of brown and rainbow trout. The lower section below Avery Creek has brown, brook, and rainbow trout. The East Fork of the Pigeon River, a native brook-trout stream, also offers excellent fishing.

The only large developed area on the byway is the city of Brevard, county seat of Transylvania County. Established in 1861, the city is the home of Brevard College and the Brevard Music Center, one of the nation's leading summer music camps. The music center offers more than 50 musical programs and public concerts from mid-June to mid-August, with everything from classical music and pops concerts to operas and Broadway musicals.

Although there are several access points, the official beginning of the scenic byway is on U.S. Highway 276 near Brevard, a few hundred feet beyond the stone columns that mark the entrance to Pisgah National Forest. An exhibit contains a map that highlights points of interest along the route. Brochures, maps, and information about area attractions are available about a mile farther up U.S. Highway 276 at the ranger station-visitor center. A side road just beyond the visitor center leads to English Chapel, a Methodist church founded in 1869 and still used by area residents and visitors. It is the only structure that remains of a small community that used to be in the area.

Sycamore Flats is a large picnic area on the banks of the Davidson River. You can wade in the river and enjoy the shade of the numerous sycamore trees that grow along the bank.

Davidson River Campground, with 161 forested or grassy sites, is the largest and busiest camping area along the byway. Davidson has hot showers and a trailer dumping station.

About five miles west of the starting point, a side trip on Forest Road 475 follows the Davidson River away from U.S. Highway 276 and leads to the Pisgah State Fish Hatchery, open daily for tours. The state Wildlife Resources Commission operates the hatchery and raises thousands of rainbow, brook, and brown trout from eggs. When the trout are between seven and nine inches long, they are released in general trout waters throughout the western part of the state.

Several hiking trails are accessible from Forest Road 475. Your best bet is the 3.1-mile trail that leads to the summit of Looking Glass Rock, a granite monolith that glistens with seeping groundwater. In winter, the water freezes on the rock's smooth face and reflects the sun like a mirror, or looking glass. Views from the top of the rock are spectacular and include Cedar Rock, the Blue Ridge Parkway, and the Pink Beds.

Peregrine falcons were reintroduced to this area, and in summer they nest and raise their young on the rock cliffs of Looking Glass Rock. You may also see an occasional golden eagle soaring overhead.

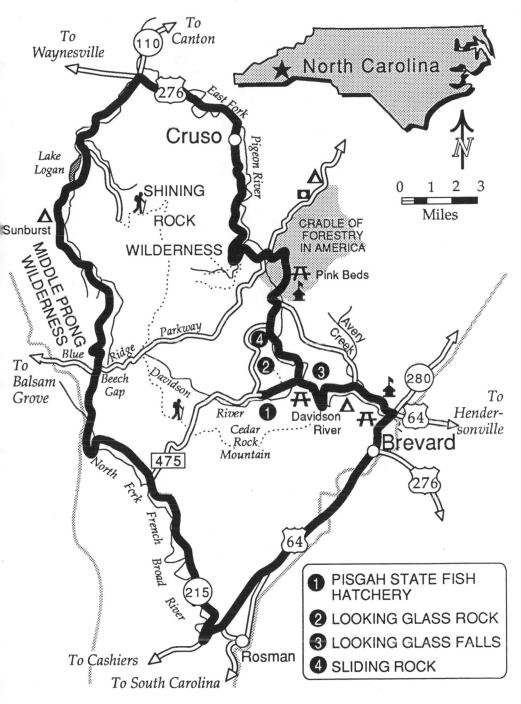

46 FOREST HERITAGE SCENIC BYWAY

To Waynesville

To Canton

110

276

East Fork

Cruso

Pigeon River

North Carolina

★

N

0 1 2 3
Miles

Lake Logan

SHINING ROCK WILDERNESS

Sunburst

MIDDLE PRONG WILDERNESS

CRADLE OF FORESTRY IN AMERICA

Pink Beds

Parkway

Blue Ridge

Beech Gap

Davidson

4

Avery Creek

2

3

280

To Balsam Grove

River

Cedar Rock Mountain

1

Davidson River

64

To Hendersonville

475

North Fork French Broad River

Brevard

64

276

215

To Cashiers

Rosman

To South Carolina

❶ PISGAH STATE FISH HATCHERY

❷ LOOKING GLASS ROCK

❸ LOOKING GLASS FALLS

❹ SLIDING ROCK

Sliding Rock gives visitors a wet thrill along the Forest Heritage Scenic Byway. Robert B. Satterwhite photo.

Just beyond the fish hatchery road is Looking Glass Falls—one of the most scenic and best-known falls in the eastern United States. Water tumbles over a massive overhanging shelf about 30 feet wide into a deep pool 60 feet below. You can park and walk to the bottom of the falls via stairs.

At Sliding Rock, the next stop on the byway, a sheet of water cascades over a 60-foot-long, gently sloping, slick-as-glass rock, creating a natural water slide. Watch from an observation deck, or don cutoffs and a T-shirt and join the hundreds of others on the slide. It's hard to resist. Be prepared for a breathtaking plunge into the icy pool at the bottom of the falls. The water is cold even during the hottest months. The slide is open from Memorial Day through Labor Day. There is a bathhouse, and lifeguards are on duty from 10 a.m. to 5:30 p.m. daily.

The Cradle of Forestry in America is a National Historic Site that commemorates the birthplace of scientific forestry and forestry education in the United States. This area, located just beyond Sliding Rock, has a visitor center, exhibits, interpretive film show, gift shop, snack bar, and two walking trails. The Biltmore Forest School Campus Trail is a one-mile paved path that goes by the restored and reconstructed buildings used by the first forestry students at the turn of the century. The Forest Festival Trail, also paved and one mile long, features early 1900s forestry exhibits, including a 1915 Climax logging locomotive and steam-powered sawmill. The Cradle of Forestry is open May through October from 10 a.m. to 6 p.m. A nominal entrance fee is charged.

The last major point of interest on U.S. Highway 276 is the Pink Beds Picnic Area. This mountain valley is covered with thick growths of native rhododendrons, mountain laurels, and flame azaleas. Blooming season runs from spring to summer, with peak bloom time in June. Visitors come from miles around to marvel at the splendid display of floral blossoms.

The byway continues northwest on U.S. Highway 276 and intersects the Blue Ridge Parkway. Below the parkway, the route crosses the East Fork of the Pigeon River, where a trailhead offers three footpaths into the Shining Rock Wilderness. The byway leaves the national forest and descends along the East Fork of the Pigeon River to Cruso, a small mountain community in Haywood County. According to local legend, the area was named by the community's first postmaster who had just read *Robinson Crusoe.*

A few miles beyond Cruso, the Forest Heritage Scenic Byway loops south on North Carolina Route 215, still following the river. Lake Logan was created in 1932 to supply water to the papermill. It is privately owned. A few miles farther, Sunburst Campground is located right on the river. Sunburst has drinking water, picnicking, hiking, and fishing.

Past Sunburst, the byway passes between the Middle Prong and Shining Rock wilderness areas, which were logged in the 1920s. Major forest fires in 1925 and 1942 burned extensive acreage. Today the region is covered with small trees and rhododendrons.

The highway climbs past several pretty waterfalls along the West Fork of the Pigeon River to Beech Gap, elevation 5,340 feet. Here the byway again passes under the Blue Ridge Parkway. Views along this section are spectacular, but the road is winding and has few pulloffs.

Beyond Beech Gap, the road follows the North Fork of the French Broad River through mountain pastures and forest. Several area trout farms supply fish to restaurants. South of the Blue Ridge Parkway, Alligator Rock juts over the byway, and North Carolina Route 215 ends at its junction with U.S. Highway 64. Travel north on U.S. Highway 64 through the countryside to Brevard. The byway passes through the middle of town, past the courthouse and Brevard College campus. Traveling just a few miles north then completes the scenic byway loop.—*Robert B. Satterwhite* □

47 OCOEE SCENIC BYWAY
Cherokee National Forest   Tennessee

General description: A 26-mile route past a lake and through the rock bluffs of the Ocoee River Gorge, with a side trip up Chilhowee Mountain.

Special attractions: White-water rafting, excellent fishing, lakes, hiking trails.

Location: Southeast Tennessee on the Cherokee National Forest, east of Cleveland. The byway follows U.S. Highway 64 on national forest lands between Cleveland and Ducktown, and it includes Forest Road 77, a spur road from Highway 64 north to Chilhowee Recreation Area.

Byway route numbers: U.S. Highway 64 and Forest Road 77.

Travel season: Year-round. Roads can be extremely icy in winter.

Camping: Two national forest campgrounds with showers, restrooms, picnic tables, and water. One with a trailer dumping station. Campgrounds open April 4 through mid-November. No hookups.

Services: All services in Cleveland. Marina, food, phone, and lodging at Lake

Ocoee and Ducktown, plus several small grocery stores with gas along U.S. Highway 64.

Nearby attractions: Red Clay State Park, Hiwassee State Scenic River, Appalachian Mountains.

For more information: Cherokee National Forest, 2800 N. Ocoee St., P.O. Box 2010, Cleveland, TN 37320, (615) 476-9700. Ranger District: Ocoee Ranger District, Route 1 Box 348D, Benton, TN 37307, (615) 338-5201.

Description: Ocoee Scenic Byway was the first designated national forest scenic byway in the nation. U.S. Highway 64, two-lane and paved, winds through the Ocoee River Gorge, and the byway includes a spur trip up Chilhowee Mountain on Forest Road 77 to Chilhowee Recreation Area. Vistas from several turnouts are exceptional. Traffic on Highway 64 can be heavy, particularly in the summer. Elevations range from 838 feet at Lake Ocoee to 2,200 feet at Chilhowee Recreation Area.

Summer visitors can expect variable weather, with temperatures ranging from the mid-70s to the mid-90s. The area is humid and has an average annual rainfall of 52.6 inches.

Cleveland, 15 miles west of the byway, is a mostly industrial city of 29,400 people. Driving east from Cleveland, your view includes Big Frog Mountain in the background and Chilhowee and Sugarloaf mountains in the foreground. The first overlook is on the dam that creates Ocoee, also called Parksville Lake. The 1,950-acre lake is entirely surrounded by national forest. It has a marina, swimming beaches, campsites, a boat launch, fishing, hiking trails, and drinking water available.

Ocoee Inn and Marina has boat gas, food, phone, and lodging. Nearby Parksville Beach, at the lake's edge, offers restrooms, open grassy areas and shady benches.

About midway down the lake, just east of the Ocoee Ranger Station, you can turn north on Forest Road 77. A steady three-mile climb leads through a forest of shortleaf and Virginia pines; scarlet, chestnut, and red oaks; dogwoods; maples; sourwoods; and black locusts. As this spur road climbs Chilhowee Mountain, the views change from tunnel-like corridors to magnificent vistas. Parksville Lake, Sugarloaf, and Gazebo overlooks afford you views that stretch more than 40 miles west across the Tennessee Valley to the Cumberland Mountains and 15 miles south into the Cohutta Mountains of Georgia. Parksville Lake Overlook has a short loop trail that provides an opportunity for easy day hiking. Sugarloaf Overlook has barrier-free picnic tables.

A visitor to Chilhowee Overlook 125 years ago could have witnessed armies marching toward one of the most decisive conflicts of the Civil War at Chattanooga. A sign at this overlook provides more information. A Civil War interpretive site, where evidence of an 1865 skirmish was found, is also along this spur road. Farther along, Gazebo Overlook was built during the Depression by the Civilian Conservation Corps. The overlook provides shelter from which to look out toward Benton.

The Chilhowee Recreation Area has a large campground with 88 sites. There is a small lake for fishing and swimming, a picnic area, amphitheater, and hiking and bicycling trails. The half-mile Forest Walk Interpretive Trail leads through this area rich in Cherokee Indian history. Other trails lead to Benton Falls, and one passes the edge of the Rock Creek Gorge Scenic Area.

Rafters prepare to launch on the white-water stretch of the Ocoee River, adjacent to the Ocoee Scenic Byway. Dan Cook photo.

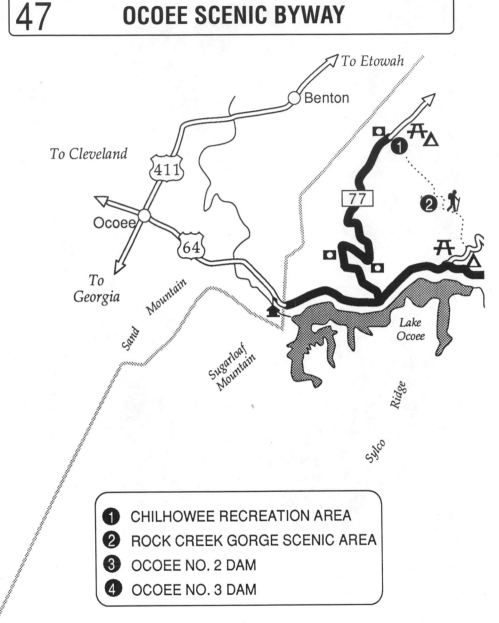

1   CHILHOWEE RECREATION AREA
2   ROCK CREEK GORGE SCENIC AREA
3   OCOEE NO. 2 DAM
4   OCOEE NO. 3 DAM

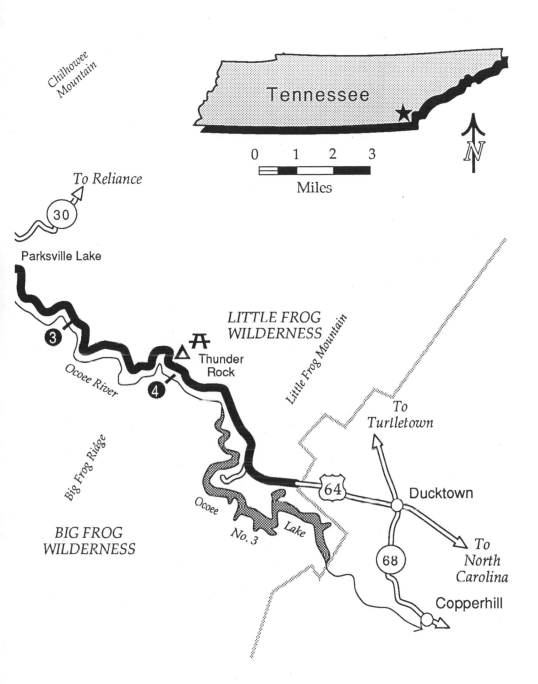

Chilhowee
Mountain

Tennessee

0   1   2   3

Miles

N

To Reliance

30

Parksville Lake

LITTLE FROG
WILDERNESS

Little Frog Mountain

3

Ocoee River

Thunder
Rock

4

To
Turtletown

Big Frog Ridge

Ocoee

No. 3   Lake

64   Ducktown

BIG FROG
WILDERNESS

68

To
North
Carolina

Copperhill

Hikers should be on the lookout for wildlife. Some of the more commonly seen animals are whitetail deer, black bears, raccoons, opossums, beavers, wild turkeys, chipmunks, and squirrels.

Flora in the Chilhowee area includes pink lady slippers, sky-blue dwarf irises, white wood anemones, pink-tinged trailing arbutuses, and bright red berries of Jack-in-the-pulpits.

The area traversed by the Ocoee Scenic Byway is characterized by numerous elongated ridges with intervening valleys, all trending in a northeast-southwest direction. This is the result of folding and fracturing that took place during a mountain-building episode 230 to 260 million years ago. The rocks are metamorphic and most visible in the gorge section of the byway.

Returning to U.S. Highway 64, continue east and take advantage of several scenic pullouts along the lake. There is a boat ramp, then picnicking, swimming beaches, drinking water, and toilets at Mac Point, encountered just before the highway enters the Ocoee River Gorge. The rock cliffs make a striking background for the Ocoee River, which is a premier location for white-water rafting and kayaking from late March until early November. The byway through the gorge is very congested on summer weekends.

The six-mile gorge section of the byway is characterized by rock outcrops, cliffs, and colorful foliage in autumn. The road is quite narrow, but has some pullouts for safe viewing of the natural features and for watching river activities. Continuing east, the byway passes a rafting put-in and a flume line diversion dam.

The Tennessee Valley Authority No. 2 powerhouse is located just east of the rafting take-out point near Thunder Rock Campground. Tennessee Power Company constructed a hydroelectric power complex in the gorge around 1912, TVA took it over in 1939, and the entire complex is now on the National Register of Historic Places. Look for the flume which snakes its way around the bluffs of the gorge for almost five miles.

Upon leaving the gorge, the byway passes another powerhouse. This one is fed by a large pipe that carries water through an underground tunnel from a reservoir tucked into the mountains more than two miles away. The byway passes the dry streambed of the Ocoee River on the south and the Little Frog Wilderness on the north. Boyd Gap has an overlook from which you can see the Big Frog Wilderness Area.

Ducktown and Copperhill, both linked to the copper-mining industry of the past, are located on the eastern end of the byway. The old Copper Road through Ocoee River Gorge was completed in 1853 and used for transporting the high-grade ore in horse-drawn wagons to the railhead in Cleveland. The ore was the primary source of copper for the Confederacy during the Civil War. A smelter in the vicinity of Ducktown and Copperhill was established in 1878 and is now a museum. From the museum, you can see lunar-like Copper Basin. In the distance is Copperhill and the more modern smelter's stacks. The background mountains are on the Chattahoochee National Forest in Georgia.—*Dan Cook* □

General description: A 38-mile loop alongside streams and waterfalls and through forested hills to the top of Brasstown Bald, the highest mountain in Georgia, and then down again.

Special attractions: Colorful autumn foliage, outstanding views, a scenic Bavarian-style town, Brasstown Wilderness, Raven Cliff Wilderness, mountain streams, waterfalls.

Location: North Georgia on the Chattahoochee National Forest, northwest of Toccoa. The byway is a loop that follows Georgia Route 17/75 from Helen north to an intersection with Georgia Route 180 near High Shoals, turns west on Route 180 to its intersection with Georgia Route 348, and then goes south on 348 back to Helen.

Byway route numbers: Georgia Routes 17/75, 180, and 348.

Travel season: Year-round, with occasional temporary closures for winter snow removal.

Camping: One national forest campground with drinking water, toilets, picnic tables, and fire grates. No hookups. Two nearby state parks with more than 180 sites, hiking trails, picnic tables, fire grates, toilets, drinking water, hookups, and a trailer dumping station.

Services: All services in Helen and in nearby Blairsville, Cleveland, and Hiawassee.

Nearby attractions: Anna Ruby Falls, Hiawassee drama and country shows, Lake Chatuge, Lake Winfield Scott, Track Rock Gap, Unicoi and Vogel state parks.

For more information: Chattahoochee National Forest, 508 Oak St., Gainesville, GA 30501, (404) 536-0541. District Rangers: Brasstown Ranger District, P.O. Box 9, Highways 19 and 129 South, Blairsville, GA 30512, (706) 745-6928; Chattooga Ranger District, P.O. Box 196, Clarkesville, GA 30523, (706) 754-6221.

Description: Showcasing some of the most spectacular and diverse scenery in Georgia, the popular, paved Russell-Brasstown loop lies entirely within the Chattahoochee National Forest.

Expect temperatures ranging from as high as 95 degrees in summer to as low as zero in winter. The weather on Brasstown Bald and the peaks along Russell Highway (Georgia Route 348) is more severe; the highest recorded temperature was 84 degrees and the lowest a frigid minus 27 degrees.

The scenery is exceptional throughout the route. Travel along the Richard Russell Highway portion is fairly light except in autumn, when colorful leaves draw spectators in droves. Other portions of the roadway are regularly traveled highways. Elevations vary from 1,600 feet to Brasstown Bald's 4,784 feet.

The route begins at fairy-tale-like Helen, a cocoon-to-butterfly story of ingenuity on the part of its citizenry. Once a sleepy sawmill town, it underwent a transformation in the 1960s. Buildings were given a Bavarian look, and tourism increased in this pretty mountain community.

The headwaters of the Chattahoochee River, which flows south to the Gulf of Mexico, are located near Helen. The river, generally crystal-clear, provides

Mountain music entertains visitors at the gift shop in the Brasstown Bald parking lot.
Dan Cook photo.

top-notch trout fishing downtown. A trout festival is one of several annual Helen events.

Unicoi State Park is three miles north of Helen via Georgia Routes 75 and 356. This is a delightful side trip from the scenic byway. The park has 80 campsites. Just above the park, in the Chattahoochee National Forest, you can reach Anna Ruby Falls via an easy, paved half-mile footpath from the visitor center. An observation deck offers a striking view of the twin falls of York and Curtis creeks. It is surrounded by a 1,600-acre scenic area.

Driving north along winding Georgia Routes 17/75, you will see beautiful views of forested hills and mountains. Andrews Cove, five miles north of Helen along Andrews Creek, has camping, fishing, and hiking. Five miles farther north, out-of-the-way High Shoals Scenic Area has a one-mile hike past five waterfalls.

Fauna of the Chattahoochee National Forest includes whitetail deer, black bears, wild turkeys, opossums, grouse, squirrels, foxes, groundhogs, and raccoons. Flora includes rhododendrons, mountain laurels, flame azaleas, dogwoods, serviceberries, sourwoods, and many species of wildflowers. Tree species range from sturdy pines, poplars, and hemlocks to majestic oaks.

Less than half a mile north of the High Shoals turnoff, the byway turns west onto Georgia Route 180. Six miles away is the intersection of 180 and Georgia 180 spur, a 2.5-mile steep route leading to the Brasstown Bald fee parking lot. The interpretive bookstore there is open seven days a week from Memorial Day through October. You have the option of either hiking the steep trail half a mile to the visitor center atop the mountain or paying a small fee to take a shuttle. The visitor center has a slide program and interpretive exhibits that tell about the area, as well as an observation deck with a view of four states.

Short day-hiking opportunities include two trails that leave from the parking lot: the 4.5-mile Jack Knob Trail leads to the Appalachian Trail at Chattahoochee Gap, and the 5.5-mile Arkaquah Trail goes west to Track Rock Road. Both trails are moderately difficult.

The name Brasstown Bald is derived from the Cherokee Indian word itse'ye. It means "new green place" or "place of fresh green." It applied particularly to a tract of ground made green by fresh vegetation after having been cleared of timber.

Geologists believe this section of the Blue Ridge Mountains is more than 300 million years old—older than the Rockies. On the north side of Brasstown Bald are communities with a distinct geologic substrate—fields of angular rock or blocks of rock with little visible subsoil. The large, angular boulders were split by the action of glaciers in the Pleistocene age. The areas, mostly north-facing, may date back at least 10,000 years.

A number of "balds," a description for treeless mountaintops of the area, stirred Indian thoughts. According to legend, a terrible monster disturbed the peaceful Cherokee nation long ago. It carried away the children of the villages, and the Indians were unable to capture or kill the beast. They cleared the mountaintops of all timber in order to observe the flight of the beast. Later the den of the marauder was located in the cliffs of a mountain. Two braves ascended the tallest hemlocks and were horrified to observe the brood of young beasts to which the monster had been feeding the children. The Indians then sought the aid of the Great Spirit, who sent down a bolt of lightning to destroy the monster and its brood. The Indians offered thanks to the Great Spirit and

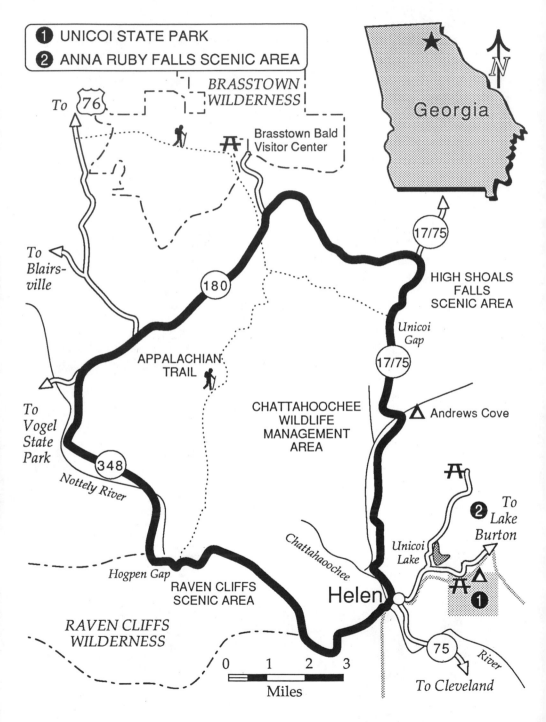

48 RUSSELL-BRASSTOWN SCENIC BYWAY

① UNICOI STATE PARK
② ANNA RUBY FALLS SCENIC AREA

BRASSTOWN WILDERNESS

To 76

Brasstown Bald Visitor Center

Georgia

To Blairsville

180

17/75

HIGH SHOALS FALLS SCENIC AREA

Unicoi Gap

17/75

APPALACHIAN TRAIL

Andrews Cove

To Vogel State Park

348

Nottely River

CHATTAHOOCHEE WILDLIFE MANAGEMENT AREA

② To Lake Burton

Unicoi Lake

Chattahoochee

①

Hogpen Gap

RAVEN CLIFFS SCENIC AREA

Helen

RAVEN CLIFFS WILDERNESS

0   1   2   3
Miles

75

To Cleveland

River

in turn received a promise that never again would the mountaintops be covered with timber.

Returning from Brasstown to Georgia Route 180, the route west provides some lovely pastoral views for eight miles before connecting with the Richard Russell Scenic Highway, Georgia Route 348. The first four miles travel south through farm county on the headwaters of the Nottely River. After reaching the national forest boundary, the byway proceeds up the mountains to Hogpen Gap, which is the Blue Ridge Divide separating the water draining into the Tennessee River on the west and the Chattahoochee on the east. Stop at the overlook on the north side of the road just before the top for a view of the visitor center atop Brasstown Bald. The drainage just below is called Lordamercy Cove for its steep and rugged landscape.

The Appalachian Trail, a 2,100-mile footpath from Georgia to Maine, crosses the byway at Hogpen Gap. It also crosses the byway between Helen and Hiawassee at Unicoi Gap.

The remaining segment of the scenic byway follows Georgia Route 348 east toward Helen. The national forest land on the south side of the highway is part of the Raven Cliff Wilderness Area. Several fine day hikes are accessible. Raven Cliff Trail goes 2.5 miles into the wilderness area to Raven Cliff Falls; the hike is moderately difficult. The Dukes Creek Falls Trail winds .8 mile from the parking lot into Dukes Creek Gorge to the falls. This trail is steep.

Complete the byway loop by returning to the town of Helen.—*Dan Cook* □

49 OSCAR WIGGINGTON MEMORIAL SCENIC BYWAY
Sumter National Forest   South Carolina

General description: A 14-mile highway through the wooded foothills of the Blue Ridge Mountains.
Special attractions: Excellent trout fishing, National Wild and Scenic Chattooga River, hunting, trout hatchery, Ellicott Rock Wilderness, scenic waterfalls, hiking trails, Oconee State Park.
Location: Northwest corner of South Carolina on the Sumter National Forest, east of Greenville. The byway begins at the Oscar State Park and runs north to the South Carolina-North Carolina state line.
Byway route number: South Carolina Route 107 and S.C. 413.
Travel season: Year-round. Occasional temporary closure for ice, generally in January or February.
Camping: One national forest campground with picnic tables, fire grates, and flush toilets. One state park with 140 sites and hookups. Additional national forest campgrounds nearby.
Services: Groceries and gift shop in Oconee State Park. All services in nearby Walhalla, Seneca, and Clemson, and in Cashiers, North Carolina.
Nearby attractions: Lakes Jocassee, Keowee, and Hartwell; Clemson University; Whitewater Falls; Cherokee Foothills Scenic Highway; abandoned railroad tunnel.
For more information: Sumter National Forest, 1835 Assembly St., 3rd floor,

Strom Thurmond Federal Building, Columbia, SC 29201, (803) 765-5222. District Ranger: Andrew Pickens Ranger District, Star Route, Walhalla, SC 29691, (803) 638-9568. Oconee State Park, Star Route, Walhalla, SC 29691, (803) 638-5353.

Description: Located in the extreme northwest corner of South Carolina in the gentle foothills of the Blue Ridge Mountains, the Oscar Wiggington Scenic Byway is known as the gateway to the mountains. The paved, easy-to-drive two-lane road ascends from 1,778 feet to 2,900 feet, and it has frequent scenic turnouts and recreational opportunities.

This area is cooler and wetter on a year-round basis than the adjoining Piedmont section of South Carolina. From December through March, low temperatures average in the 20s and highs in the 50s. April, May, and October have temperatures in the 40s through 70s, and June through September average in the 60s to 90s. Expect rain on 87 days of the year, with January, February, March, and July the wettest months.

In the early days, Cherokee warriors came through the area on their way to conquer the Piedmont tribes. The high plateaus and mountains were the last strongholds of the Cherokees in South Carolina before they moved out in 1792, after signing a peace treaty.

The Sumter National Forest boundary is north of Walhalla on Route 28. At the boundary, you will find the Stumphouse Ranger Station, which has visitor information, and the Stumphouse Tunnel and Park. You can walk 1,600 feet into the pre-Civil War, never-completed railroad tunnel as it winds into the solid granite mountain. It was abandoned in the 1850s due to lack of money. The tunnel was used at one time by South Carolina's famous agricultural college, Clemson University, to cure the renowned Clemson Bleu Cheese. Walls of the curing room are still visible. The tunnel and adjacent park are on the National Register of Historic Places.

Near the tunnel is Issaqueena Falls, rich in Indian legend, and a pleasant five-mile hiking trail along an abandoned railroad bed.

Two miles north of the ranger station, turn north onto South Carolina Route 107. Two more miles lead to Oconee State Park and the beginning of the scenic byway. Oconee State Park is one of the gems of the South Carolina state park system. Tucked away in wooded areas that border a crystal-clear, 20-acre lake fed by two cool mountain streams are family rental cabins and a 140-site campground. All campsites have water and electrical hookups and modern restrooms with hot showers. A store at the entrance to the camping area has groceries, film, souvenirs, and camping supplies. Square-dancing, clogging, nature trails, and programs by park naturalists highlight park activities.

The forests here are composed predominantly of white and loblolly pines, hickories, and red and white oaks. During the autumn, the byway is crowded with visitors who come to view the vivid foliage colors. Peak viewing is around mid-October. Spring visitors are attracted to the showy display of flowering mountain laurels, dogwoods, and rosebay and catawba rhododendrons.

Birdwatchers enjoy spotting red-tailed, sharp-shinned, and Cooper's hawks, American kestrels, bluebirds, mockingbirds, Carolina wrens, wood thrushes, and cardinals. Wildflowers include trilliums, sunflowers, asters, butterfly weeds, and fawn's breath.

Visitors are welcome to view the operations at Walhalla National Fish Hatchery, along South Carolina State Highway 107. Larry Cribb photo.

A side trip on Tamassee Road follows an old trail used by the Cherokees to get to Lake Cherokee. This is also one of the points where the Foothills Trail crosses Highway 107. This 43.3-mile hiking trail rambles across the upper part of South Carolina and links Oconee State Park with Table Rock State Park via Whitewater Falls. It crosses some of the most rugged, beautiful terrain in the Carolinas.

Cherry Hill Campground has 22 sites in the trees and a bathhouse, drinking water, fishing and hiking opportunities, picnic tables, fire grates, and a trailer dumping station.

A half-mile farther is Moody Springs Recreation Area. In addition to the picnic grounds and toilet facilities, there is a spring that some local people believe has medicinal properties.

A side trip on Burrells Ford Road leads three miles to a shallow portion of the Chattooga River, where a wagon road crossed the river. The powerful Chattooga, which has been designated a National Wild and Scenic River, descends almost 2,500 feet in its 50-mile length. The river is the western boundary of the Sumter National Forest and the state line between South Carolina and Georgia. There is excellent fishing for brown and rainbow trout, challenging boating and rafting, and beautiful hiking trails along the banks. Floating is permitted on a 28-mile stretch of the river. Information on canoe rentals and guided trips is available at the ranger station.

Part of the Appalachian Chain, the Blue Ridge Mountains were formed some 320 million years ago when the continental plate that contained Africa collided with the continental plate that contained North America. The collision thrust a section of the earth's crust skyward to form mountains that were as high and majestic as today's Himalayas. For the past 200 million years, these plates have been pulling apart and the Appalachian Mountains gradually

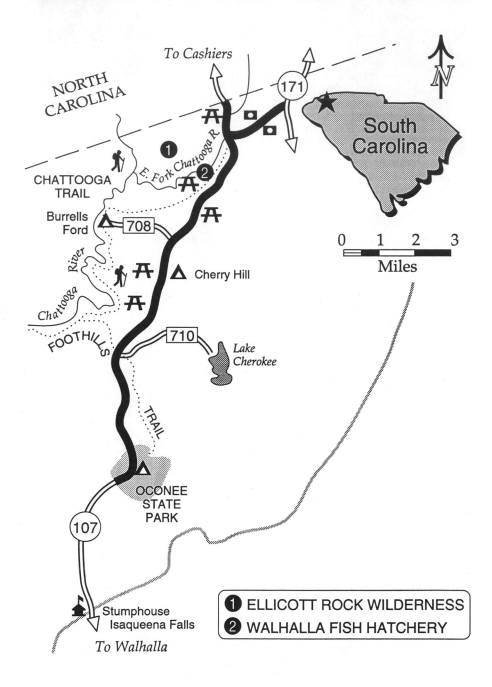

To Cashiers

171

NORTH CAROLINA

N

South Carolina

1

E. Fork Chattooga R.

2

CHATTOOGA TRAIL

Burrells Ford

708

Chattooga River

Cherry Hill

FOOTHILLS

710

Lake Cherokee

0 1 2 3
Miles

TRAIL

OCONEE STATE PARK

107

Stumphouse Isaqueena Falls

To Walhalla

1 ELLICOTT ROCK WILDERNESS
2 WALHALLA FISH HATCHERY

wearing away. This pulling apart has also formed the Atlantic Ocean. There are igneous and metamorphic rocks here, such as mica schist and granitic gneiss.

Burrell's Place is a roadside picnic area, and a mile farther is the entrance to the Walhalla National Fish Hatchery and the Chattooga Picnic Area. The winding two-mile road down the side of the mountain features exciting hairpin turns and an excellent look at the forest. Near the parking lot, a footbridge leads over the East Fork of the Chattooga to the fish hatchery, where you can see brood stock of rainbow and brown trout. The hatchery raises millions of trout fingerlings annually, and the U.S. Fish and Wildlife Service stocks streams in South Carolina, North Carolina, and Georgia with these fish.

Another path out of the hatchery parking lot leads into Ellicott Rock Wilderness, which contains giant old-growth eastern hemlocks and white pines. Some tower more than 200 feet high. Rhododendrons and mountain laurels abound, and the forest feels much like a rain forest. On a summer day, it can be 15 to 20 degrees cooler here than in the surrounding territory.

This trail gives the opportunity to journey a quarter-mile into real wilderness. The Ellicott Rock Wilderness was named for a surveyor hired to locate the disputed border for South Carolina, North Carolina, and Georgia. In 1811, he chiseled his mark in a rock at the survey's ending point on the South Carolina bank of the river. The trail runs right along the beautiful stream that is the East Fork of the Chattooga River.

A breathtaking view is available at the Wiggington Cutoff. Two overlooks about a quarter-mile off the byway are high above Lake Jocassee. About three miles farther down the side road, you reach pretty Whitewater Falls.

Sloan Bridge Recreation Area is the last picnic area on the byway before the South Carolina-North Carolina state line. South Carolina Highway 107 travels through a beautiful mountain landscape and offers a look at the mountain culture of the lower Appalachian Mountains.—*Larry Cribb* □

---

50 APALACHEE SAVANNAHS SCENIC BYWAY
Apalachicola National Forest *Florida*

General description: A 31-mile paved highway through pine forest, riverine systems, and savannahs.

Special attractions: Camping, hunting, fishing, abundant wildlife, wildflowers, unusual plants, Fort Gadsden State Park.

Location: Northwest Florida on the Apalachicola National Forest, south of Chattahoochee. The byway follows County Road 12 from the national forest boundary south of Bristol south to its intersection with County Road 379, then 379 south to Sumatra, and south again on Florida Route 65. The byway ends just north of Buck Siding at the national forest boundary.

Byway route numbers: County Roads 12 and 379, Florida Route 65.

Travel season: Year-round.

Camping: One state park and three national forest campgrounds with water, picnic tables, fire grates, and flush toilets. No hookups.

Services: All services in Bristol, Blountstown, Apalachicola, Eastpoint, and Carrabelle.

Nearby attractions: Torreya State Park, historic Gregory Home, Apalachicola River, Mud Swamp-New River Wilderness, Bradwell Bay Wilderness, Florida National Scenic Trail, Ochlockonee River, Lake Talquin.

For more information: National Forests in Florida, Woodcrest Office Park, 325 John Knox Road, Building F, Tallahasee, FL 32303, (904) 942-9300. District Ranger: Apalachicola Ranger District, Highway 20, P.O. Box 579, Bristol, FL 32321, (904) 643-2282.

Description: Set in the pine forests and savannahs of the Florida panhandle, the Apalachee Savannahs Scenic Byway runs roughly parallel to the imposing and historic Apalachicola River. The two-lane highway is paved, and there are frequent access roads of graded dirt or clay that are sequentially numbered. Traffic is light and the highway well-maintained. The landscape is composed of southern yellow pine forests, savannahs, cypress stands, and abundant wildflowers in season, such as milkworts, bachelor buttons, grass pinks, coreopsis, blazing stars, and black-eyed Susans.

Summer visitors should be prepared for temperatures in the 90s and 100s, high humidity, and frequent rain. Spring and fall are more moderate, and winter travelers may encounter lows in the 30s and 40s in January and February.

Bristol is a small, rural community near the Apalachicola River. The scenic byway begins seven miles south of Bristol on County Road 12, at the national forest boundary. One mile south of the boundary, Camel Lake Recreation Area offers excellent camping opportunities on the banks of a small scenic lake surrounded by cypresses, oaks, and pines. There are 10 campsites, a swimming area, a boat ramp, picnic tables, and public restrooms. Fishing for bass and bream is good, and dove hunting is permitted in season.

Farther south on the byway, the thick pine forest is interspersed with bay and cypress swamps. The forest provides habitat for many wildlife species, including black bears, deer, wild turkeys, squirrels, bobcats, alligators, foxes, oppossums, and gopher tortoises. The latter burrow in the ground, creating underground refuges for many other species. The red-cockaded woodpecker, an endangered species, prefers to nest in mature longleaf pines. Showy orchids and lilies, as well as carnivorous insect-eating pitcher plants and bladderworts, grow in the boggy treeless areas called savannahs.

An unusual activity practiced in the forest is a rural technique of worm gathering called grunting. A wooden stake is driven into moist soil and rubbed across the top with a heavy piece of iron. This transmits underground vibrations that drive worms to the surface. The technique provides anglers with plenty of worms for bait.

After crossing Big Gully Creek, drive less than a mile to the intersection of County Road 12 and County Road 379. The byway continues south on 379. A side trip west on Forest Road 133 leads to Big Gully Landing, the first in a series of public boat launches. Fishing is good for bass, bream, and catfish in Big Gully Creek, which also provides access to the Apalachicola River.

Continuing south on 379, you pass a quaint, deserted church and cemetery,

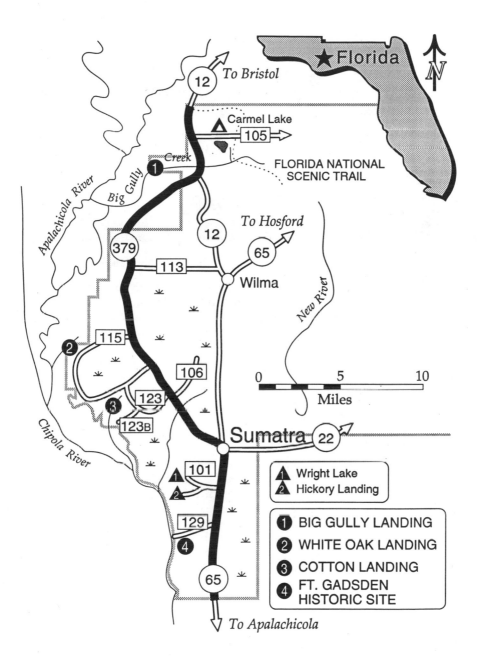

The Apalachee Savannahs Scenic Byway provides many access points to the Apalachicola River and other waterways of the Florida panhandle. William A. Greer photo.

as well as vast expanses of broom sedge and a few miles of private, agricultural land. The tilled fields offer a marked contrast to the tall stands of timber that line the road within the national forest.

The byway has frequent access roads that branch to the east and west. County Road 379A leads west two miles to a fee boat launch into the Florida River, part of a system of creeks and rivers that feed into the giant Apalachicola River. Just south of 379A is Forest Road 115, which goes to White Oak Landing on the River Styx. The three-mile drive on 115 travels past a series of rather quaint campers and trailers, offering a rare view of life in rural Florida off the beaten path. The route skirts the north end of Big Cypress Swamp. Huge cypress stumps rise from the boggy area near the road, where an interpretive sign indicates a "Hydric Hardwood Swamp."

Farther south on 379, the vista opens up. Large savannahs, maintained treeless by prescribed fires, are bordered by pine stands on the east and west. Forest Road 123 leads west four miles through thick palmetto underbrush full of birds and wildlife. The landscape is subtle, and fresh green ferns cover the forest floor in burned areas. The route ends at Cotton Landing, which has four campsites, picnicking, and toilets available. Fishing and canoeing are fun in Kennedy Creek.

The next side trip is Forest Road 106. This graded road offers particularly good opportunities for viewing a wide variety of wildflowers and insectivorous plants. Here pitcher plants, Venus flytraps, sundews, bladderworts, and orchids grow in abundance and can be photographed with ease.

The byway offers dramatic views of stands of dwarf cypresses near the highway. Three miles south of Forest Road 106, the tiny town of Sumatra has a one-room post office, a church, several residences, and one convenience store with restroom and phone. The byway then follows Florida Route 65 south.

South of Sumatra, a side trip west on Forest Road 101 leads to Wright Lake and Hickory Landing recreation areas. Hickory Landing has 10 campsites set in a mixed pine and hardwood forest close to the stream bank. The boat launch accesses Owl Creek, where you can fish for bass and bream. Wright Lake has 25 sites in the tall pines adjacent to the lake. Swimming, canoeing, and fishing are fun in the crystal-clear waters of Wright Lake.

The last side trip leads west on Forest Road 129 to Fort Gadsden State Park. Interpretive exhibits depict the history of Fort Gadsden and the part it played in Florida's history. The fort was particularly important because of its strategic location on the Apalachicola River, a major transportation route during the Civil War. Today contours in the ground indicate the location of the fort on a bluff overlooking the river. There is a covered picnic area, a restroom, and a small outdoor museum with artifact displays and a lighted diorama of the fort. Literature about the fort is available at the site.

The entire area is underlain by limestone bedrock, probably from the Miocene age. This area along the Apalachicola River has been inhabited by Native Americans for 10,000 to 12,000 years. Arrowheads and pottery shards found in fields and along river and creek banks must be left there, to preserve our heritage.

The byway ends just north of Buck Siding, a mere bend in the road at the national forest boundary. Motorists continuing south and west will pass through the fishing town of Eastpoint, and then Apalachicola, a town well worth a stop. It has some fine Victorian architecture and the John Gorrie Museum. The recently restored Gibson Hotel, dating from the 1880s, is in the center of town and offers food and repose with an excellent view of Apalachicola Bay.—*William A. Greer* □

About the Author

Beverly Magley is a free-lance writer from Helena, Montana. Her articles are published frequently in *Montana Magazine*, and she has written several natural history field guides for children. Ms. Magley is happiest in the outdoors, and she has backpacked, bicycled, rafted, and cross-country skied in such varied locales as the United States, Europe, and the South Pacific.

Recreation Guides from Falcon Press

The Angler's Guide to Montana
The Beartooth Fishing Guide
The Floater's Guide to Colorado
The Floater's Guide to Montana
The Hiker's Guide to Arizona
The Hiker's Guide to California
The Hiker's Guide to Colorado
The Hiker's Guide to Hot Springs
  in the Pacific Northwest

The Hiker's Guide to Idaho
The Hiker's Guide to Montana
The Hiker's Guide to Montana's
  Continental Divide Trail
The Hiker's Guide to Utah
The Hiker's Guide to Washington
The Hunter's Guide to Montana
National Forest Scenic Byways
The Rockhound's Guide to Montana

Falcon Press is continually expanding its list of recreational guidebooks using the same general format as this book. All books include detailed descriptions, accurate maps, and all information necessary for enjoyable trips. You can order extra copies of this book and get information and prices for the books listed above by writing Falcon Press, P.O. Box 1718, Helena, MT 59624. Also, please ask for our free catalog listing all Falcon Press books and calendars.